a *girl* named *Lovely*

One Child's
Miraculous Survival
and My Journey to the
Heart of Haiti

Catherine Porter

Published by Simon & Schuster
New York London Toronto Sydney New Delhi

SIMON &
SCHUSTER
CANADA

Simon & Schuster Canada
A Division of Simon & Schuster, Inc.
166 King Street East, Suite 300
Toronto, Ontario M5A 1J3

This Simon & Schuster Canada edition February 2019

SIMON & SCHUSTER CANADA and colophon are
trademarks of Simon & Schuster, Inc.

For information about special discounts for bulk purchases,
please contact Simon & Schuster Special Sales at 1-800-268-3216
or CustomerService@simonandschuster.ca.

Library and Archives Canada Cataloguing in Publication

Porter, Catherine, 1972 December 26–, author A girl named Lovely /
Catherine Porter.
Issued in print and electronic formats.
ISBN 978-1-5011-6809-3 (hardcover).—ISBN 978-1-5011-6811-6 (ebook)
1. Haiti Earthquake, Haiti, 2010. 2. Earthquake relief—Haiti. 3. Haiti—
History—21st century. 4. Porter, Catherine, 1972 December 26–
—Travel—Haiti. 5. Avelus, Lovely. I. Title.
HV600.2010.H2P67 2019 363.34'95097294090512
C2018-902309-0 C2018-902310-4

Interior design by Lewelin Polanco

Manufactured in the United States of America

1   3   5   7   9   10   8   6   4   2

ISBN 978-1-5011-6809-3
ISBN 978-1-5011-6811-6 (ebook)

To Graeme, Lyla, Noah, and Lovely.

Contents

Lovely's Household

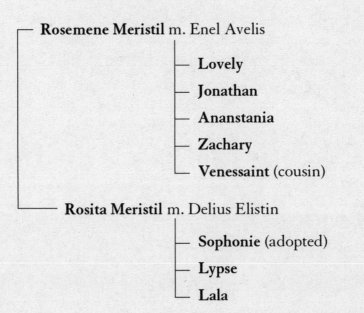

Rosemene Meristil m. Enel Avelis

- **Lovely**
- **Jonathan**
- **Ananstania**
- **Zachary**
- **Venessaint** (cousin)

Rosita Meristil m. Delius Elistin

- **Sophonie** (adopted)
- **Lypse**
- **Lala**

Prologue

In the late afternoon of January 12, 2010, an earthquake struck Haiti near the town of Léogâne, twenty-five kilometers outside the country's already destitute capital, Port-au-Prince. The destruction was unlike anything the world had seen since World War II: as many as 300,000 people killed, another 300,000 injured, 1.5 million made homeless. The carnage was caused not just by the earthquake, which was 7.0 on the Richter scale, but also by decades of neglect and poverty. Haiti was then—and remains—the poorest country in the western hemisphere, a place where one-third of children were malnourished and half were illiterate. People had built illegal concrete homes in the capital's valleys and hillsides with cheap material and no oversight. Now those buildings killed them. The earthquake was indiscriminate, though: it destroyed the homes and hospitals of the rich, too. The country's premier luxury hotel, the Montana, collapsed like an accordion, killing more than one hundred staff members and guests—many of whom had arrived just minutes before from the airport, which itself was damaged. An hour after the first undulating tremor, night fell over the country like a blackout blind, and locals relied on the lights from their cell phones while desperately clawing by hand through the rubble for their loved ones. The first international help flew into the Dominican Republic, on the other side of the island, and then drove across the border. What started as a trickle became a flood, and Haiti would soon claim a second title: the recipient of the world's largest international aid effort, an accolade that would in time reveal itself to be a mixed blessing. But in those first fragile days after the earthquake, hundreds of people were dug out from the wreckage, to the cheers of rescue crews. Each one was considered sacred.

Six days after the earthquake, a two-year-old girl—covered in dust and crying for her mother—was hauled out from a broken home.

Her name was Lovely, and she would become sacred to me.

Part 1

Chapter 1

The End of the World

It felt like the plane was landing in the middle of the ocean.

Peering out a window, I could see nothing but vast blackness. There were no white lights dotting the edges of the runway, no brightly lit terminal buildings in the distance, and, beyond that, no twinkling city lights. Just blackness, then *bump*: we were on the ground.

But the voice over the plane's loudspeaker confirmed that we had in fact arrived at our destination: the devastated city of Port-au-Prince.

It was 10:00 p.m. on January 23, 2010, eleven days after the earthquake. Somewhere out there in the darkness were hundreds of thousands of bloated corpses, severely injured people, and armed thugs who were using the chaos to loot, rape, and exact hideous revenge by burning their enemies alive in the streets. I'd seen pictures of the latter, taken by my colleague, photographer Lucas Oleniuk, and splayed across the front page of our newspaper, the *Toronto Star*. They had kept me awake for the past couple of nights, ever since my editor had phoned me during lunch and asked if I wanted to go to Haiti.

"Of course," I'd said without pause. I was a columnist at the newspaper, but my dream was to become a foreign correspondent. This was my big break. But I'd been quietly freaking out since that moment. What if I was kidnapped by one of those thugs? What if I witnessed a public lynching? Would I be able to handle the Civil War–era amputations to remove gangrenous limbs that my colleagues had reported were taking place in tents around the city?

I packed in our basement the night before my planned departure as my two little kids looked on from the couch. This would be my longest separation from them. Was I being an irresponsible parent, leaving them to travel into danger? Would I return injured or broken? But if I didn't go, how could I ever forgive myself? Most days, I felt emotionally stretched between two worlds as a working mom; now that tug-of-war between ambition and duty felt as though it would snap me in half. When I couldn't find my freshly purchased Lonely Planet guide to the Dominican Republic and Haiti, I started frantically tearing apart my bag and sobbing uncontrollably. I was having a full-fledged panic attack. My kids cuddled me on the couch and recited the soothing words I always told them: "Everything will be okay, Mommy."

Adding to the sticky fear that clenched my stomach and muffled my lungs was performance anxiety. Every journalist is crippled by self-doubt most of the time. We all think we've somehow managed to patch things together thus far, but that it's only a matter of time before everyone else figures out that we are winging it. Would this be the trip that revealed all my failings? Would I crack under the pressure and be forced to call my editor blubbering and begging to be brought home? Would I get scooped by all the competing journalists and miss the big stories?

A cheer went up in the plane around me. I was at the back of an Air Canada relief flight, surrounded by mostly female airline staff who had been trained as caregivers to soothe survivors after airplane "incidents"—scares or, worse, crashes. For them, this trip was about delivering aid to their colleagues in Haiti and bringing Haitian orphans, whose international adoptions had been expedited by the Canadian government, back to their new homes in Canada.

The volunteers wore matching beige T-shirts with the word "Hope" printed in English, French, and Kreyòl ayisyen —Haitian Creole, one of the country's two official languages—on the back. They had spent most of the ride bouncing excitedly between seats, snapping photos of one another and passing out chocolates and home-baked muffins.

"What we are doing is greater than all of us," their upbeat leader, Duncan Dee, had announced over the plane's loudspeaker before takeoff.

Duncan was the chief operating officer for Air Canada, which had become Canada's official emergency aid transporter after the Southeast Asian tsunami four years earlier. He was short, with cropped black hair and glasses that amplified his round face. This was his third aid mission, after Indonesia and Hurricane Katrina, and already it had a special significance.

A few nights before, Duncan had watched a Canadian Broadcasting Corporation (CBC) newscast from Port-au-Prince featuring a child getting sutures without anesthetic at a bare-bones medical clinic. The child's screams moved Duncan to tears and haunted him. He was a devout Catholic with two children of his own.

"I couldn't not do anything, knowing I would be in Port-au-Prince forty-eight hours after that child was screaming," he said. He'd picked up his phone and emailed Peter Mansbridge, the anchor of the flagship CBC newscast The National, who directed him to a reporter in Port-au-Prince. Within an hour Duncan had connected with a volunteer at the makeshift clinic who provided a long list of needed supplies.

Over the past two days Duncan and his volunteer crew had criss-crossed Ottawa, personally collecting wheelchairs, generators, and diapers. Except for one type of antibiotic, they had picked up every last thing on the list. They were high on compassion and buzzing from the endorphins of altruism.

"It's a privilege for us to do this. We are helping people who have nothing," Duncan said.

Back in economy class, I and my colleague Brett Popplewell, a reporter with the *Star*, were the only ones who were getting off. We weren't here to save lives or help in any tangible way. We were here to witness whatever horrors were unfurling in the darkness and report it to our readers back in Canada.

I nervously checked my bag one more time to make sure I had everything: my pens and notebooks, camera and laptop. I tapped my waist, where I was wearing a money belt filled with my passport and a thick wad of American dollars I'd packed to pay for drivers, translators, and a hotel room, if I could find one.

I began to shuffle my way to the airplane exit, a sense of dread growing with each step. My breath was shallow, and nausea gripped my stomach. As I was leaving, the Air Canada agent who'd been the most buoyant and enthusiastic called out to me: "Good luck."

Outside, the air was thick and warm, like a damp wool blanket. The smell of burning rubber filled my nostrils. It was dark except for the headlights of a giant pickup truck that had rolled right up to the plane, and the white glow of a television camera.

From atop the metal staircase, I could see Duncan's round face illuminated in the camera's glare below. The same CBC reporter who had inspired him to help was now interviewing him.

A knot of people moved in the shadows nearby. When I reached the ground, I quickly learned most had arrived to pick up the emergency supplies Air Canada staff had carefully collected.

These weren't professional aid workers, though. They seemed to be just a bunch of random people who, like Duncan, had watched the news and been inspired to help Haiti in person. I would come to call them catastrophe missionaries.

"We've been setting up tents, holding babies, seeing a woman give birth," said a thirty-year-old man from New Jersey wearing a baseball cap and baggy shorts. "It's been the craziest two days. We rode in on the back of a dump truck to get here. We brought bags of lollipops to give to kids. We were jumping rope with them today."

When I asked him his job, he said his fiance was in medical school. I raised my eyebrows. Seriously, what good did he think he was doing skipping with kids in an earthquake zone? I at least had a job to do here. He was just some yahoo who'd come for a strange thrill. I figured he would cause more harm than good. But I scratched everything he told me down in my notebook, hoping my pen was working in the dark. The best cure for performance anxiety is action, and interviewing someone—anyone—was calming.

The man pointed out his group's leader, a tall, slim, and slow-talking information technology specialist from Manhattan named Alphonse Edouard. Alphonse had been vacationing in the Dominican Republic when the earthquake struck and had rushed over the border with two duffel bags of hastily purchased medical supplies. He'd met up with members of the Dominican Republic Civil Defense and some Greek doctors, and together they'd set up a medical clinic on the edge of an industrial complex near the airport. It was Alphonse who had sent Duncan the list of needed supplies.

"I'm still pinching myself. I can't believe the plane is actually here," Alphonse said. "The people of Haiti really need the relief."

At the clinic, doctors were seeing dozens of patients a day, treating fractures and delivering babies. As I scrawled down his words, I heard something that made me stop. His clinic was taking care of a "miracle baby," a little girl named Jonatha who had been dropped off six days after the earthquake. The girl had survived all six days under the rubble alone. He figured she was one and a half years old.

"We'll have to do something for her," he said. "Her parents died."

Six days without water—that seemed a miracle indeed, particularly for such a small person. My kids, Lyla and Noah, were three and one, and they wouldn't make it a single day without food or water.

Even when we were stepping out for a quick errand, I packed as though we were going on a two-day canoe trip with an assortment of snacks in various containers and multiple brimming sippy cups.

I had to find this girl. Alphonse directed me to something called "Sonapi."

"Go to the *Trois Mains* and turn right," he said. I had never been to Haiti before, so the directions meant nothing to me, but I figured locals would know what he was talking about and lead me there.

As we were talking, boxes were being off-loaded from the plane onto the warm tarmac. I spotted my bulky camping knapsack among them. I hauled my bag up onto my back and asked an Air Canada employee if she could tell me the direction of the hangar. She stretched out her finger and pointed under the plane.

With Brett beside me, we shuffled under the hulking belly of the giant Airbus A330 in the direction the airline employee had indicated, hoping that we'd bump into the hangar. We were immediately enveloped by the darkness. I couldn't see a thing. I was still scared, but there was a slight loosening of the coils in my stomach. In a few hours I was going to head out and find that orphaned girl, wherever she was.

When the sun rose the next morning, the view was devastating.

Port-au-Prince was built around valleys that had once been verdant with trees. At first glance, it also seemed that there were waterfalls flowing down the hills around the city. A closer look revealed that the white wasn't spray but concrete blocks that had spilled down the valley, one small house smashing the next.

Jumbled piles of concrete lined both sides of the street. The buildings were flattened, tipped over, reduced to skeletons of rebar and wood. Some offered clues to their former lives: a Yamaha sign resting atop a mess of rubble, a large wooden cross with Jesus rising before a jumble of bricks and broken stained glass windows.

So many of the buildings were broken that the ones left standing were easy to spot. They stood out. They resembled dissected carcasses. Here I could see the rows of dusty desks up on the third floor of a sliced-open building, and there the baby bassinets of a medical clinic.

We passed the country's largest cathedral, called locally the Port-au-Prince Cathedral, which now resembled a Roman ruin: no roof or stained glass, just pillars and bare walls. And there were the three white domes of the presidential palace. The central one had collapsed like a sunken marzipan cake.

A vast camp spread around the palace in what had once been the city's version of Central Park and Times Square combined—a dozen small parks dotted with graceful trees and statues of revolutionary heroes. Before, this was where locals would meet at the end of the day to eat ice cream or do their homework beneath the streetlamps. During the annual carnival, it was where the parade and dancing took place. Now every inch of ground was clogged by homemade tents fashioned from bedsheets. I could make out a children's play structure, with a slide and a ladder in the distance. People had camped out on its upper platform, where kids were meant to line up for their turn down the slide.

People lay on the streets all around, under sheets or tied-up tarps. Others rummaged through the rubble, heaving hammers and digging with their bare hands. Signs made with spray paint flashed from walls and hanging sheets: *We need food. Water Please. S.O.S. We need help. We need help. We need help.*

I scrawled down notes as I toured the city, trying to get my bearings. But just as I fixed my eyes on one broken thing, another leapt into view. I felt like a kid in a haunted house, overwhelmed and distracted. It was too much to take in.

Brett and I were the second team of reporters from our newspaper to arrive, relieving our colleagues who had rushed into the country a couple of days after the quake and were now strung out and exhausted. They had already reported on the death and destruction. Our assignment was to document what came next: the aid and presumably, the first steps of healing.

But the devastation was so overpowering, it was hard to imagine moving on from it. How could anyone heal from this type of damage?

We stopped in at a police station near the airport, which had become the Haitian government's temporary headquarters, since most ministry buildings had collapsed. The only sign of any government, though, was the long-faced communications minister, Marie-Laurence Jocelyn Lassègue, sitting alone at a table under a dusty mango tree. A piece of paper had been folded to make a nameplate in front of her, with the word *Presse*.

"We need tents, medicines, nurses," she said forcefully in perfect English. It was as if I'd pushed the play button on her monologue, and she rushed on without breaking or even breathing. "The NGOs don't look at the government's priority, and they need to be better coordinated. The majority of the population is women and they lost everything. It was already very hard for them to live. It seems the jail was opened, and there have been many rapes. We need soldiers to protect them and put lights up in the camps."

When I left the station, I was immediately swept up in the next matter; it was all I could do to keep up. But I would soon learn just how prescient Minister Lassègue's words were.

All morning, I had been emailing Alphonse, the volunteer coordinator, trying to get better directions to the clinic where the miracle girl was being cared for. He had repeated the same two things: "Sonapi" and "*Trois Mains*."

Even before the earthquake, Port-au-Prince was an easy city to get lost in. Few of the warren-like streets had names, let alone signs. To find their way, locals used landmarks to give directions: Go to this supermarket, say, turn left, and when you get to the big house with three satellite dishes, turn right. But most of the usual landmarks were now gone, so even locals could spend hours trying to find their way around town.

When I asked our driver if he knew "Sonapi" or "*Trois Mains*," he shook his head. He was new to Port-au-Prince.

Passing the airport, however, we circled a roundabout with a statue in its center. When I looked out the window, I saw it: three joining metal hands. *Trois Mains.*

Just beyond the statue was a large wall with a big blue metal gate, guarded by United Nations soldiers in flak jackets and blue helmets. Over the gate was a sign: PARC INDUSTRIEL MÉTROPOLITAIN, SONAPI (Société Nationale des Parcs Industriels).

What I found on the other side of that gate looked more like a disorganized campground than a medical clinic. Set around a muddy patch of grass and a brick courtyard were a smattering of tents: silver camping domes, large, heavy canvas shelters, and a big army-green party tent, now full of the Air Canada supplies. Chickens and a rooster scratched in the spaces between them.

The place was eerily quiet. The buzz of activity and crowds of injured patients I'd expected from Alphonse's description were conspicuously absent. Sundays, it turned out, were convalescence days for the Greek doctors who worked with the large medical NGO Médecins du Monde. The clinic was officially closed.

A few volunteers milled about, including Alphonse, who walked over to greet me.

"You're here!" he said warmly. "Let me introduce you to Jonatha."

The miracle child was sitting under the shade of a tree in the center of a crowd of adorers. She was small, with birdlike bones—barely taller than my one-year-old, Noah, but with the coordination of my three-year-old, Lyla. Her hair was fluffing out from a neat row of cornrows that someone had lovingly tended to.

She was sitting on a small ledge, between adults, dressed in a white tank top that slid off one shoulder, a pink corduroy skirt that was also too big, and a plastic pink play cell phone that hung around her neck on a cord.

She did not look like a refugee who had lost everything and survived hell. She looked healthy and happy, as though she were spending another afternoon in the sandpit at a local park. I watched her snatch the baseball cap off the head of one of her adult admirers and plop it teasingly on her own head.

She repeatedly returned to the side of a woman with an auburn bob and brown crinkly eyes named Michele Laporte. A retired psychiatric nurse from Montreal, Michele had flown to the Dominican Republic two days after the earthquake to meet her daughter, and together they had rushed over the border by bus. She called the decision an impulsive "cry of the heart." She had never done anything like this before.

Michele had spent her first few days setting femur and tibia fractures on the ground, often without anesthetic.

"How can people suffer so much?" she asked wearily.

Then, six days after the earthquake, Jonatha arrived.

The clinic was in such chaos then, no one noted where the ambulance was from.

"We don't even know how many patients we had this week," Michele said.

The Greek doctors examined Jonatha and were shocked to find no broken bones, no open wounds, not even any scratches. The only things physically wrong with Jonatha, medically speaking, were long-term malnutrition and giardia, a common digestive tract parasite; neither condition a result of the earthquake. But, psychologically, she was distressed. She curled up in the fetal position and cried for days, refusing to talk except when calling out weakly for her mother.

Michele had decided, simply, to hold Jonatha constantly, keeping her on her lap during the day and curling around her at night. She'd become a human rescue blanket, transmitting warm love from her body into the child's, and it had worked. Jonatha had stopped crying the day before I arrived. She had started to speak again, too. That morning she'd had another breakthrough: while Michele was sorting medication in their tent, she heard a noise behind her, and turned to find the little girl shaking a pill bottle like it was a rattle.

"She made a smile," Michele recounted. "It was illuminating. I thought she would never smile again."

Most survivors are pulled out of the wreckage within the first twenty-four hours of an earthquake, disaster experts say. Adults are unlikely to survive more than three days without water. For children, it is even less. Michele couldn't fathom how Jonatha survived, but she assumed the same grace had not spared her parents.

"Will we ever know?" Michele said.

While I listened to the story, I casually studied Jonatha, looking for signs of what she'd been through. A volunteer brought over a Styrofoam container of food, and she was eating like a linebacker: shoveling rice and beans into her mouth, sucking the meat off the ribs, and then crunching the bones and swallowing those, too.

Michele took hold of the container to pull it away, and Jonatha gripped it firmly and narrowed her eyes. Her eyes were dark and exacting, like those of an old woman the world could no longer trick. There was a toughness in this kid I didn't see in my children. Is that what had kept her alive all those days under the rubble? What horrors had she witnessed? Had someone sung songs of comfort to her, like I often sang to my children, or had she heard nothing but the moans and cries of despair? I hoped her mother had held her for a time before passing away.

Tomorrow, Jonatha's small life was about to be upended again. After ten days Michele was going back home, as were many of the other catastrophe missionaries. Who would care for Jonatha?

"We don't want to take her to an orphanage. They are all broken rubble. She needs stability," Michele said. "But what can we do?"

Less than an hour before, I had been under the UNICEF tarp, set up in the United Nations compound just down the road from the airport. The UN camp resembled a set for the 1970s television series *M.A.S.H.* Many agencies' headquarters had been destroyed, so they had set up under dusty tarps with hastily scrawled signs poking from the gravel outside.

There, I learned UNICEF had established three clandestine safe houses around the city for children who had lost their families. Sitting beside Michele, I emailed a contact at UNICEF about Jonatha. He replied within minutes: an officer would be by soon.

"Do you think the care there will be good?" Michele asked. "There are a thousand families in Canada who would want her. I hope she ends up with a good family and can take painting classes and ballet and do all the things our kids get to do."

I hadn't been in Haiti for a full day yet, but from what I'd seen that morning and what I'd read about the country, I doubted the care at the safe houses would meet such high standards. After all she had been through, Jonatha seemed destined for an internally displaced persons camp or a broken orphanage, which in Haiti rarely came with school, let alone ballet lessons. Looking down at the petite girl, I was overcome with pity. It was incredible she had survived, but for what? She'd lost her parents and now she was going to be abandoned again.

I checked the time. I had to go. My deadline was looming.

I crouched down and said good-bye to the little girl the way I did to my kids' friends: with a pat on the shoulder. As I walked away, I looked back to see Michele lead her away by the hand for a washroom break. Her pink corduroy skirt slid down her backside, revealing a pair of diapers.

I met a lot of little kids over the next few days. Kids living under tarps in the street; shoeless kids lining up for bottled water; filthy homeless kids locals disparagingly called "street rats" who darted in and out of traffic offering to clean windshields for pennies.

Some had uplifting stories. The day after visiting Jonatha, I came across one six-year-old girl on a bed in the middle of the street. It was surrounded by dozens of others and protected from the sun and rain by tarps, converting the road into a giant communal room. The girl's aunt was combing her hair in preparation for her first outing since the earthquake. A Dominican charity had organized a camp for the kids on her street. I rode in a truck with them to a large house with a walled-in yard, where they sang songs and did jumping jacks. It was a rare moment of joy, one that a select lucky few seemed able to embrace. Most of their stories were heavily stitched with despair.

Later that day, a giant hospital came into view through the car window, and I asked the driver to pull over. It was the public hospital for Delmas, a suburb of Port-au-Prince, called Hôpital Universitaire de la Paix. The earthquake had cracked it but not leveled it, and inside the main courtyard, staff were conducting their first post-earthquake meeting. The parking lot and patch of grass outside were crowded with patients lying on gurneys and mattresses. Many had been discharged but had no homes to return to, so they fashioned their own rooms with sheets and green hospital room dividers.

Inside, I met an obstetrical nurse from Spain who, upon hearing I was a journalist, ushered me into the hospital's birthing room. The room was cavernous and bare except for a metal table set in its center. Upon it lay a large woman, entirely naked. She was in the midst of labor, grunting and gasping for air. Between her legs, I could see the crown of her baby's head pushing out.

"Among all this catastrophe is this beauty," the nurse said. Then he pulled out his digital camera and started flipping through photos of dead babies he'd delivered after the earthquake.

It was all surreal. In Toronto, if I had wanted to witness a labor for a story, it would have taken days of bureaucratic approvals, waiver forms, and stringent communications procedures. Here, I was waved in casually, and this woman's most vulnerable, intimate moment was simply a backdrop. The mother in me was repulsed. I had given birth to both my kids without pain medication, and I knew how agonizing and intense it was. The thought of some stranger popping in unannounced in the middle of any of it was infuriating. But I was that strange journalist, and I was there for a reason.

My initial fears about missing stories for the paper were unfounded: they were on every street corner, each one more compelling and alarming than the last. The only challenge was picking which ones to focus on. Did I stop at the mound of rubble that had once been a school, where an excavation team was pulling out four decomposing bodies of dead students? (I did.) Or did I go to the nearby Digicel building, the city's tallest tower, where the company's staff was having a giant prayer service on its ground floor? (I did that, too.)

At the back of my mind, Jonatha lurked. I worried not only what would happen to her in the long run but what today or tomorrow would bring. Her crew of adorers seemed kind and well-meaning, but only the Greek doctors and the Dominican Republic Civil Defense volunteers reported to an official organization. The rest were a ragtag group who had flown to Haiti on a compassionate whim and glommed together by chance. What if one of them was there on false pretenses? No one had screened them, and no one was keeping tabs on them.

In the scramble of patients coming and going, volunteers arriving and departing, and Michele leaving, how long would it take for someone to notice that Jonatha was missing? The thought of my own kids in her situation filled me with anxiety. The following day, when the blue Sonapi gate flashed on the side of the road, I asked my driver to pull over. I, too, was suffering a "cry of the heart."

I found Jonatha wandering between the tents in a sundress, happily eating a banana with Michele following behind her. The retired nurse had delayed her departure by a couple of days to continue caring for the girl. In the meantime, another orphan—a twelve-year-old boy named Carlos—had shown up. Both were reported to the Haitian government. Relieved, I pushed on.

I was sharing a hotel room with Brett and Lucas, who had decided to remain in Haiti for another week. The hotel was full, packed with aid workers, along with journalists from Fox and ABC News who had converted the rooftop patio into their command centers, complete with hulking satellite dishes and humming generators.

The hotel was located at the top of a steep cobblestone driveway high up a mountain of Pétionville, Port-au-Prince's rich lofty suburb, which offered television reporters a great backdrop for their evening newscasts. The city below looked beautiful from this distance, all the destruction softened by the glimmering Caribbean Sea. In fact, if you lay on one of the patio chairs by the pool, you would have no reason to believe something terrible had happened and that the city was in the grips of misery.

Our room was on the ground floor, and we left the glass patio door open at night so we could rush out in our pajamas if we were awoken by another earthquake. Inside, there was a wooden chest of drawers that we'd filled with granola and protein bars from Canada. For days, that's all I ate. There were two double beds, and the men graciously offered to bunk together so I had one to myself. We barely slept. Instead, we spent most of the night scrolling on our phones through stories from other news outlets, too jacked up on adrenaline and raw emotion to talk much. But by 6:00 every morning, after a few fitful hours of sleep, I was climbing back into a car, heading out with my laptop over my shoulder and bulging money belt around my waist to report.

The reporting was exhilarating. I never knew what story I would find, and invariably whatever story I stumbled upon was more gripping than any other I'd covered before.

Early one morning I went to the national soccer stadium to stand in a women's food line. Rationing centers had turned into thrashing mosh pits in the past couple of days, with peacekeepers frantically trying to command control by liberally dousing the crowds with pepper spray. So the World Food Programme had decided to distribute rice only to women, figuring they were less likely to riot and more likely than men to feed their families.

It was barely 7:30 a.m., and already hundreds of women were in line, holding each other's hips to guard their places and chatting excitedly. I quickly learned that life for women in Haiti is hard in a way most North Americans can't imagine. Most are single mothers who have to pay for everything: water, school fees, hospital visits. They have no real national system of welfare, and spousal support is laughable. Many more die in childbirth than anywhere else in the western hemisphere, and the rate of rape is terrifying. Since the earthquake, many women were now sleeping under cotton bedsheets, with no protection from the criminals who escaped the central prison.

But the feeling in the line wasn't despair. It was giddy from relief that they were going to get food and the small scrap of power they'd been given. We were surrounded by men. At the front of the line were United Nations soldiers, sitting atop their hulking tanklike armored personnel carriers. They were dressed for war in camouflaged fatigues and helmets, and they rested giant guns on their laps. Beside and behind, angry Haitian men prowled like coyotes on the hunt. They shouted that they wanted coupons for rice and shoved women out of their paths. The women shared stories and held on to one another, but their conga line shifted nervously and flicked toward the traffic on the dusty adjacent road.

I was pinched between a very pregnant woman dressed simply in a white nightgown and Paulette Paul, a forty-nine-year-old woman whose lined face and gray cornrows made her look decades older. Her right arm was in a cast; she'd broken it while fleeing her crumbling house. Her husband had been badly injured and they had ten children to feed. She held two empty rice bags and hoped that, finally, this time she'd leave with them full. It was at least her fourth attempt to get food.

As we were talking, the nervous energy around us boiled over. Shrill whistles sounded. I looked up and saw that the UN distribution trucks were slowly pulling away. Soldiers on the ground were using their riot shields to push the women back and clear a way through. A wave of bodies rolled toward us. Paulette and I turned and began to shoulder against the women behind us to get out of the way. We rushed onto the road, beside cars that were stuck in traffic, but the scene ahead made us stop dead. Between two idling cars, three men were fighting. We watched as one lassoed the arms of another behind his back. The third man pulled a silver gun from his pocket and brandished it in the air.

My heart thundered in my chest. Instinctively, Paulette and I locked arms at the elbow and leaned into the river of women barrelling down on us. We shouldered our way to the front of the idling car and then dashed across the road to a gas station.

Once we were safely behind the pumps, we turned to see what had happened.

It was as if my vision had slowed, and I could watch the scene in distinct photos. The silver gun rose up and struck the pinned man against one cheek. It was brandished again and struck him against the other cheek.

Then it was over. The man with the gun got back in his car and drove off.

I never saw what happened to his victim.

I returned to the government headquarters. They had built a covered dais in the yard of the police station from which ministers could deliver official reports to the press. I watched Haitian president René Préval declare that the country needed many more tents, only to be contradicted moments later by the American lead on relief efforts, Lewis Lucke, who said plastic sheeting would be much better for temporary housing. Who was in charge of the country?

When I left the press conference, the *Trois Mains* appeared through the car's windshield. I was working with a new driver by then, a man with long, neatly manicured fingernails named Jefferson, as well as a young English teacher named David, who was translating for me. I asked them to pull over so I could go check in on Jonatha.

The clinic was humming with patients this time. There was a row of heavily bandaged men sitting in wheelchairs under the tree where I'd first met Jonatha, and a long line of women holding babies leaking out from one of the manila tents where the Greek doctors were doing examinations and diagnosing mostly fevers, diarrhea, rashes, and malnutrition. The acute trauma had passed now, making all those supplies brought down by Air Canada useless. The medical team was now greeting dehydrated and feverish children. They had a whole new wish list, starting with baby Tylenol.

I found Jonatha dressed in a little purple sundress, sitting on a thin mattress under a tree. She was eating again from a Styrofoam container, this one brimming with macaroni and cheese. Michele had left, I learned, and a heavyset Dominican woman had been tapped to watch over the little girl.

In fact, a whole new group of catastrophe missionaries had arrived since my last visit. There was a political science student from Boston, a French fisherman, and a life coach from Mexico who had flown into flood zones in Venezuela and rescue camps in Argentina. The life coach had been working with Jonatha every day, getting her to play and separate from Michele so she wasn't traumatized by the Montreal nurse's departure. He thought she was improving.

"She needs parents now," he said.

Two UNICEF workers had arrived to collect Jonatha, but the volunteers refused to let her go with them.

"They didn't have any identification," the French fisherman said. "We can't give her to anyone."

This struck me as richly ironic and reassuring at the same time. Jonatha's safety net was stronger than I'd feared.

When the little girl looked up at me, she offered no glimmer of recognition. Her dark eyes fixed on me flatly, then returned to her lunch. She wasn't a charmer, like my daughter, Lyla, who always plays to the crowd. She wasn't happy-go-lucky and oblivious like my son, Noah, either. She was hard-baked, weary, and incredibly self-possessed. This crowd of adults was flocking around her because, to them, she represented the country's fragility—a helpless human rescued from the rubble. But to me she seemed more to reflect the country's weary resilience. She was a survivor.

She wasn't the only one in the makeshift medical clinic. A group of fifty children were also wolfing down macaroni and cheese nearby. They were from a damaged orphanage and now lived under a tarp on a nearby field. None of them was as clean or well-dressed as Jonatha. A few wore sandals that were at least two sizes too big, and others had no shoes at all. I watched them line up quietly next to the row of

wheelchairs to wait for a pickup truck to take them back to the orphanage, and wondered if Jonatha would be joining them soon.

I set off down a cobblestone road, heading deeper into the Sonapi
industrial complex. Before the earthquake, it had been the country's
premier sweatshop zone, filled with factories making T-shirts for
Western companies. Now the factories were not operating, but ca-
tering trucks hummed around them. A small Canadian flag fluttered
from a spindly tree on the edge of the road, and I wandered past it
and up a footpath to where five turbaned men sat in plastic chairs in
a circle under a tarp, grating ginger and washing kidney beans for
dinner. They were volunteers with Sikh United who'd come from
Brampton, a suburb of my hometown Toronto, more than a week
ago, to cook 2,500 free meals a day. I was stunned.

"God gave us a lot," said their leader, a truck driver. "Why
wouldn't we share with somebody who has nothing?"

That seems like the obvious response of a human being faced with
the suffering of other human beings. Even the New Jersey boy, whom
I'd dismissed as a yahoo upon stepping off the plane, had good intentions and loving instincts. But the cardinal rule of journalism is to
remain objective, which means staying emotionally detached and not
getting personally involved. Our job, we say, is to record stories and
recount them honestly in all their gruesome and delightful fullness,
without bending or influencing them. We are witnesses, not actors,
in the world.

That's how it works on paper, at least. In practice, I was finding it
difficult. Every day I was beseeched on the street by people asking for
èd—the Kreyòl word for aid. They were hungry; they asked me for
food. They'd lost their livelihoods; they asked me for work.

I repeated the same refrain: "I am a journalist, not an aid worker.
I don't have money. I don't have jobs. I don't have food. I am here to
tell your stories."

Usually they nodded in resignation but asked me to jot down their names and cell phone numbers, *just in case*. When I gave my business card to one man who was among the lucky few to get a temporary job shoveling up the rubble downtown, I was immediately swarmed by his colleagues. They all stuck out their hands, demanding a business card. Despite what I told them, they all hoped I would help them somehow.

The problem was, I didn't believe my own words. I could feel my money belt along the flat of my belly, still thick with American cash, and in my bag was a fistful of granola bars. I *could* help them, but my job demanded that I not.

While every other *blan*—foreigner—I'd met had dropped his or her life to rush here and assist in some way, I had to make the conscious decision, time and again, not to offer even the smallest help. In theory, I knew the stories I was writing would contribute to the larger cause by inspiring Canadians to pay attention and hopefully send money. But in the moment, those abstract thoughts were poor comfort. The guilt and horror piled up inside me like the jumbled debris that clogged the roads.

My normal way of dealing with stress is to shove my feet into running shoes and set out for a hard run. But I hadn't brought my running shoes, and even if I had, I couldn't imagine running alongside the mounds of rubble, past people sleeping on the road. So I started to bum cigarettes from other journalists and wealthy Haitian businessmen staying at the hotel after filing my stories.

I'd smoke them on the hotel patio, ten kilometers and a world away from the darkened city below.

Days later, I was standing outside a pale yellow house in a dense neighborhood with Jony St. Louis. He was a physiotherapist and a translator for a local clinic that included the country's only prosthetic limb workshop. This had been his home before the earthquake.

From the outside, it looked like the building hadn't suffered too much damage—just cracks in the walls, a few gaping holes. But, peering through one, I saw a kitchen on the first floor that Jony explained had come from two floors up. The outer walls had stayed standing, while the floors inside had collapsed like descending cards in a shuffling deck.

Jony had lived in the basement with his wife, Annia, who was a doctor, and their two young kids. On the afternoon of the earthquake, Annia returned from the hospital, sent their children upstairs to play at the top-floor neighbors', and lay down in bed for a quick nap.

Two stories of concrete and furniture collapsed atop her.

Jony was across the city at the time, working with a stroke patient in her home, when the three adjacent houses all came crashing down. He described how, after calling the patient's son to let him know she was fine, he jumped on his motorcycle and raced home. The streets were full of unconscious and bleeding people. Ten minutes from home his motorcycle stopped dead, so he abandoned it and ran.

"With each breath, I said 'My wife, my daughter, my son,'" he said.

It was dark by the time he reached his home, so he used the light of his cell phone to guide his way to the spot where his home had stood. There, he dug for Annia with the help of some boys from the neighborhood soccer team he had coached.

Before Jony guided me to the spot where he'd dug, we needed to prepare for the sickly sweet smell of death. A young girl had died in the upstairs bathroom, and her body was still there, decomposing. Around the city, I'd seen people walking with minty toothpaste smeared below their noses to block out the smell of death all around them. Jony had an upscale version of that: peppermint oil. He handed me the bottle and I wiped it on my upper lip, wondering at how the most grotesque rituals become pedestrian in such a short time.

The houses in most neighborhoods of Port-au-Prince were packed tightly together, which explained how so many people died. You fled your crumbling house only to be crushed by the one falling next door. There was barely enough room to walk between Jony's house and his neighbors', and the path was now a course of jumbled hunks of concrete shards and cinder blocks. At the corner, we turned down an even tighter alley and stopped halfway down the width of the house, where there was a hole at the base of the wall. Strewn around it were items of Jony's former life, yanked out as his team made its daunting progress: his six-month-old daughter's peach baby blanket and a white sandal, two blue ties, an electronic piano. Jony squatted and picked up a small family photo album, flipping through its pages of happy memories. I crouched beside him and leaned in to peer into the hole. In the dark, I could make out the wooden board of a baby crib.

The night of the earthquake, Jony could hear Annia's faint voice calling for their two-year-old son, Semi. He and his team had pounded with a hammer and clawed with their hands, calling to her, asking her to knock against the ceiling that was pressed against her face. When they finally reached her eight hours later, one of the boys slid through the tunnel on his back and pulled her out.

"I carried her out to the road like a baby," Jony said. "She couldn't move her legs."

He rushed her to the closest hospital, the same one where I had seen the woman giving birth, but he'd found its dark grounds filled with innumerable patients and few doctors. So he took Annia to his mother's courtyard. After three days, Annia told him she still had not peed. She needed a catheter.

He turned the city upside down looking for one, all to no avail. Annia died that night, likely of renal failure.

"Her family thinks I didn't do enough," he said. "I should have brought her to a hospital in the Dominican Republic. . . . I can't sleep. I never drank alcohol before, and now I drink a lot of rum at night. That helps me to forget."

I often cry when interviewing people who are emotional themselves. Sitting beside Jony, I wept not just with sympathy but with horror. I imagined what it meant to be buried alive. To be conscious that your life was ending but to remain trapped and unable to do anything about it. I thought about the heroics of Jony's neighbors, risking their lives to enter the house while aftershocks rattled and threatened to maim or kill them, too.

The futility of it all was haunting. All that effort, to be left with nothing but guilt and uncertainty. What, I wondered, was a human life worth?

I left Port-au-Prince ten days after I arrived. Brett and I were loaded onto a bus at the Canadian embassy and driven down one of the city's main boulevards toward the airport. As we passed the statue of three hands, I craned my neck to see the blue gates of the industrial district where Jonatha was likely still living. I didn't have a chance to say good-bye to her.

Most of my fellow passengers were Haitian Canadians, dressed in their Sunday best for the trip. They wore straw hats, flowery sundresses, and suits. We walked in a long line onto the airport tarmac and boarded the giant gray Canadian military plane up its back ramp, as though we were trudging into Moby Dick's open mouth.

Inside, the plane was stripped of all its guts; all that remained was a rim of metal seats along the walls and the cold metal floor on which we all sat, strapped into place by long belts that stretched across many laps before being ratcheted down. Our luggage towered under a net behind us.

The noise of the engine as the plane reversed was tremendous. It sounded, I realized, like an earthquake. The women around me raised their hands over their heads and began to pray and scream. The whites of their eyes flashed. For a moment it seemed like they were reliving the horror of that evening. They were all traumatized.

Before I'd left that morning, I had done a final interview with Gaëlle Delaquis, the Canadian embassy employee coordinating my evacuation. Her nails were immaculate, her high-heeled shoes expensive, and her thick, dark hair pulled into a glossy ponytail. She was the picture of poise; I felt like a slob in my hiking boots and baseball hat.

As we shared a cigarette on the back steps of the embassy, she told me her story of the earthquake. She was driving home from work when the road had transformed into a roiling river. She managed to maneuver the car to her street, where she found every house destroyed except for hers. Her neighbor was on the road screaming hysterically. The woman had just stepped out to buy some lemons, leaving all four of her kids at home, and now they were all buried beneath the remains of her house. Gaëlle rushed to her garden shed to look for tools, but she found only shovels and a "girly hammer." Still, for four days, she and her neighbors dug for the children until their voices stopped calling out. In the end, they pulled out only dismembered arms.

I realized Gaëlle's immaculate appearance was a conscious attempt at control. On the inside, she was a broken mess. Her story, like every other one I'd heard over the past ten days, was intimately raw and emotionally overwhelming. I felt honored she trusted me with it. Each story was an intimate gift. I told myself I had the responsibility to use them well.

Some of my dispatches from Haiti had made the front page of the newspaper. I hadn't missed anything; on the contrary, I'd dug up good stories and delivered them on time. I had always wanted to be a foreign correspondent, and here I had proved to myself and my bosses that I could do it. But that's not what I thought about, sitting on the cold floor of the plane, surrounded by refugees and traumatized survivors returning to their second home in Canada.

After telling me her story, Gaëlle pointed her manicured finger across the grounds of the Canadian embassy to a security guard.

"That woman over there," she said. "She comes here every day smiling in her uniform. She lost her family and is living on the street."

Gaëlle's point was that in the mountain of tragedy that was Haiti right now, she was relatively unscathed. Others had it worse and were bravely holding up the appearance of normality, so Gaëlle tamped down her despair and did the same.

I ripped open my knapsack. Before I had left Toronto for Haiti, I had rushed out to the outdoor equipment store and hastily bought a thin sleeping bag and a tent, in case I couldn't find a hotel room and needed to sleep outside. Both were still sealed in their packages.

I dug both of them out and handed them to Gaëlle.

"Give her these," I said.

I didn't report on that woman's story. In fact, I never spoke to her. So this simple act of kindness was not breaking any journalism credos. But it buoyed me.

I felt, for a brief moment, like I wasn't just a cold tape recorder indifferently capturing the sounds of suffering. I was a member of the human family, reacting with love and kindness.

That thought warmed me on the cold flight home.

Chapter 2

Personal Aftershocks

I stayed in bed for days. I was physically shattered. I had hardly slept in Haiti, but it was the emotional exhaustion that knocked me out upon returning. I felt drugged. I'd wake up at 11:00 a.m., look up at the shards of winter light that had evaded the drapes and slashed across the ceiling of my bedroom, roll over, and sink back into sleep. Sometimes Noah would escape our nanny and clamber upstairs to my room, appearing beside the bed, smiling, his loose curls softly haloing his head. The trip to Haiti had been our longest time apart.

"Mama," he'd say, and I'd pull him under the duvet for a brief cuddle until he got bored and bounded off again in search of a ball or hockey stick or, preferably, both.

When my bladder left me no choice, I counted the seconds it took to swing my legs over the edge and stumble down the hall to the bathroom. Thirty-five was the magic number. That's how long it took to cut off an arm, crush a woman napping after work, smother a whole family. That was how long the earthquake had lasted.

The flight back to Canada had been only three hours, but I was traveling back to another world: one where fifty-story buildings stood impervious to danger, children were bundled up in snowsuits and carried off to drop-in centers, and radio DJs listed their favorite breakfast cereals, not the names of the missing and the dead.

Certain images saturated my foggy brain. A Haitian woman inside a sweltering tent, leaning heavily on a physiotherapist while attempting to stand on her remaining limb for the first time since the earthquake. But instead of her it was my father sitting there helplessly, his powerful right leg a stump, his bulky right arm missing. I imagined his humiliation and loss and fear. How does someone rebuild themselves after losing half their body?

I pictured arriving at my house at dusk to find it standing in a lagoon of rubble, then rushing to my garden shed in search of tools. I would resort to my cell phone for light, too, if the power lines snapped. I imagined hearing the voices of my neighbors' children, and then, slowly, those voices fading to a muffle.

I was haunted—not just by the horrors I had witnessed, but by the fragility and helplessness of life they had exposed. The world I knew ran on purpose and principle. We tell our kids that if you are kind and good and work hard and don't rack up too much debt and don't do drugs, things will turn out all right. Ours is a world with ambulances and socialized medicine and building codes. For the first time I'd seen how indiscriminate and unfair death could be, and I understood that it doesn't matter how much studying you've done late at night or how many charities you've built or lives you've saved: your skull will crack just the same as a serial rapist's. Life was unpredictable, nonnegotiable, and indifferent. In thirty-five seconds the world—for me—had transformed into a scary, cruel place.

My daughter Lyla's fourth birthday was swiftly approaching. I imagined her trapped beneath the bricks of our home, crying and calling for me and her father. How scared she would be in the dark, all alone, and confused that no one was coming to help. How would she pass the time over six long days?

After a week in bed, I returned to work.

The *Toronto Star* was the biggest newspaper in the country. Its newsroom was bigger than a football field, crammed with gray desks buried beneath piles of papers, bulky computers, and dying plants. No matter what time of day, fluorescent lights blinked overhead. When big news was breaking, the floor vibrated with stress and excitement. But on regular mornings, when reporters were out collecting stories and editors had not arrived yet, it was quiet.

I was a social justice columnist, covering issues of women's rights, poverty, hunger, climate change, and mental health. But at heart I remained a reporter. I rarely pontificated from afar; I preferred to see things close-up and in person. I'd usually spend equal time meeting people in the center of a story—illegal immigrant women facing deportation, poor people at food banks, environmentalists in the field—and studying the broader issues in the library, reading reports or talking to experts. I baked my opinions slowly, but once I formed them, I'd go hard.

It was not a place with time or patience for brooding. Editors were always focused on how to fill the next paper and satiate the ravenous Internet. They wanted to know what I was going to file next.

So, I got to it. My first column after returning was about stupid city bureaucracy. I met with the members of an active neighborhood group that had been banned from using a pizza oven they'd built themselves in their local park because of the city's fearful lawyers. It was a good column—tight, energetic, pointed. But, in the wake of where I'd just been, it seemed trivial.

The saving grace: many Canadians were also transfixed by Haiti. As a country, we had donated more to relief efforts after the earthquake than we'd donated to any emergency before: C$154 million over one month. Of that, C$128 million was matched by the government, adding up to C$282 million. That made Canadians the second biggest donors to aid agencies in Haiti, as a country, after the Americans. But when you took our small population into account, we gave the most per person.

Even Canadians who had never heard of or thought about Haiti before were consumed by the horror of what had happened there. The fact that Canada's beloved and dynamic head of state, Michaëlle Jean, had been a Haitian refugee made people feel a connection to the country.

The park activists who led me to their pizza oven asked me about Haiti. So did the women breastfeeding in a clinic that faced closure that I wrote about in my next column. Even the women's shelter residents, who were scared police raids might lead to their deportation, asked me about my trip to Haiti.

They all wanted to know the same things: what I had seen, how people in Haiti were faring, and whether the money they'd sent was helping. I started to begin my interviews unusually—by talking more than listening. I would describe the scenes that played in a loop in my head: the buildings in heaps that were laced with intimate clues of the lives they once cradled; the parks crowded with tents made from bedsheets; and Michele Laporte sleeping curled around Jonatha's trembling body at night. Help was arriving; the country just needed a lot more of it. Invariably, my voice would crack and I would start to cry. I could hardly make it two hours without leaking, which embarrassed me. Reporters are often typecast as hard-shelled and unflappable. I was failing terribly to maintain that image.

A dear friend of mine is a psychiatrist. She explained that talking about what I'd seen, as uncomfortable as it felt, was therapy. If I wasn't having nightmares or anxiety attacks, then I wasn't suffering from post-traumatic stress disorder. I needed to use my own "natural support networks" and heal by talking, she instructed.

So I did. I talked to everyone who asked me about it. Soon I expanded the discussions to groups in my neighborhood.

My family and I were lucky to have a supportive community

around us. Most summer nights, the kids on our street congregated on our tiny front lawn, which offered the only grassy playground. Their parents would sit on our steps and share glasses of wine. Soon after I returned from Haiti, one of those neighbors arrived on my doorstep with a plastic container of homemade cookies and a plan. She had rented out a local church for an evening. Would I do a public talk about Haiti?

It was the first of a number of requests that came in from schools, universities, women's groups. I said yes to all of them. Despite the discomfort I felt at becoming emotional in public, I was relieved. Talking about Haiti released some of the guilt I had carried back with me on that evacuation plane.

When I recounted what I'd seen, I became more than a passive observer of horror. I was an active responder. It allowed me to make a financial difference by donating my honorariums to the charities I'd seen working in Port-au-Prince. But, just as important, I was able to show people that love, as much as money, was needed to save lives.

During my trip, I visited amputees who were being fit for new prosthetic limbs. Inside one silver-domed tent on the grounds of a broken hospital, I found a burly, gray-haired American volunteer with a handlebar moustache playing his harmonica. He was another catastrophe missionary, like Alphonse Edouard. Professionally, this man was a silkscreener and photographer, but he'd come down to Haiti to sing to people.

My first reaction was cynical, just as it had been to the jump-roping New Jersey boy. I dismissed him as well-meaning but naïve. I had assumed that he would do more harm than good—tripping up the real lifesavers, sucking up supplies and space, distracting attention.

But I was learning that there is more than expertise involved in saving lives. I had no doubt that Michele Laporte's cuddles had saved Jonatha. Similarly, in the tent that day, I watched the woman dance in her gurney to his music. Her leg was shattered. She was facing a long, difficult recovery. But, for this moment, she was happy. She raised her hands above her head to clap, and smiled widely.

"When the Lord gets ready," he sang, "you got to move."

I had started out thinking that Good Samaritans got in the way. But people like this man showed me I was wrong. They offered a kind of spiritual medicine.

Near the end of February, I was invited to my local church to speak in place of the Sunday sermon. The minister interviewed me before the congregation. We sat in big, comfy chairs in a pool of crimson light cast by the church's large stained glass window.

The wooden pews below us were packed with people—not just any people, but wealthy, activist-minded people. The United Church has a social justice bent, and this one is located in the heart of Rosedale, Toronto's leafy, old-money neighborhood. Some members of the congregation are so rich, they have heated driveways so that they don't need to shovel after snowstorms. If anyone had the money to help Haiti rebuild, it was the members of his congregation.

My voice remained calm and poised for most of the twenty-four-minute interview. Then, at the end, the minister asked me for advice.

"What should the congregation do for Haiti?" he asked.

I cracked and began to leak again. Because, in truth, I didn't know.

I had done the first part of my job: witnessing death and despair in a disaster zone. But I hadn't done the second part. I knew almost nothing about Haiti's history or politics. I knew little about disaster relief. Sure, I had seen some charities working on the ground, but I hadn't studied them. I didn't feel knowledgeable enough to formally endorse them. I couldn't direct people to Haitian civil society, either: in my time in Haiti, I met only one Haitian NGO, working on women's rights. I had no formal call to action prepared; I had only my own version of a bedsheet spray-painted with SOS.

My crying saved me from having to answer directly.

"I'm not here with answers. This is the way I feel I can help, by talking about Haiti," I told the people packed in pews before me. "This congregation has the brains, the financial means, and the spirit to help, too."

Any journalist would have called my response a dodge. If I was
going to speak about Haiti, I would have to learn more about the
country.

Haitians themselves were only just starting to take stock of the damage and figure out an answer to the question of what they needed.
More than two hundred Haitian bureaucrats, businesspeople, and
politicians, along with an army of international experts, were holed
up with borrowed laptops in a hotel in Pétionville, the upper-class
suburb of Port-au-Prince where I'd stayed with Brett and Lucas.
In mid-March they produced a document with the official title
"Post-Disaster Needs Assessment." Everyone working on it called it
simply "the plan."

It was a clear rush job in desperate need of a good editor—
massive, scattered, in places contradictory and flat-out wrong. There
were 114 pages of charts, bullet points, and figures mixed in with
snippets of history, philosophy, and aspirational plans. It was an early
indication that there were too many cooks in the kitchen of Haiti's
reconstruction.

But it did give the first vague overview of what damage had en-
sued after the earthquake. The worst was the human destruction:
Around 1.3 million people were living in temporary shelters. Many
were in camps in one of the four affected regions, but some 600,000
people had fled to the countryside.

The damage to infrastructure was equally alarming, since much
of the country's population and investment had been crowded in
the capital, close to the earthquake's epicenter. Eighty percent of the
country's university buildings were destroyed, along with one-fifth of
the country's schools. More than half of the country's hospitals were
in the devastated area near or in Port-au-Prince, and most were badly
damaged, including Haiti's largest and only teaching hospital. Haiti's
only international airport and port were badly hit. The presidential
palace, parliament, law courts, and most of the government ministry

buildings were reduced to rubble. Some 105,000 homes were destroyed and double that damaged.

In total, "the plan" estimated 40 million cubic meters of rubble needed to be removed—enough to fill 16,000 Olympic-sized swimming pools.

Then there was the economic damage. Before the earthquake, 80 percent of the country's industry, commerce, and banking were located in the capital. Much of that was now in ruins. "The plan" estimated 8.5 percent of the country's existing jobs would be lost because of the earthquake—and this in a country where one-third of people were officially unemployed.

All of this put together added up to US$7.9 billion lost—"equivalent to 120 percent of the country's GDP in 2009," according to the report.

While the international community seemed to accept all this, a clear sticking point became the death toll. What had started around 40,000 a couple of days after the earthquake was pegged at 170,000 by the Haitian government by the time my evacuation plane took off in February. Not long after my return to Toronto, the official number given by a Haitian minister had climbed to 230,000. By March, the Haitian government was estimating that 300,000 people had died.

A team of researchers financed by the US Agency for International Development (USAID) later concluded the death count was much lower, at most 85,000. But their report was quashed by the agency itself because of "inconsistencies." The United Nations used the figure 220,000 and the Haitian government eventually settled on the curiously exact 316,000.

The truth was, no one really knew because no one had been counting, nor could they. Dump trucks carried the bloated bodies from the overflowing morgue at the city's main broken hospital and trundled them north of the city to a desolate place that had long served as the country's paupers' fields, as well as a dumping ground for political victims of past rulers. It was called Titanyen—a word that made many Haitians shudder. There, the bodies were thrown into giant pits and buried quickly, often before they could even be identified. Community leaders in many neighborhoods also dug mass graves for their own residents, but no one from the central government was overseeing those.

The issue quickly became political: the greater the number of deaths, the greater the call for assistance in rebuilding would be.

What everyone could agree on was that the earthquake's damage was unprecedented. The Inter-American Development Bank called it "the most destructive natural disaster in modern times . . . vastly more destructive than the Indonesian Tsunami of 2004 and the cyclone that hit Myanmar in 2008."

Naturally, such an unprecedented disaster called for an unprecedented international response.

But the plan included only a few concrete recommendations, like constructing six hundred new kilometers of roads. Mostly, it was frothy with first-world dreams: universal health care, universal access to primary school, organic farming, and a decongested capital.

The Haitian government's sister document, called *Action Plan for National Recovery and Development of Haiti: Immediate Key Initiatives for the Future*, was supposed to lay out more specifics. But it was equally detail-anemic.

The earthquake, the document said, would give the country a "fresh start." The country needed to be decentralized, with national airports, ports, hospitals, and industrial parks built outside the capital. It called for a national malnutrition prevention plan and school canteens that would offer students free lunches.

Finally, it requested US$11.5 billion in international donations—part for the eighteen-month emergency phase, and the bulk for the next ten years of reconstruction. Both the redevelopment and the donor money would be overseen by a board made up of Haitians and foreigners representing the donor countries. This was meant to sidestep concerns of corruption and replicate the successful commission that had rebuilt Aceh, Indonesia, after the 2004 tsunami.

"The plan" was released with much fanfare at the end of March

during the International Donors' Conference Towards a New Future
for Haiti, a one-day conference hosted by the United Nations in New
York City. The theme of the conference was a line, coined by former
American president Bill Clinton, who would become the co-chair of
the Reconstruction Commission: "Build Back Better."

The world's leaders and representatives gathered that day did
not disappoint. More than fifty nations and organizations pledged
a total of US$5.3 billion in immediate aid and US$9.9 billion over
ten years. Canada was the third biggest national donor that day, after
Venezuela and the United States, promising US$400 million over two
years. That made Haiti, the Canadian government liked to repeat in
its press releases, "Canada's largest aid beneficiary in the Americas."

Sitting beside United Nations leader Ban Ki-moon in the United
Nations unofficial uniform of a dark suit, Haitian president Préval
thanked the little countries for their little contributions and the big
countries for their big ones alike.

"It's a movement of heart. It's a witness that Haiti is not alone,"
he said in French. "And I say, in the name of Haitian people, 'Thank
you.'"

The night before Lyla's fourth birthday party, she was banging her
pink winter boots mindlessly against a metal shopping cart as we
inspected the aisles of a bulk store for pink jelly beans and purple
Skittles.

The scene was equal parts devotion, overwork, and poor planning. It was already past her bedtime, but she wanted a castle cake,
complete with turrets and standards and pink and purple candied
walls, and I was determined to make it.

As a working mom, I often beat myself up over the time I was not
spending with my kids. However proud I was of my mom's career
as a book publisher, I remembered resenting all the volleyball games
and swim meets she had missed because she was at work. I was determined to avoid doing the same thing, which meant I was often

haggard, bitching at a subway delay or arriving sweaty and panting at a dance recital. It was why I was making a birthday cake from scratch, instead of just buying one.

My trip to Haiti had intensified my guilt. I now missed Lyla and Noah even when we were together. I jumped into the bath with them at night, where we played crabs with our hands until the bubbles had long dissolved and the water had grown cool, and I crept into their bedrooms at night to breathe in their smell while they were sleeping. Had Jonatha's parents kissed her in the hour before the earthquake? Every moment suddenly felt painfully important. I started to work from home a couple of times a week—typing on my bed, since my office doubled as their playroom in the basement—so I could sit with my kids at lunch and hear them playing around the house.

We took a vacation to Florida with much of our extended family. I had brought novels with me but I hardly opened one that trip, spending the time instead laughing at things my kids did. At one point Lyla walked right into a wedding ceremony on the beach, stationing herself a few feet behind the bride and groom so she could hear every word. The couple was too polite to shoo her away, and finally I composed myself enough to casually pull her aside. I figured that enough of the couple's wedding photos would include my daughter in her big yellow floppy sun hat and bathing suit.

But even as I fell deeper in love with my precious family, my longing to return to Haiti grew stronger. I craved the adrenaline of a day's work there: the unpredictability of what would happen, the detours, the surprising discoveries, the rawness, the extreme emotions.

My conscience pulled me back, too. I felt a responsibility to the people I had met in those tumultuous weeks after the earthquake— people who had trusted me as a messenger to the world with their bruising stories. To them, I was likely just another *blan*—foreigner— who appeared briefly in the fog of their sorrow. But I relived their stories in my mind every day.

What had happened to Paulette Paul, the woman I had met in the food line? What about Jony St. Louis, the physiotherapist who had rescued his wife, only to watch her die three days later? And what of Jonatha? Who—if anybody—was taking care of her now? Was she still living under a tarp in a field with fifty other orphaned children?

As impotent as I felt, an outsider looking in, I was compelled to bear witness again. So, on April 13, three months and one day after the earthquake, I found myself heading down to Port-au-Prince on another Air Canada plane—this one a regular commercial flight.

I felt calmer this time. I'd done my homework, grooming the Web for news on Haiti's reconstruction and digging into the library and bookshops. I was better equipped and understood more about what I was getting myself into. At least, that was what I told myself.

Chapter 3

Building Back Better

Pure joy greeted me through the metal gates of Fleurs de Chou primary school. Hundreds of little girls dressed in beige tartan tunics were bouncing in their black Mary Janes like squash balls, singing at the top of their voices. "*Regardez! Regardez!*"—"Look! Look!" they sang, louder and louder and louder, until the noise filled up all the space in my lungs and rattled my rib cage. They were dressed immaculately, as though they were heading to the theater for the afternoon—hair oiled, braided, and neatly pulled into pigtails, which were tied up like presents with floppy white ribbons that matched their lacy socks.

"*Regardez! Regardez!*" The girls' bows flapped up and down while they bounced to the song.

I was definitely looking, mouth ajar. It was too much to take in—the joy, the noise, the shell of a building. The only thing left of Fleurs de Chou was the exterior walls. The rest had been destroyed in the earthquake and carted away. The children were singing from behind rows of wooden desks set out in an empty courtyard. Their only shelter was some white canvas screens donated by Plan International—a large global development organization that had brought me here, presumably to show Canadians where their donations were going. I wondered if the singing and dancing had been staged for me.

But then, after the song subsided, a teacher stood up in front of the crowd with her back to me, raised her hands, and *boom*, they started again—a new song, more dancing, hundreds of little arms waving and waists twirling.

Haitians didn't need to fake their emotions from the earthquake; they were raw and huge and personal, indifferent to outsiders. This was what true happiness looked like. The reason the kids were so happy would seem surprising to many Canadian children: they were back in school.

The mood of the entire city had reversed since I left two months before. Instead of being tinged with despair, Port-au-Prince felt like a bubbling cauldron of optimism and industry. I spotted the change minutes after stepping off the plane. The airport was operating! My first arrival, when I finally found the building in the dark, I almost tripped over the sleeping customs officer, who was curled against a long wooden desk that blocked the entrance of the arrivals hallway like a river dam.

Now there was a band of troubadours inside a wooden arrivals hall, where three customs officers sat in freshly built plywood boxes, waiting to stamp passports.

On the streets outside, the SOS sheets had been replaced with colorful canvases: bold, African-style paintings of market women, hung up on walls and fences like makeshift galleries. The most telling sign of life returning, though, was kids in uniforms and backpacks walking along the edges of the streets en route to school. The government had restarted the school term that week, and many schools had reopened in fields under tarps and on the cleared footprint of their former selves.

Fleurs de Chou was the first I visited. It had been a massive primary school in the nearby town of Croix-des-Bouquets. Before the earthquake, it housed 1,500 students in two adjacent two-story buildings. One was *kraze* by the earthquake, as the Haitians said. Smashed. The other was still standing but badly cracked. Luckily, the school hadn't been offering night courses to students, so the building had been empty when it collapsed.

This was the second day of classes, which principal Marie Florvie Dorestan admitted would be just songs and games for the first week.

She had written to the mayor's office asking for help to rebuild her school. But, after weeks of waiting and hearing nothing, she had decided to do it herself. She sacrificed her savings and borrowed money to hire a forty-person crew to remove the rubble and salvage what furniture and equipment wasn't destroyed.

"The kids were just walking around the neighborhood. They told me they wanted to come back to school. Their parents wanted them back at school," Marie said in Kreyòl.

Many of her students would no longer be able to pay their monthly tuition fees: they were living in tents; their parents had lost their jobs or means of working. It was unlikely Marie would be able to pay their teachers—at least, not without going more into debt.

The government had promised to compensate principals like Marie, but she doubted that would ever happen. Fleurs de Chou, like 85 percent of the schools in Haiti, was private. The government barely managed to pay the principals and teachers at the public schools at the best of times. Now they had bigger problems.

But Marie worked anyway.

"I'm helping my country in the way I can," she said.

It was her contribution to Haiti's recovery.

The city was awash in help: aid workers, university volunteers, American missionaries in matching T-shirts that said things like *Help Haiti* and *Mission Haiti*. Once in the city, you could spot them from afar, for everyone seemed to have rented the same white SUVs—the symbol in Haiti for white aid workers and wealth. The few hotels still functioning were filled with them.

I hadn't expected this and had foolishly left my hotel booking until the week before. What tourist in their right mind would be visiting the ruins of Port-au-Prince? I called every hotel I knew about in town, but none had space for me. One receptionist told me the rooms had been blocked off for the entire month by an aid group. I hadn't appreciated how lucky we'd been on the last trip to secure a hotel room.

Out of desperation, I emailed a Canadian doctor who had been traveling to Haiti for ten years. She directed me to a guesthouse run by her organization, Healing Hands for Haiti, a nonprofit that worked with amputees and other disabled and injured Haitians. While the organization's workshop was damaged, its guesthouse survived the earthquake and the grounds were beautiful—lush, crowded with pawpaw and mango trees—and there were two resident chickens, Mark and Emily, that scooted through the antique house and outdoor patios.

I dropped my bag in the room I would be sharing with four other people and jumped back into the car, hoping to get a tour of downtown before sundown, which in Haiti comes like a falling blind. But just outside the guesthouse gates I was introduced to another sign of Haiti's rousing life and aid influx: *blokis*. The perfect Kreyòl word for gridlock. Traffic in the city had been bad before the earthquake—the result of stuffing 3 million people into a place built for fewer than 1 million without expanding the road system. But the growing mounds of rubble that house and business owners were sweeping onto the roads had made things infinitely worse. The two-lane Avenue John Brown that weaved past the guesthouse was choked with cars and packed *tap-taps*—Haiti's version of buses, effectively pickup trucks with benches thrown down the back and metal awnings painted brightly and decorated with hopeful mottos like *Jesus watch over us*.

I wouldn't make it downtown and back in two hours, let alone see other parts of the city. So I shortened the tour to a single stop: the nine-hole Pétionville golf course ten minutes up the road.

Before the earthquake, the golf course had been the playground of the country's rich elite. It was the only one in the country, set among large barricaded properties, their walls dripping with bougainvillea and guarded by men with shotguns. Overlooking the golf course were a clubhouse, where members came after work for a drink, and tennis courts. This was the other Haiti—the one of comfort and culture and American Ivy League education.

The evening of the earthquake, thousands of survivors escaped from their crowded, *kraze* neighborhoods and came here—a place they deemed safe because of its open space. There were no lethal buildings nearby, no poorly constructed walls that could fall down and crush you in one of the many aftershocks.

I had visited the golf course many times on my first trip to Haiti. The unplanned camp was a study in group dynamics under extreme stress: men lying prone and blank-eyed; women bathing their pot-bellied children in the now fetid brook; a small hospital; and three church services a night, with hundreds of people waving their hands in the air and singing. It was a reporter's treasure chest, bursting with stories of personal tragedy and triumph.

Two months later I walked over the hill from the golf course clubhouse and arrived to a town the size of a healthy Ontario suburb. Some 60,000 people were living there in homes built out of blue and orange plastic tarps. Many had been upgraded into miniature sheds using scraps of corrugated metal. Some, I noticed, even had wooden doors with padlocks. There was a veritable sea of them, clumped shoulder to shoulder as far as I could see.

The rivulet paths that once wove between and through tents were now planned, bustling thoroughfares lined by sandbags. A main road was now lined with *timachann*, or market vendors, who wore giant straw hats and sat on stools behind their wares—charcoal, fish, coconuts, padlocks. Small *boutiks*—stores made from wooden shelters selling radios and cell phones—had been erected, too. Down the center of the road, a man pushed a cart topped by a giant block of ice that, for a few Haitian gourdes, he shaved into a paper cone and doused with whatever sweet syrup you wanted from his collection of bottles.

There were barbershops with swivel chairs and saloon mirrors, beauty parlors offering hair extensions, and even small restaurants with lace tablecloths and flickering televisions powered with stolen electricity from nearby lines. I peeked through a crack in the door of Cine Paw, a makeshift movie theater that charged 10 gourdes (24 cents US) for a seat to every night's screening.

Signs of help were everywhere, too. The hospital at the crest of the hill had grown. It now had an X-ray center and a dental clinic. It had been joined by another four health clinics below. I walked by a little primary school set up under a tarp, complete with blackboards and yellow and red wicker chairs. Sanitation crews pushed wheelbarrows full of garbage up the paths. There were Porta-Potties and water spigots attached to giant water bladders.

Staked into the ground were the names of large international aid groups. They served as both street addresses and rudimentary advertisements telling passersby—particularly those with cameras—that the silver "baby-friendly tents" came from Save the Children or that the giant bladders of water and Porta-Potties were from Oxfam. All the silver and white tarps that the American director of relief had talked about were prominently stamped with either USAID for the American aid arm or simply *Canada*.

Not all the aid groups were so well established and internationally known, though. I met a wiry, bearded, ginger-haired man who introduced himself as Captain Barry. He was an American tugboat captain who had come here to help with a newly formed humanitarian organization named J/P HRO. Few in their group had experience, he admitted, but they were managing the camp.

While we were talking, Sean Penn, the Hollywood actor, walked by. He was wearing army pants and the same blue shirt as Captain Barry. I was stunned. What was Sean Penn doing here, in the middle of the country's biggest displaced person camp? He wasn't surrounded by handlers or bodyguards or cameramen—he was alone. I watched as he joined a group of people handing out mattresses to a crowd.

"Penn started the organization," Barry explained. The letters in the group's name stood for Jenkins-Penn Haiti Relief Organization. Penn, it turned out, was a catastrophe missionary who had been moved by the post-earthquake newscasts about rudimentary anesthetic-free surgeries, particularly because his own son had recently recovered from brain surgery.

Penn's friend offered to help him start up a charity. He then chartered a plane with supplies and assembled a team of doctors and other volunteers. They all ended up here, on the golf course, living in tents on the tennis courts.

The light was fading. I had to go. My last glimpse of the golf course city was of Sean Penn wading into a fight over a mattress. I watched incredulously as he stepped between two arguing men, his hands raised.

Jonatha was never far from my thoughts during all of this. As soon as I had a spare moment, I set off in search of her. I returned to the Sonapi compound, but when I pulled through the gates, I was greeted by an empty parking lot. There was no sign of the clinic—no tents, no medical equipment, no patients—just a single uniformed guard asleep in a chair. He jolted awake but was of no help. The temporary clinic was gone, he confirmed. But he didn't know where it had moved or who might know. It was as if I had dreamed it all up.

I set off for the United Nations compound, hoping that the UNICEF office would have a record of Jonatha. The communications person I had spoken to on my last trip was long gone. In fact, nearly all the aid workers I'd met in January had left. Aid workers generally rotate in two-month shifts in emergencies so they don't burn out, I learned, which meant the few contacts I had made months before were of no use.

When I found the head child protection officer, she told me that out of the more than 750 children the agency had registered as "un-accompanied," only 75 were reunited with their families. She didn't know if Jonatha was among them.

Haiti did not have a formal system of foster care or children's aid. Poor parents from the country sometimes send their children to relatives or friends of relatives in the big city, hoping they will enroll them in school. In return, the children are expected to work as domestics, cleaning and cooking for the family. They are called *restavèks*, which literally translates to "stay withs." *Restavèks* were notoriously abused. I hoped Jonatha was not among them now.

I decided to walk around and see if I could glean any useful information or story leads. Reporting work often seems like deep-sea fishing. You cast out a bunch of hooks in hopes that a few will snag something.

While one part of the compound felt like an internally displaced persons' camp, a whole other established part resembled a small university campus, with paved roads and treed walkways curving between white low-slung buildings, each with their own plaque—UNDP, UNFEMME, OCHA, IOM. I learned that every morning the different departments got together for a press conference. That seemed like a good place to start.

When I think back on that press conference, I shake my head at its obvious symbolism. First, there were only a handful of reporters there, and those who were assembled were all foreigners. But, more importantly, all the speakers delivering updates were foreigners, communication attachés from various arms of the United Nations. Not a single one was Haitian. And they conducted the news conference in English, a language that few Haitians outside the foreign-educated elite could speak. The press conference could have just as easily taken place in Bath or Regina or some small town in New Hampshire.

Haitian development workers and community leaders, it turned out, had a hard time getting into the heavily guarded United Nations compound by the airport. While I was immediately waved in with my press badge, grassroots community leaders and humanitarians with local NGOs complained they weren't told about the meetings, didn't have the proper ID passes to get in, or couldn't spare the time to travel through the city's *blokis* to make it to the United Nations compound. That meant they weren't participating in the vital "cluster meetings" where aid organizations shared information and, in theory, coordinated their actions. There was the protection cluster, the education cluster, and the "wash" cluster, which was aidspeak for water and sanitation.

Already it was becoming clear that despite the government's appeal for assistance and their hand in writing the recovery plan, the execution of aid and recovery was being led by foreigners.

At the press conference, I learned that the looming crisis of the moment was the pending rainy season. Many areas of the city were at great risk of flash floods, which threatened to sweep away earthquake survivors in their ramshackle homes. Over the next few days, UN organizations would be moving 2,500 people to new temporary homes in planned camps. The next move was in two days, from the Vallée de Bourdon. I took down the directions to the community—go up Avenue John Brown, turn on Rue Garnier, head down to the bottom of the valley, and then walk along the river—and immediately set off.

Jefferson, the driver I'd hired in January, had gone back to his full-time job driving for the Canadian embassy. He'd sent me a friend of his, Jean, to both drive and translate. Jean's only qualification for the job was his command of English, which he spoke with a Washington, DC, slang. He was a deportee—a Haitian who had spent many years living and working illegally in the United States until he was pulled over for a small traffic violation and promptly arrested. He told long stories about his time in prison with other illegal workers from around the world, all waiting to be sent back to their home countries. He'd borrowed one of Jefferson's cars, and it was clear, once we started driving around, that his grasp of Port-au-Prince geography was barely better than mine.

Thankfully, Rue Garnier was marked with a street sign—one of a precious few I had spotted in Port-au-Prince. It was a steep switch-back dotted with massive potholes that stopped abruptly at the foot of a forest.

We got out of the car and followed a worn path beside a thin stream, through a mango grove, and past a group of topless women washing themselves and their laundry. A giant black pig waddled by, ruffling through mounds of old plastic bags and pop cans. Garbage collection is spotty, especially in the poor neighborhoods, so ravines are unofficial dump sites in the city.

When the path ended, Jean and I walked through the stream in our flip-flops. Finally, the *bidonvil* appeared.

Bidonvils are Haitian slums. They are scattered throughout the city, atop hills and deep in valleys. They universally feature tightly packed, boxlike concrete houses, separated only by footpaths. You can rarely drive through a *bidonvil*; you have to walk, and often—like here—the path will squeeze so tightly between ramshackle houses that you need to swivel your shoulders and sidestep through them. These are what Haitian planners call "archaic developments"—full of the poor who moved to the city from the countryside in search of jobs and who have rented some unused land to build a small house on.

"*Blan! Blan!*" kids screamed after me as we made our way down the path through the community.

We walked past the shells of tiny one-room homes that had been re-duced to jumbled concrete platforms. Tarps were strung up and metal siding hammered together to form slapdash walls. Stairs led up into the air: all of the second stories had collapsed. I snapped a photo of a man standing knee-deep in rubble, a metal cup in one hand and a toothbrush in the other. He reminded me of a heron standing in a lagoon.

The path ended at the river, which was wider and deeper here. I approached a house ringed by plants in old tomato tins and knocked at the gate.

An artist with thick black-rimmed glasses emerged to talk to me. Just as he began to tell his story about moving, I felt a hot rush in my bowels.

I had to go to the bathroom. Right then.

This panicked moment will be familiar to many backpackers. It's your body's warning signal that you have eaten something your weak, antiseptic digestive system cannot process, and it's about to open all the emergency latches, forcing you to spend hours or days in the bathroom until your system is completely flushed and clear again. I had minutes to reach a toilet. Otherwise I would shit my pants.

Sweat pooled at my temples, along my hairline, at the back of my neck. The artist continued to talk, but it was like I was watching him from underwater. I had stopped listening. My rabid-dog mind raced around, sniffing out possibilities: Should I ask to use his toilet? It would likely just be a hole in the ground; could I bear to crouch over it for twenty minutes and then face him again? I thought about running back up the stream and trying to find a quiet pocket of the forest. No, I couldn't do that, either. Was there a school nearby that would have real flushing toilets, and would they let me in?

My eyes were casting about when two people from the Healing Hands guesthouse appeared directly across the stream from me. I felt like a shipwreck survivor who had just been tossed a lifeline. I excused myself, waded across the stream, and climbed up the bank and into the guesthouse's forested grounds.

I had traveled an hour by car and foot from my guesthouse only to arrive a few meters away. This was the universe's way of teaching me how much I had to learn, not just about the workings of aid, but about Haiti.

It was also an act of grace. I made it to my shared bathroom just in time.

The next day, I set out in search of Corail-Cesselesse, a new planned settlement about twenty kilometers north of Port-au-Prince. We took the two-lane Route Nationale 1 out of the city, cutting through the shacks of Cité Soleil until they were outnumbered by banana trees. As Jean and I drove into dusty scrubland of Haiti's central plateau, dotted with long-fingered cacti reaching from the ground like claws, we passed two kids riding a donkey bareback. We had shed the congestion of the city for a bare, forlorn, windswept desert. There were hardly any houses here.

We saw the new settlement from the distance: row after row of glaring white tents in the shape of half barrels set out on the flat ground without any trees or posts between them. It looked like a bomb-testing site in New Mexico.

We found the camp manager writing on whiteboards under a large tarp. "You have good timing," he said. "The president is on his way here now."

Sure enough, about a half hour later, I watched a line of beige armored vehicles snake their way up the dirt road, spilling clouds of dust and startling a group of donkeys. Behind them came a convoy of Land Rovers with tinted windows.

Out of one, as promised, stepped René Préval, the Haitian president, in a dress shirt and suit pants. Out of another emerged Sean Penn. He looked like he'd been backpacking around India for a year, with a T-shirt, khakis, baseball hat, and aviator sunglasses. Finally, out came Edmond Mulet, the head of the United Nations in Haiti.

Haitian reporters I had not noticed before appeared instantly with their television cameras and tape recorders, huddling around the men, who delivered impromptu speeches.

The UN chief called the new neighborhood "an example for the rest of the world." Pulling his hat off to expose a bad henna treatment that had turned his hair red, Sean Penn proclaimed, "We see very tangibly the beginning of something that could be real hope in Haiti."

President Préval was much less celebratory. He perhaps knew what locals were already saying about the camp: that it was a set on a baking desert in the middle of nowhere. "We are doing our best. You have to be patient," he said into the raised microphones. It had been two years since Hurricane Katrina destroyed much of New Orleans, and rebuilding had yet to really begin there, he pointed out. "It's not that easy to create good conditions right away. . . .

If it's difficult for countries that are richer than us, it's going to be more difficult for us."

With that, the president set off for a tour, surrounded by dozens of fawning followers and television cameras. Sean Penn trailed behind, not one camera or microphone before him. He was anonymous here, just another *blan* come to help. I found myself walking beside a tall, thin, bespectacled man who turned out to be a fellow Canadian. He introduced himself as Nigel Fisher and told me he had recently been seconded from UNICEF Canada to come here and help conduct the post-disaster needs assessment. Our meeting was a stroke of luck: less than two weeks later, Nigel was named the country's top humanitarian—Haiti's deputy special representative for the United Nations, in charge of all their projects as well as coordinating the thousands of foreign nongovernment groups and the plans to strengthen the Haitian government.

In journalistic parlance, he was a killer source.

I managed to jot down his phone number and email address before my third lucky break of the afternoon arrived in the form of a distant figure. I peered at him, wondering if my eyes were mistaken. No, it really was him! Jony St. Louis! I ran toward him, shouting his name, and wrapped him in an unexpected hug.

I wouldn't say he was unhappy to see me. But he was surprised. I'd been carrying his haunting story with me every day for two months like worry beads, remembering his wife trapped on her bed and the heroics of his neighborhood soccer team. At the same time he'd been focusing his energy on survival. He hadn't given our conversation that day a second thought.

Still, it felt wonderful to close this one loop. His two children were living with a relative in the countryside. He was involved with a circle of local medical interns who met regularly to talk about the earthquake, and that was helping. And he'd landed a new job with World Vision, the largest NGO in the world. He was in Corail-Cesselesse researching what programs the organization might run there.

The plans for Corail-Cesselesse were fantastic on paper. They included elementary schools, community gardens and kitchens, and three health centers. In a few months the tents would be replaced by T-shelters, the buzzword among aid workers for transitional homes. Made of cement fiberboard and corrugated metal, they were intended to last about a decade, until more permanent housing could be built. There was even the promise of factory jobs from a new industrial park slated to open nearby.

An hour or so later, after the president's SUV doors had slammed shut and his entourage had pulled away in a cloud of dust, I was quietly interviewing a family at the entrance to their sweltering tent, when Sean Penn appeared before me.

"Can I get your help?" he asked.

My help? Really? I had asked the Hollywood actor for an interview earlier and he'd sloughed me off. Now he was back, but not for me. He wanted Jean to translate something for him into Kreyòl.

Penn stayed behind to inspect the new camp, without any security guards or hangers-on. Most of the people moving to Corail-Cesselesse were coming from the Pétionville golf course camp, which he was managing, and he wanted to make sure that this camp was all that he was promising them. He led Jean and me to another tent and pointed to a tarp attaching it to the next. "This is not safe," he said. "If a fire starts in one tent, it could spread to the other." Jean dutifully translated this to the tent's new occupant, a young man sitting on a set of stereo speakers who looked up at us quizzically.

So I got the chance to interview Sean Penn after all. Haiti, for him, was not just a cry of the heart. It offered him liberty. I typed my story for the next day's newspaper on the drive back to the city.

Later that week, I got a call from the child services agent working on Jonatha's case. What he told me was so incredible and confusing, I asked him to repeat it a couple of times. I hadn't misheard: the little girl had been reunited with her parents. She was living with them up in the mountains southeast of the city.

I was dumbfounded. Everyone at that clinic a couple of months ago had been so sure Jonatha was orphaned, and I'd believed it, too. Plus, the girl I'd met was named Jonatha, but the agent kept referring to her as "Lovely." I suspected we had our little girls mixed up.

The agent agreed to take me to her. She was living in Fermathe, a town up in the mountains famous for a fort built by revolutionary Alexandre Pétion soon after Haiti's independence two hundred years ago. As Jean drove me up the twisting two-lane highway, each turn seemed to confirm my suspicion that we were heading toward somebody else's happy ending. It felt like we had crossed the border into a whole new country. The air was cool and fresh, not humid and tinged with exhaust and burning garbage, and the road was shaded by trees. The houses grew more and more enormous, each of them decorated with satellite dishes. Jean pointed out President Préval's walled mansion on the side of the road. As we climbed higher, the flashes of countryside were strikingly beautiful—vibrant green in patches, descending steeply down the mountainsides. How was it possible that Jonatha, a little girl who was malnourished, came from this kind of wealth?

We left the main paved road for a treacherous rocky path, where a whole other Haiti came into view—one that seemed frozen in time from the 1930s. Little kids without shoes pushed bike tires down the edge of the road, and farmers looked up from thin patches of corn they were digging at with scythes. There were cows tethered to trees and chickens racing along the edges of the road.

We pulled up to a small stone house with a veranda bordered by a neat trim of purple flowers. But instead of taking us inside, the agent led us down a little gravel path that skirted around the house. There, we came to a tin shed wrapped in a USAID tarp, just like the ones that had been erected around the golf course. I stepped into the muddy yard and there she was: the little girl from Sonapi, the girl I knew as Jonatha, her hard, suspicious eyes peeking at me from behind the legs of a small woman. It was really her!

Her mother, Rosemene, kissed both of my cheeks. On her hip

she was carrying a large toddler. She introduced him as Jonathan. *Jonatha*.

The realization hit me: aid workers assumed this little girl was saying her own name. In fact, she had been calling for her little brother. Her name was Lovely.

Some plastic chairs were pulled out and we sat in the dirt yard in the shade of a banana tree. I took Rosemene in: she was thin but strong, with a beautiful broad face and wide apple cheekbones. Her voice was high and she spoke rapidly, words spilling out of her joyously like a burbling brook. The love she had for her children was palpable. She bounced Jonathan on her knee and Lovely leaned into her lap as Rosemene told me the story I was desperate to hear.

The family came from Fort National—a downtown *bidonvil* close to the National Palace. The afternoon of the earthquake, Rosemene was nursing a stomachache at home with her kids while her husband, Enel, was out working, selling sugarcane from a wheelbarrow. Rosemene dropped Lovely off next door to watch cartoons with her best friend, Gaëlle, and then she lay down with Jonathan. They were roused by the sound of a large truck passing by. It was the *goudougoudou*—the new onomatopoeic word Haitians had created for the earthquake. The ground below Rosemene bucked and she was pitched to her knees. Dust clouded her eyes. She managed to get up, grab Jonathan, and rush outside just before the building collapsed.

Her neighbor's two-story home, where Lovely had been watching television, had crumbled.

Hysterical, Rosemene joined the throngs of people coursing through the streets, frantically searching for loved ones, all to the soundtrack of wailing, calls to Jesus, and screams for help. With Jonathan on her hip, Rosemene added her voice, shouting for her husband, Enel. She found him on a road before the sunken National Palace. It was dark by then and they settled among the thousands who crowded into Champs de Mars for the night. The next day they came here, to Fermathe, where Rosemene's sister, Rosita, lived with her husband, a lanky farmer named Delius Elistin—like many Haitians, he went by his last name—and their two children, an adopted daughter, Sophonie, and a son, Lypse.

For days Enel stayed down in the city, walking around the rubble of their old home, straining futilely for any sound or sign of Lovely. They thought she had died, and Rosemene spent her time weeping and praying. Then, six days after the earthquake, a neighbor called to say Lovely had been dug out. She was alive! The word was she'd been taken to a hospital, but no one knew which, so over the next couple of weeks Enel and Elistin descended into the city daily, checking at hospitals, embassies, and radio stations for word or sign of her. But there were hundreds of little medical clinics opened around the broken city at the time. The chances of finding their girl were slim.

It was thanks to Haiti's incredibly effective system of spreading news that Lovely was located. Almost everyone in the city had a cell phone, which it seemed they never turned off, answering calls in the middle of the night because that was how they got crucial alerts, be it about an approaching riot or the chance at a job. Sure enough, a neighbor called Rosemene to say he'd been to a clinic at Sonapi near the *Trois Mains*, where he'd seen Lovely.

Early the next morning Rosemene boarded a crowded *tap-tap*, nervously descending the mountain, wondering if her neighbor was wrong and her heart would be broken again.

When she finally pushed through the blue metal gates of the industrial zone and found the makeshift medical clinic out on the cobblestones, there was her daughter, surrounded by a group of *blans*. Lovely looked up at her, pointed, and told the woman who was carrying her, "Look, there's my *manman*."

Rosemene was overcome with relief and joy. She waved her arms in the air, calling, "Glory to God."

The *blans* at the clinic wouldn't let her take Lovely home, though. They wanted proof Rosemene was truly the child's mother. So Enel went back to their childhood homes near Jacmel to look for baby photos of Lovely, while Rosemene traveled back and forth to the clinic each day, riding three separate *tap-taps*, to see her daughter and hold her. The child services agent planned to do a DNA test, but after a few visits watching the two of them together, it became clear they were mother and daughter. He signed the papers and considered the case his most unlikely success.

"We were lucky because Rosemene found us herself," he said.

While we spoke, Lovely danced around the yard, returning time and time again to kiss Jonathan, who was a large, chubby baby. She chirped a song about a little baby drinking milk from his bottle and tickled her brother, who squirmed, smiling. It was the most playful I had ever seen her. Then she climbed onto my lap and took the pen I'd been writing notes with out of my hand. She began to scratch lines on my reporter's notepad.

"*Gade!*" she announced. "Look! I'm doing something. I'm drawing. *Gade! Gade!*" When Rosemene reached to pull her away, Lovely's little brow furrowed and she swatted her mother, shouting, "Get out of here. I'm writing!"

She wasn't cute, but she was endearing, and there was something special about her. It was her iron core. Her friend Gaëlle had died, Rosemene said, along with Gaëlle's grandmother. Lovely must have watched them perish or seen their unresponsive bodies nearby. I wonder how her two-year-old brain had processed it all.

"Does Lovely talk about the earthquake?" I asked Rosemene.

"Yes, *anpil*—a lot," she said. "She says she was under the concrete for so long. And someone helped her, bringing her food and water."

Who was that?

Rosemene leaned toward me from her perch and said, with her light chirpy voice, "It was her guardian spirit." That's how Lovely survived unscathed six days under the rubble while thousands of people died from blood loss, toxic shock, and dehydration.

I do not believe in guardian spirits or divine intervention. But the explanation didn't seem ridiculous. My logical mind could not explain the fact that this two-year-old survived many days longer than was medically possible. Something had kept her alive.

Before I left, Rosemene scooped up Jonathan and placed him on my lap beside Lovely for a photo. While Jean snapped the picture, Rosemene snuck behind him and popped out on either side to wave and make her children smile—just like I did with my kids. In fact, I could see my own family in them. I had two children, about the same ages as Lovely and Jonathan, and if something terrible happened to me and my husband, the first person we'd turn to was my sister.

On my way down the mountain to the broken city below, I ruminated over Lovely's story. Just that morning I had interviewed a midwife downtown. She'd arrived late and seemed scattered, unable to answer my questions, until she abruptly apologized and explained that she'd lost her husband and two children in the earthquake and had not been able to concentrate since then.

Lovely and her family were so very lucky; they'd survived hell. But they were now living in misery. I poked my head into the dark, crudely built shed where they slept. It was a dismal scene: two cots and a mattress on the dirt floor. Eight of them slept there at night: not just Lovely's nuclear family—Rosemene, Enel, and Jonathan—but her aunt, Rosita, her uncle, Elistin, and her cousins, Sophonie and Lypse, as well. When it rained—which it did often during the rainy season—a river coursed through the bottom of the shed, forcing them all to stand. I couldn't imagine living like that. It wasn't a life; it was survival.

Before the earthquake, Rosemene worked as a *timachann*, selling small packets of spaghetti and bouillon cubes from baskets on the side of the road. She couldn't read or write, nor could Enel. They had both left school after just a couple of years. But Rosemene had dreams for Lovely. Her daughter's friend, Gaëlle, had been two years older than her, and she'd attended school regularly. She was the one who taught Lovely how to hold a pen and "write" her lessons. Rosemene had planned to send Lovely to school, and for two months before the earthquake she tucked money into a can each day to go toward that. The can was long gone, with all their other possessions and dreams.

Rosemene told me one other thing. On April 27, Lovely would turn three. They weren't planning a celebration, because, as she put it, "*pa gen kòb*." It was a refrain I'd heard often: *I don't have money.*

My family recently celebrated my son Noah's second birthday in Florida with presents and cake. It seemed to me Lovely should have that, too. A loose plan began to form in my mind. My plane ride out of Haiti was April 28. I would take a day off on Lovely's birthday and drive a party up to her shed. Maybe I could offer another surprise present, one that would make Rosemene happy: a year's school tuition. How much could that possibly cost?

A number of readers contacted me with the same idea, responding to my regular columns about Haiti in the *Star* with offers to send money to enroll Lovely in school. As I thought more about my plan over the next day, I augmented my original idea. Lovely hadn't been the only girl in her little compound. There was her eight-year-old cousin, Sophonie, and her four-year-old neighbor, Jenanine. If I was going to pay for Lovely's school, I surely should pay for their tuition, too; that seemed only fair. Otherwise, we might sow jealousy and create more problems than we solved. I also felt we should help Rosemene get her small business going again so she could support her family and start saving money in a new tin can.

I'd volunteered with a development agency for a year in northern India before I was married, and the concept of providing people with livelihoods rather than things had been drilled into me. I wrote an email to the readers who'd contacted me, proposing that we pay the girls' tuition for two years and give Rosemene US$100 a month for six months—long enough, I figured, to get her grounded and going again. They all wrote back in agreement.

On Lovely's birthday, my last day in Port-au-Prince, Jean took me on a morning shopping spree around Pétionville. We inched our way through the clogged streets to visit a half-empty toy store where I bought dolls and a soccer ball, a bookstore where I got pens and some notebooks, the grocery store for cookies and juice, and a bakery, where I purchased a cake.

When we arrived at Lovely's home, she and her family were

waiting for us. Enel was there, too—thin, shy, and very young look-ing. He was, in fact, more than five years younger than Rosemene. He had taken a day off the job he'd found, clearing rubble from a yard down in Port-au-Prince, for the special occasion. They wanted to reg-ister the kids in school first and party later. So all of us crowded into the car and we bounced back down the same dirt road past a small cemetery to stop before a simple elementary school hidden behind a wall. The classrooms were set around a concrete yard with a naked basketball hoop and a flagpole. Peering through the screen windows, I saw kids in uniforms sitting in long rows at desks, student art taped to the stone walls, and teachers standing at blackboards, leading les-sons.

This was a school run by the Baptist Haiti Mission. The tuition was subsidized by the church, but, even so, many families were not able to pay the reduced fee for their children—including Sophonie, the principal informed me. I pulled out my money belt and paid her outstanding bill, as well as next year's fees.

Waiting in the courtyard, Rosemene shook her head adamantly when I told her I would happily enroll Lovely there, too. Rosemene had her heart set on a different school. We all piled back into the car and slowly bumped up the rutted road, the kids bouncing like pop-corn in the back seat. Farther up the mountain, we turned down a thin road that snaked between houses and a field of corn and stopped abruptly at a maroon gate.

The school didn't look like a school in the Western sense. It was a large house with a big parking pad. There was no playground equip-ment, but the walls were decorated with cartoon characters. A group of kindergarten children sat on small wicker chairs in the courtyard, where their teacher led them in a song about *cochons*—French for pigs. The little girls were wearing red tunics and many had white bows and plastic barrettes in their hair. The boys wore tartan red shirts and red shorts.

The administration office was at the end of the courtyard under a heavy concrete overhang. There we met the *directrice*, a round woman with painted nails, a starched white dress shirt, and a firm handshake. She took us on a tour of the classrooms on the ground floor while reciting the curriculum and learning objectives in classic French. Despite the earthquake, her students' parents were still paying tuition, which was more than double what it was at the previous school we'd visited.

This was a school for middle-class kids, I realized. I assumed that was why Rosemene had picked it. She must have thought the education was better, and I figured she would know best.

A secretary in the office pulled out an old-fashioned wooden stamp and a blue ink pad and proceeded to pound each registration form with authority and flourish. This was my first taste of the bureaucratic rituals the Haitians retained from their former French slave owners, whom they'd driven off the island more than two hundred years ago. The secretary then pulled out a roll of tartan fabric and cut enough to make four collared shirts—two for Lovely and two for Jenanine. The girls would start school as soon as their uniforms were tailored.

It seemed a perfect development plan, clean and simple. I look back on that afternoon today with both tenderness and weariness. I didn't expect to see Lovely again; I only imagined her sitting among those perfectly coiffed, doll-like children, singing her heart out about pigs. I had no idea if she would succeed or not, and I honestly didn't think I'd find out. I figured the newspaper's interest in and budget for Haiti would expire soon, so it was unlikely I'd be back again in the near future, if ever. Still, I was filled with joy. It felt wonderful to give an open-handed, no-strings-attached gift. What I was doing was as much for myself as it was for them. After all the horror I had passively witnessed and all the cries for help I had pushed away, here was one small but meaningful way I could respond not as a journalist but as a human being.

Many foreign correspondents are renowned for their exaggerated personalities and drinking or drug addictions, and I think I now know why. Passively witnessing tragedy and injustice is corrosive to your soul. The mantra that a journalist's objective work is important as a record, and the principle that it often heralds larger changes, is true. But in that moment of witnessing deaths and hunger and violence you know you can personally stop, even for just one person, well, philosophy doesn't offer any tonic. You feel like an accomplice to a crime. Kevin Carter, a South African photographer who documented famine in Sudan in 1993, famously spent twenty minutes framing a photo of an emaciated girl, Lovely's age, curled in a barren field under the hungry gaze of a nearby vulture. Carter later said he was waiting for the vulture to spread its wings, but it never did and he eventually chased it away. The girl didn't die that day—she later got up and walked to her parents on shaky legs. The photo won Carter the Pulitzer Prize—the Olympic gold medal for journalists. But he also came under withering criticism for choosing to spend that precious time framing his photo rather than helping the child. The decision haunted him and he died by suicide soon after.

After the party that afternoon, I handed Rosemene a US$100 bill and told her my plan. I stated clearly that I'd pay for Lovely's school for two years. Then it would become her responsibility again. I couldn't help forever, and I wanted to set my boundaries clearly. I wasn't a fount that Rosemene could sip from whenever she needed money. But my grandmother had been a refugee, leaving Hungary on foot with my mother after the 1956 revolution. She often said, "Life happened to me." I hoped the money would help Rosemene regain some control over her family's life—that they could make choices rather than constantly react to greater forces.

More than anything, I hoped that, after the unimaginable horror she had endured, Lovely would get the chance to thrive.

Rosemene was exuberant. "Thank you, thank you, thank you," she chirped in her singsong voice, hugging me good-bye. "I will pray for you."

I was exuberant, too. It was the best—and only—day off I had taken in Haiti.

Chapter 4

Crossing the Line

A couple of weeks later, I was buckling my seat belt in the back of an American Airlines plane, heading again to Port-au-Prince. Beside me was my boss's boss, the *Star*'s publisher, John Cruickshank, who was coming down for three days. He wasn't the only one with me, either: Michael Cooke, the paper's top editor, was sitting farther up in the airplane.

"What do you want to see while we are there?" I asked John.

"Whatever is most useful to you," he responded, smiling at me from his seat. "I'm in your hands."

My eyes widened. It was unprecedented to have a publisher join you on an assignment—not just for me but for any journalist I knew. That in itself made me nervous. Up until now, I'd been blissfully ignorant of the trip's objective. Now that I knew it was to support my greater plan, I had another reason to be nervous: I didn't have one yet.

The three of us were there because of the column I had written about my last day in Haiti. Upon returning to the newsroom, I burst into my favorite editor's office and told her all about Lovely's birthday party. I clearly wasn't thinking straight: I'd broken the cardinal rule of journalism, and here I was happily telling my boss. But she didn't admonish me; in fact, she convinced me I should write a column about it. "You are supposed to take positions and be partial," she said. "It's an incredible story. I think you should tell it."

The response from readers was instant and enormous. The first email message arrived within minutes of the story going up Friday night. It was titled, "It was a Lovely thing that you did :)." Within an hour, dozens of other readers had written to say they wanted to do the same thing: enroll destitute kids like Lovely in Haitian schools.

By Monday morning, I'd received 160 emails from readers demanding to join what many called "the project," and they kept on coming. When I got to work, the first donation check—written out to me personally, to direct wherever I thought best—was already waiting at my desk. It was for C$100.

The diversity of the readers reaching out was remarkable. There were chartered accountants, translators, day care workers, school principals, provincial bureaucrats, and shelter workers all begging to help me. While some were well-off, many disclosed they were single parents or retired pensioners on small, fixed incomes but that they wanted to pull something from their thin budgets.

Mondays were usually crunch days for me, when I had to research and write a column in just eight hours. Clearly, it wasn't going to be a regular Monday, and I wasn't going to write about something new; the day was going to be spent replying to emails. But what to say?

My response was the standard one most journalists offer: "I am not a development worker. I suggest you send your money to one of the organizations I saw working in Haiti, including Médecins Sans Frontières [Doctors Without Borders], Oxfam, and Save the Children." But already I'd found those lines wanting. A weary skepticism about large international charities and development organizations emerged in the emails. Many readers feared that much of their money would be soaked up in overhead and that, by donating through me, they could be sure all the money would go directly to help Haitians. They trusted me.

That put me in an awkward situation. In my column I'd declared the long-standing code of journalists—impartiality at all costs—foolish. So how could I hide behind it now? I had decided to personally help; was I going to block other people from doing the same?

I didn't have any answers. But I was sure about two things. First, I had to be very careful with the money arriving. The *Star* had its own credit union, four floors below the newsroom. I went there, opened a new account, and deposited that C$100 check into it.

Second, the newspaper had to decide if it did have a project in Haiti, and, if so, what it was. I couldn't make that decision alone. I proposed to Michael Cooke that he come down to Haiti with me for the weekend to see what the pitfalls and possibilities were. He jumped at the idea, and the next thing I knew, Michael, John, and I were on our way to Port-au-Prince.

I spent much of the flight fretting. This was not a role I was used to. I was an expert at finding stories, convincing people to talk to me, asking critical questions, and writing—all of which were gloriously independent and solitary activities. For the next three days I would have to act as a secretary, social convener, and tour guide in a city that was not just physically devastated but dangerous.

I hired Jean again to drive us around and translate. Over the phone I implored him to get one of Jefferson's good, roomy cars with air-conditioning. He promised that he had. But a few minutes out of the airport it was clear he had been lying.

Jean greeted us, standing in the sweltering Haitian heat in his trademark jeans and extra-large T-shirt that hung down to his knees. He led us across the street and stopped before a white, mud-splattered, rusty jalopy. It was so low-slung that Michael and I had to hunch down to squeeze into the back seat, our knees and elbows jumbled together. There was no air-conditioning, so we hastily rolled down the windows.

To start the car, Jean punched a metal button on the dashboard.

After a few failed efforts it sputtered to life and we pulled out of the muddy lot, creaking past the airport grounds, which were now jammed with tents and makeshift shelters.

A few minutes later, as we mounted a hill, the car's engine died. The smell of burning plastic wafted up from under its hood. Suddenly we began rolling backward.

Jean pounded on the metal button like a cardiac nurse, and the engine coughed back to life. He then proceeded to do a nine-point turn, halting traffic on all sides and startling the *timachanns* with their wares set up on the edges of the road, until we were heading back downhill to where we started. But even with the generous boost of gravity, the engine's burbling didn't last long. Soon, Michael and John were out on the street, pushing the car to the side of a busy four-lane road, past a dozen motorcyclists all lounging on their bikes.

I pulled out my phone to look at a map. From what I could tell, we were in one of the city's red zones, where aid workers were warned not to stop without security. Many convicted gang members had escaped the city's central prison during the earthquake and were still at large. Reports of armed robberies outside of banks and kidnappings had been circulating, including one about two Médecins Sans Frontières nurses who had been held hostage for six days. What if we were attracting the wrong kind of attention?

I implored Michael and John to take off their suit jackets and hide them in the trunk.

"Let's walk down the street and rent a car," Jean suggested meekly. In hindsight, that wasn't a bad idea. But I had never seen a car rental place in Haiti, and whatever faith I'd put in Jean as a guide had completely drained. I'd have to figure this out on my own—and fast.

Desperately scanning the street, I spotted a white jeep with two large black letters down its side: UN. I raced across four lanes of traffic and knocked on the window. The driver rolled down the window languidly. My French was rusty, but I got my predicament across to him.

"Where are your bosses?" he asked suspiciously. I pointed to where Michael and John were standing by the trunk of the car. The

United Nations officer nodded his head, rolled up his window, and opened the door of his car. "Follow me," he said, and he strode across the street with purpose.

The officer halted before the crew of motorcyclists near us. It turned out that the motorcycle drivers were not shady layabouts or would-be kidnappers but taxi drivers. Here I was asking a UN officer to find me a taxi when in fact we were surrounded by them.

One of the men on a bike was a police officer, dressed in uniform. The UN officer struck up a conversation with him while I waited to the side. "He will help you get a car," he said, before charging back to his vehicle.

The police officer stepped out into the street and began to flag down cars.

I negotiated a ride in a van that was so beat-up, the door was held together with duct tape. Once we were inside, I noticed that the gas gauge needle was at zero. I doubted if we would even make it to our hotel at the top of Pétionville.

Along the way, the driver pulled into one gas station after another. At each one he was waved away. The city was facing a gas shortage. The island has no gas reserves itself—it imported all of its gas from Venezuela—so such shortages weren't uncommon. The tanker was late again.

I masked my anxiety by acting like a cheerful tour guide for John and Michael, pointing out the giant pigs and markets until we pulled up the hotel's steep cobblestone drive. Either God had chosen to be merciful or the driver's gas meter was broken, but we arrived. I gladly handed over the fare and climbed wearily out of the van.

My role reversal was complete by noon the next day. My two bosses were gleeful children under my command. John was wearing my baseball hat to protect his head from the Haitian sun, and Michael had taken to calling me "Mommy."

We ventured into Cité Soleil, the country's most dangerous

neighborhood, with a crew of middle-class Haitians who'd been inspired by the earthquake to help their fellow countrymen. Every Sunday they cooked up giant pots of food and distributed it to the neighborhood's residents. Police officers accompanied our convoy into the heart of the slum, where we stopped in a large dirt field.

I had passed through Cité Soleil before on my way out of the city, but I'd never dared to get out of the car. What I saw now was worse than anything I'd seen in Port-au-Prince, even though the area had been left relatively unscathed by the quake.

The houses around us were rusted tin sheds, set shoulder to shoulder around a large dirt yard. A crowd of children was milling around, most of them dressed only in rags and some completely naked. Few had shoes. They looked like refugees, but they hadn't lost anything in the quake; this was how they'd always lived.

The children quickly arranged themselves into long lines, ordered from shortest to tallest, to await their portion. Their patience and discipline was heartbreaking.

A visibly pregnant woman in line approached me. She looked exhausted; her face, eyes, shoulders all sagged. Her hair was unbrushed and she was barefoot. In her arms she carried a tiny baby.

I couldn't find Jean, so I asked one of the volunteers to translate for me. The woman, who was just sixteen, asked if I'd take her unborn child; she already had two babies and couldn't afford them, let alone a third child.

My translator was a twenty-one-year-old college student. She asked for a piece of paper from my notepad and scribbled down the woman's cell number. I figured she was planning on helping this girl with money or clothing. But that wasn't it at all.

"I'm going to ask my friends to see if anyone is looking for a baby," she said.

I was speechless. What kind of poverty would make both these things possible—that a person would give up her child to a complete stranger she'd met on the street, and that the complete stranger's first impulse was to take the child?

I realized that Lovely's living condition was not an anomaly in Haiti but the norm. And that whatever project the *Star* did here, it risked becoming a version of handing out containers of macaroni—helpful to some people for a short time but not much in the grand scheme of things.

The rainy season was in its full-throated rhythm. Most afternoons, dark, woolly clouds rolled in and unleashed a torrent of water— sometimes for just an hour and other times for much of the night. The clouds had already gathered by the time we made it out of Cité Soleil and started climbing toward Lovely's home. It felt good to shed the city's filth and be embraced by the green of the mountainside. Historically, Haiti had been the most productive colony of not just France's empire but of all the colonial empires, because of the fertility of the soil and productivity of slave labor. When kidnapped African slaves escaped the sugarcane plantations, French troops found it diffi- cult to chase them through the dense forests of mahogany and cedar. That was hundreds of years ago. Most of the country's trees had long been cut down for charcoal. But as we climbed the mountain and passed under the majestic umbrellas of a few, I got a sense of what the country once looked like.

When we arrived, the family was waiting for us. Lovely's neigh- bor Jenanine—whom I'd also enrolled in school—raced toward me and leapt into my arms. Lovely held back and looked at me coyly. She did not wear her heart on her sleeve.

After introductions were made, we settled down in the yard. As I looked around, I saw a shelter made from corrugated metal that I hadn't noticed on my first visit. Inside, there was a fire pit where Rosemene's sister, Rosita, made all the family meals. Just beyond it were a few meager fields of corn and pumpkins, which Rosita's hus- band, Elistin, farmed.

John had stuffed his bag with gifts for the kids: books, crayons, and a soccer ball. He pulled them out and handed them to Lovely's parents. Michael doled out Skittles to the children.

And then we sat there, wondering where to start. In the past, my visits folded along the hard spine of purpose—to get the story or to enroll the kids in school. But here we were, three privileged white people from a world they could not imagine, coming simply to say hello. It was awkward.

To break the silence, I asked Rosemene to tell us the story of the *goudougoudou* again, and she did, with her two kids jumping on and off her lap.

When the rain broke, crashing down in plum-sized drops, Elistin hurried us into the room where his family had lived before the earthquake. He didn't own it; he was the custodian of the land, and his payment came as free rent. There was a single bed, a chest of drawers, a wooden side table, and a rod hanging from the ceiling that acted as a wardrobe for Elistin's shirts. A single lightbulb hung down, illuminating the room. There was barely enough space for all of us, but we squeezed in, our hosts giving us the chairs and sitting themselves on the bed.

Quietly, I told Rosemene I had to go to the washroom, and she motioned for me to go around the building we were in. I dashed outside in search for what I assumed was an outhouse. I was wrong. There was nothing there, not even a hole. So I squatted under the eaves of the tin roof and went pee like I did when I was camping.

When the conversation inside the cinder-block room came to its natural end, everyone shook hands and I kissed both Lovely and her mother goodbye. I handed Rosemene her second US$100 installment. I had intended to send it by Western Union, but delivered it in person instead. Looking around one last time, I realized Lovely and her aunt and uncle's daily life was like a camping trip. And that, like the daily lives of the residents of Cité Soleil, it had nothing to do with the earthquake.

The next day John and I went to the Canadian embassy for a meeting with a political attaché. I'd heard that the first thing a foreign reporter should do on entering a country is get an off-the-record briefing from a diplomat. It was immediately clear why. Sitting in the ambassador's air-conditioned office, he gave us a hearty crash course on the country's issues, ranging from overcrowded prisons to the country's lack of land title system to a political system based on patronage and beset by bribery. The flip side of a country with such immense problems was that there were immense opportunities to do good—as long as it was done well. That was the big catch. Much of the aid that came to Haiti caused more harm than it relieved.

Before the earthquake, the city had two new private hospitals. They had both served primarily the rich—people who could afford to pay their fees—but, still, they were promising signs of private investment and homegrown development. A doctor in one had recently performed the country's first kidney transplant. After the earthquake, a lot of foreign doctors had come to volunteer their services—which was good. But many had stayed, and now they were treating patients with ailments that had nothing to do with the earthquake. As a result, the private hospitals had lost many of their paying patients and their staff, who had been lured away by international NGOs offering larger salaries than what the local hospitals could pay. One of the two hospitals had already closed down and the other looked doomed to the same fate. It was a clear example of what the diplomat called "catastrophic aid."

From there, we went to a school in Morne Lazarre, a hilltop neighborhood that had been decimated by the earthquake. The school's principal, Rea Dol, had become a local hero, heading out in her brother's truck to buy food and deliver it to her neighbors the day after the earthquake.

The school was called SOPUDEP—an acronym that translated to Society of Providence United for the Economic Development of Pétionville. Like most private schools in Haiti, it was run out of a former family home. Most of the classrooms were squeezed into bedrooms, and the narrow halls were meant for a handful of people to pass one another, not hundreds.

Rea had a heart-shaped face and a booming laugh she unleashed often, particularly when discussing chilling things. Laughter, she told me, was her antidote to misery. That and social activism. The school was bursting with more than 550 students, all of whom were poor and half of whom didn't pay any tuition.

"How are you able to fund the school, then?" I asked Rea.

She told me about Ryan Sawatzky, a thirty-three-year-old amusement park designer from Orillia, Ontario, a town an hour from my home. He and his father had arrived in Port-au-Prince three years before the earthquake with plans to raise money for computers in the school. But after a student had fainted from hunger at their feet, they had decided to fund a lunch program instead. Their commitment had continued expanding, and now they were paying the salaries of all fifty staff as well as funding the lunch program. The world seemed incredibly small again.

"Every day I pray for him," Rea said, clapping her hands and looking up at the sky. "Ryan is a *bon bagay*."

Rea's school provided the inverse lesson to the pregnant girl in Cité Soleil: one person, or maybe two together, couldn't change the world, but they could certainly improve a part of it and change the lives of many people. Rea had unwittingly provided me with the formula for an impactful project the *Star* could launch in Haiti: one part foreign money, two parts local activism. I wondered how we could apply the same thinking to help Lovely's family get their life back in order.

The day after visiting Rea, I was back on another plane with John and Michael, basking in quiet victory. We had not been kidnapped, maimed in a car accident, mugged, or even humiliated and gastronomically crippled by dodgy food. We almost missed the plane because the concierge had lost the key to the safe-deposit box with Michael's passport. But that was already another humorous anecdote.

I knew both John and Michael enjoyed the trip. It was a full-throated adventure. But I wasn't sure what they had taken from it or if they'd decided on a project for the *Star* in Haiti.

A few days later I was called into a meeting in the publisher's boardroom. John was waiting inside, along with Michael and my editor. Two senior features writers who had also reported from Haiti had been summoned as well.

There, we were informed of the *Star*'s plan: the three of us would write about Haiti's reconstruction efforts through Lovely's family. They would be our personal, intimate lens on the country's dreams and efforts.

But then they announced another unusual directive: We would spend the money sent to me to pay not just for Lovely's schooling but also to cover tuition for other Haitians just like her. The money in the account was far more than would be needed for just one child, and many readers had sent money not specifically for Lovely but, inspired by her, to send other kids to school. Other readers had sent money with no instructions, and we'd use that to help Lovely's family along the way. So, if Enel needed funds to restart his business, we would give him some. If Lovely's uncle Elistin would benefit from an agriculture program, we would enroll him. As we informed readers about the theoretical and historical pitfalls and shortcomings of development in Haiti, we'd be witnessing their effects through Lovely's family. There were no clear guidelines as to what we would fund and what we wouldn't; we'd have to make those decisions along the way.

The only fixed rule for us, as journalists, was this: we would be clear and honest with readers about how we'd influenced the story we were reporting and exactly how much money we'd spent where. As a news organization, on this singular project, we'd all torn up the journalist mantra of objectivity. In its place was our new philosophy: transparency.

I left the meeting buzzing with excitement. Instead of maligning my decision, my bosses had endorsed it and joined in. That meant many more trips to Haiti for me. It also meant Lovely's chances of escaping poverty were better. It wouldn't just be me helping her now; Canada's biggest newspaper would be behind her. I pictured her standing between her parents, watching water roll past their feet in that shed. I hoped, at the very least, her life would become more comfortable.

By then, the money that generous readers had sent for the project had swollen to C$13,663 in its savings account. And it was still growing.

Chapter 5

Not Just One Girl

It was a Wednesday morning in late July 2010, and I was gingerly navigating the sharp stones that jutted from the road like shark teeth, wishing for once that I had worn hiking boots and not silver flip-flops. Threaded between my fingers were Lovely's little fingers. On her other side, her mother, Rosemene, strode with purpose beside Enel.

It was only 7:30 a.m. but the sun was already hot, beating down on the back of my neck. I surveyed the dusty road for shade. There was none—just a thin, black cow grazing on the edge of a meager field of cabbages and a home's perimeter wall crowned with barbed wire. I had peeked inside a few such compounds when their large metal gates were open to make way for their dark SUVs. There I'd glimpsed Haiti's elite—their lush green lawns, pools, and paved driveways—who were said to own more than half the country's wealth. In Haiti, extreme poverty and extreme wealth live cheek by jowl in a way that was uncommon in Canada. But while poverty was hidden back home in high-rise buildings and homeless shelters and wealth pronounced itself with big lawns and bigger houses, here the inverse seemed true: poverty paraded the street freely, and wealth was barricaded away.

Lovely was immaculately dressed in a checkered red-and-white shirt tucked into a red pleated dress. On her feet were clean black oxfords below cloudy folds of lacy white socks. Her hair was twisted into cornrow braids and adorned with white bows and red hair clips. If you'd seen her, you might have thought she was going to a christening or a birthday party in one of these mansions, but this was just a regular Wednesday, and we were walking to school.

What Rosemene went through every morning to get Lovely looking like this was exhausting to think about. She got up at 5:00 a.m. to bathe her daughter in a plastic tub she filled with cold water that she lugged from a neighbor's cistern. Then she built a campfire in their kitchen shed to boil a pot of water for coffee. To twist Lovely's hair into braids, she used the natural oil of seeds she collected from a local plant called *maskriti*, also known as the Palm of Christ, or castor.

We were three months into the two-year plan to get Lovely, now three years old, started in school. Her teachers told me she was feeling more at home in the classroom—drawing, making collages and friends, and singing along with her classmates. I'd seen her sing in the muddy yard of her home, too, marching her brother and Jenanine up and down in a line and commanding them in the French of her schoolteachers: *"Epelez maïs pour moi, je vous dites"*—"I'm telling you, spell 'corn' for me." But the school secretary also mentioned that Lovely was missing school often—one to two days a week—because she was sick. Even now, on our walk, it was clear she wasn't well. Her nose was running.

"Dan mwen ap fè m mal," she said. Her teeth hurt.

Rosemene told me everyone in the household had been felled by colds and the flu, which didn't surprise me, given their meager housing. They'd moved out of the crowded, muddy shed and into Elistin's family's room a month ago. But it was still cold and damp, and they were sleeping on a concrete floor. Washing their hands was a production—I had rarely seen them do it—so illnesses passed around quickly.

As we walked and talked idly, Rosemene carried a red cooler over her shoulder with a strap. I asked her what she had packed for Lovely's *goute* (snack). In response, she held it in the air and rattled it.

"It's empty," she said. "Every morning, I go with this empty."

By then I'd given Rosemene US$400 to relaunch her business. She was selling little bags of rice, oil, coffee, soap, and bouillon cubes from baskets in the nearby Fermathe market. But price inflation and the location were killing her. Where she used to pull in US$10 to US$15 a day in sales, she was now making just US$2 or US$3—and that was before she subtracted her costs. Part of the problem was the price of bulk items sold in the big markets in the city below had shot up, but those increases had not trickled up to the local market, where the *timachanns* charged the same price as always. Before the earthquake, Rosemene had hawked on a busy downtown street where there were lots of shoppers. Here, she was in the sticks, where many families grew their own food and market days were just three times a week. She was also convinced a bad woman in the market used spells to ensure competing vendors lost money. This was *maji*—sorcery—something I was learning Rosemene believed in deeply, despite being devoutly Protestant. The reason she'd dropped out of school in grade one, she said, was a witch had cast a spell on her, making her deathly ill for two whole years.

Lovely's dad, Enel, wasn't bringing in any money, either. He'd never been paid for the job clearing rubble, so after a month he'd quit with nothing to show for it.

That left no money for food, and Rosemene said she didn't want to eat her merchandise. In principle, this was great, as it showed her dedication. But in practice, it was very concerning.

"What did you have this morning for breakfast?" I asked.

"Nothing," she said.

What about yesterday? Did Lovely have anything to eat then?

"A Rice Krispies bar," she said. Oh, and she'd had some thin soup with plantains and vegetables from her uncle's garden.

When was the last time they ate a real meal?

"Sunday," she said. "*Diri ak sos pwa.*" Rice and bean sauce.

That was three days ago. I thought about Lovely, sucking the meat off those ribs and crunching the bones in the makeshift clinic when I first met her. The doctors there said she was malnourished. She'd been clearly making up for a couple of years of starvation. And now, she was famished again. No wonder she was sick.

A block from Lovely's school, a line of *timachanns* lined up each morning to sell snacks for parents, many of whom were arriving in cars. There were hot dogs and beef patties, plantain chips, and fried hunks of pork. The prices were cheap—just 10 gourdes (20 cents US) for a beef patty—but even that was too much for Rosemene and Enel right now. I stopped and bought enough to fill Lovely's lunch box for the day.

When we got to school, I asked the secretary what happened when children didn't have a snack. Her answer was telling: They *had* to bring food in their *bwat*. That was the normal job of parents. She lived in the other Haiti, the one with manicured lawns, where it was unconscionable that someone wouldn't have 20 cents for a beef patty.

Unlike the Baptist mission school where I paid for Sophonie to go, at Lovely's school there was no free lunch program funded by the World Food Programme. Rosemene might have assumed this school was better because middle-class children went there, and she was likely right, as middle-class parents who were educated themselves would be more demanding of the teachers. But neither she nor I had thought through the complications this choice would cause.

Since the team at the *Star* hatched the project to enroll more kids in school, I'd been interviewing education experts in the country. What I'd learned was alarming.

Long before nearly one-quarter of the country's schools—80 percent of which were in the Port-au-Prince area—collapsed in the earthquake,

Haiti's education system was badly broken. According to one Canadian education development worker, the earthquake only exposed the fragility that had been there for twenty years. "None of this is new to Haitians," he said. "It's just now everyone's talking about it."

Although the country's constitution promised free education for everyone, it funded very few public schools. Around 85 percent of the schools in Haiti were private, charging annual fees of anywhere from US$60 for a modest school to US$10,000 for a spot at the Union School, where the country's elites and expat children went. For most parents, who earned less than US$2 a day, the average cost of US$135—including books and uniforms—was more than two months of their income. It was no wonder that as many as one in four little kids didn't go to school and less than half the population was literate. Education was a luxury, like an all-inclusive vacation.

Even worse, the state didn't have the means to monitor the private schools and ensure they were safe and providing quality education. The government openly admitted there was little to no oversight. Entrepreneurs opened schools in their homes or yards all the time—typically as businesses, not community development projects—and most would not qualify as anything beyond abysmal day cares.

Advertisements for schools were splashed across the gray concrete walls that shouldered most streets in Port-au-Prince—as many as four per block. They had impressive-sounding names like Collège Le Méridien. But when I asked my latest translator—a young man named Dimitri Bien-Aimé—to call a couple of the numbers, the people who answered the phone couldn't speak French, which was one of the primary languages of instruction. *How could the schools possibly be legitimate?* I wondered.

The locals had a name for these schools. They called them *lekòl bòlèt*—lottery schools. The wisdom held that kids had as much of a chance of earning an education there as their parents did of winning the lottery.

I glimpsed many of these problems firsthand when I enrolled Lovely's cousin Emmanuel in school. He approached me after Lovely's birthday party in April and handed me a two-page handwritten letter, shyly asking to send him to school. Emmanuel was short and thin, with coal-black skin and red eyes. He looked about eighteen, but he was twenty-five. He had dropped out of school in grade eight after his father died, and he was working as an apprentice carpenter, supporting his mother and little sister, who lived elsewhere. "I loved school *anpil, anpil*," his letter said, adding that he dreamed of being a journalist or policeman. He seemed old to go into grade eight; he'd be at least ten years older than many of his classmates. But he rightly explained that being overage was not a big deal when it came to school in Haiti. When their parents were broke, children would often miss a year of school to work.

I agreed to help Emmanuel with all the arrangements. I met him halfway up the two-lane highway to his mountain home, in the town of Thomassin. From there, he led me to a house on a crowded street with a double sign out front: *College Univers Fraternel de Thomassin* and *Fleur Rose Kindergarten*. The combination of a high school and kindergarten struck me as odd, but no odder than schools running out of houses. The principal greeted us and led us inside into what felt like a messy storage closet.

There were two wooden desks, both cluttered with papers, and an old-fashioned metal handbell to ring at the beginning of class, but no computer or electrical equipment of any type. Looking up, I noticed there was no overhead light, either: the room was simply illuminated by the soft morning light filtering through a window that held no glass. The school's filing system consisted of just one shelf, jammed with papers, and an assortment of plastic bags hanging from nails in the yellow walls, each of which was decorated with passages from the Bible, scrawled by hand in green marker. *J.C. is the same yesterday, today and eternally,* one said.

The principal explained that he'd been operating the school for seven years. Before that, he'd been a civil engineer. I didn't know enough at the time to quiz him on his qualifications as an educator. Coming from a world of regulations, it hadn't dawned on me that schools might be openly running underground. I never learned if this one was sanctioned by the government or not. But I came to think of many schools in the country as "make-believe."

I paid the US$200 tuition in cash. The principal filled out Emmanuel's student card and stamped it with his school's crest with the same flourish that the secretary at Lovely's school had used. I felt uneasy. From the little I'd seen of the school, I wouldn't send my kids there. But who was I to say, as an outsider with so little knowledge of Haiti? Emmanuel was the one going to school. He was an adult, and he had specifically picked this one. The last thing I wanted to be was an overbearing Westerner who claimed to know better than the locals about their own system. Haiti was overrun by those, roaring around in their white rented SUVs. Still, uncertainty crept inside my mind: What if Emmanuel only got a make-believe education? What good would that do him? I guessed it would at least help him get to a make-believe university: the vast majority of the country's postsecondary institutions also operated without state authorization.

"Make-believe" seemed to describe a lot of Haitian infrastructure. The few stoplights in the city were ignored by drivers, who plowed right through the intersection when they flashed red. They were make-believe stoplights. Even so-called orphanages weren't always what they claimed to be. Many kids had parents who simply couldn't afford to pay for them. The parents would visit regularly, and the administration had no plans to offer these kids up for actual adoption; they just hoped to get funding from foreign aid groups to keep them there, like low-end boarding schools. They were make-believe orphanages.

But the worst offender was the country's make-believe currency: the Haitian dollar. Gourdes are the official national currency in Haiti. They come, like Canadian or American dollars, in coins and bills, most of which have drawings of past presidents or important revolutionaries on them. On my first trip to Haiti, I had stopped in a *boutik* to buy some water. The merchant told me the price in Haitian dollars, so I pulled out the gourdes I had in my pocket and carefully counted them out. The vendor looked at what I had laid out and flatly repeated the price. So I counted the money again and pushed it across the counter toward her. That's when my translator jumped in and said, "Haitian dollars, not gourdes." I dug through my pockets, looking for a different type of bill. I found only more gourdes, which, to my surprise, he picked through, adding more bills and coins to the growing pile on the counter. "That's enough," he said. He left me wondering why I had just paid five times the listed price.

It turns out that the Haitian gourde was pegged to the American dollar back in 1912 at a rate of five gourdes to one greenback. That ended in 1989, when the gourde began to float. Still, on the street and even in stores, people referred to five gourdes as a "*dola ayisyen*"—a Haitian dollar—and often quoted their prices in it. It made absolutely no sense that a whole nation would trade in an imaginary currency, requiring mathematical gymnastics, when it could simply do what most of the world does and trade in the physical currency their national bank printed. But there it was: a make-believe currency.

The more I learned about Haiti, the less I understood. But one thing became increasingly clear: the terrible state of the country's education system before the earthquake was not an exception to the norm. It *was* the norm.

"If we just think this is about the earthquake, that is dead wrong. The earthquake was a natural disaster on a structural disaster," Nigel Fisher told me over dinner at a restaurant one night in July. Since our brief in the desert camp of Corail-Cesselesse, he'd agreed to squeeze me into the ends of his hectic days.

"There is no reconstruction, rebuilding, or re-anything, because what they had before was no good," he said.

Nigel had spent the last forty years in many of the world's most miserable and frightening places: Biafra, Yemen, Afghanistan. Yet he was one of the most upbeat people I'd ever met. Haiti, however, was proving his hardest assignment to date.

With so many things broken, where did you start? There was little trust between the foreign donors, who controlled two-thirds of the country's annual budget, and the government. There were so many NGOs working in the country, no one knew an exact number or what many of the small ones were doing.

When I'd first spoken with Nigel a couple of months before, he'd estimated it would take ten years to soundly rebuild the country. Already he was pushing out that time line.

By now, the project's savings account was up to almost C$17,000, and the checks kept arriving, many of them with letters asking that I put the money toward a new child's education. I had paid for all the kids in Lovely's family to go to school. Now I had to start enrolling other children, but where? I certainly didn't want to put them into make-believe schools. How could I be sure which ones were real, offering safe, quality education at rates that poor families could afford?

I took it upon myself to draft some rules of engagement. Any school I picked had to be registered with the Ministry of Education and Vocational Training and follow its curriculum. The teachers had to be qualified. And the school had to serve students who were poor before the earthquake; the student body didn't need to be entirely poor, but the school at least had to offer them tuition through its own scholarship program. I wanted to help the country's neediest, like Lovely. But I also wanted to avoid the mistake I'd already made there by enrolling a poor child in a middle-class school. Keeping up with the Joneses was putting unnecessary stress on Lovely's family, and I feared it was more likely to lead to her dropping out in the long run.

Ideally, the school would be run by someone like Rea Dol, a community activist with a passion for social justice through education, rather than an entrepreneur who ran the school as a profit-making enterprise. But that, it turned out, was not common.

I decided to also fund some college tuitions. Aid groups traditionally focus on early education, and that was certainly the case in Haiti. But if the country wanted to rebuild and become truly independent, then it would need educated workers with professional skills to do it.

Finally, I decided that I wouldn't choose any more students myself but give that job to the school principals instead. My worry quota was already full with Lovely and her family. I didn't want to personally take on the problems of dozens of other students; I couldn't spare the time or the emotional roller coaster of it. After breaking the cardinal rule that kept journalists apart from the subjects they reported on, I needed to erect some kind of wall of my own.

My new fixer, Dimitri, became my gauge of which schools I supported and which I did not. Jean had arrived one day with Dimitri and surprised me by announcing he was his replacement in the job. The swap had turned out to work in my favor. Fixers are what foreign correspondents call their local contractors; the ones who help you "fix" things. In theory, they are supposed to be a journalist's dream tour guide, offering not just literal translations but also cultural ones, historical and political context, and contacts. Up until then, I'd hired whomever could provide the basics—literal translation and a means of getting around. Dimitri was the first who offered more.

Dimitri was tall and muscular and dressed like a typical hipster, in jeans, a T-shirt, and aviator sunglasses. By training, he was an accountant. The *goudougoudou* had destroyed the retail business where he'd worked as an account supervisor, so now he made a living in his green Nissan Patrol, just looking for a day's wage. He was waiting for his American visa to come through; his wife had moved to New Jersey and he was hoping to join her there.

It turned out he had a knack for the fixer's job. He read the local papers and listened to the radio, so he could always brief me on what was happening in the country. He had graduated from one of the country's good universities, so he had friends who worked as doctors, lawyers, and salesmen whom we called for input. He had traveled to the United States, too, so he understood what things were distinctly Haitian and could offer some cultural translation. During interviews with principals, I would often glance at him for his ruling on the school. A nod was a green light; a slight head shake meant "Let's get out of here."

I brought Dimitri with me to visit one of the colleges that I thought showed promise. We entered the courtyard of a private home that had been transformed into classrooms. Inside, we found students in white coats standing at tall, freshly made plywood desks and looking through microscopes. The patio was jammed with school equipment, and the administration staff sat at computers by the entrance to register students.

The college director greeted me in her dark living room. Her name was Gilberte Salomon. She was small, with milky eyes, short, curly gray hair she hid under a straw hat, and a gap between her front two teeth that flashed when she smiled. Her right hand curled at the wrist, the effect of a stroke she'd suffered a few years earlier.

Despite her handicap, she was still teaching. The afternoon of the earthquake, she was up on the top floor of her downtown nursing college helping a student who had stayed behind after class. The ceiling split like a halved watermelon: one side of the building fell one way and the other fell the other. She looked up and saw the blue sky.

"I said good-bye to the earth and thanks to God," she said. "But not even a little rock fell on me."

The fact that *Bondye* had spared her life after he had taken so many of her students and compatriots—well, she figured it was a sign.

"My mission is not over yet," she said, the gap appearing between her teeth.

Gilberte's mission was very similar to Rea Dol's: she wanted to alleviate the poverty she saw around her in both professional and personal ways. Her home was full of orphaned children, two of whom she'd adopted as babies, raising them together with a third biological son as a single mother.

Professionally, Gilberte had been trained as both a teacher and a lab worker. Her college, called Institut Louis Pasteur, had evolved from its origins as a collective of lab technicians. Over the years it had expanded to include pharmacy assistants and a nursing program, which became its largest. Seven years earlier Gilberte had used the profits from her college to open a Montessori school for the poor children in her neighborhood, charging parents a nominal C$64 for tuition. She named it Mutuelle Scolaire Pa Nou, which meant "education for all of us mutually." It became Muspan for short.

I had come with a plan to sponsor some of her nursing students. But she wanted me to take a look at Muspan.

From the street outside the children's school, I could make out the cartoon characters of Donald and Daffy Duck painted on the wall. Above them, a set of concrete stairs shot up into the air like a leaning chimney, leading nowhere. The concrete roof had collapsed on one side, smothering the classroom below it. On the other, it looked like a sagging pancake held up by a thin central wall. I delicately picked my way up the stairs, around smashed chunks of concrete, to the second floor. There I found classrooms that seemed like museum displays about the earthquake. They were frozen in time. Dust had settled on the long wooden desks and benches, which still sat at attention in rows. Notes were scattered on the floors. The date was written at the tops of the cracked green chalkboards at the front of the room: 12 Janvier 2010.

Thankfully, when the earthquake struck, the school day had ended, and Muspan didn't offer evening classes. No broken bodies had been pulled from here. Still, it felt like a mausoleum.

Gilberte was now running the children's school under blue and gray tarps, among the tents clogging a nearby soccer field. Peeking inside, I found kids in their green school uniforms hard at work at desks set on the dirt. They were solving problems on chalkboards and copying notes into their books. In the small kindergarten class, a teacher looked up from a pile of tests she was marking and greeted me warmly. In immaculate French, she explained that she had been trained at the École Normale Supérieure, the state university's teachers' training faculty.

I looked over at Dimitri, who nodded. *Green light*. The tour did exactly what Gilberte had clearly intended. Right then, I committed to pay the tuition for ten students, but later I upped that to thirty—enough to cover Gilberte's outstanding bills for the year. On top of that, I'd cover the tuition of four nursing students.

It seemed like an even better program than the one Ryan Sawatzky had devised supporting SOPUDEP, because in this case there was a clear end date. If I could help Gilberte get her college up and running again, she'd be able to fund her elementary school as she had before. She would no longer need me.

I recognized that might take some time, though. Gilberte had no money to rebuild her college, and the engineers she'd hired to examine Muspan's remains had told her it would cost tens of thousands of dollars to rebuild. She wrote many letters to aid groups, asking for help, but so far she'd received no answer. She also applied to the Ministry of Education and Vocational Training, to enroll in the government's program to help principals cover at least some of their costs. She'd heard nothing back from them, either.

In fact, the government had no plan for private universities. And for private primary schools they'd decided to impose standards by sponsoring students. It was essentially bribery: principals who could prove they followed the national curriculum and who agreed to send their teachers to government courses would qualify for financial support, forgoing the nightmare of chasing after parents to pay. Instead, the government would foot the bill. It seemed brilliant to me. But Gilberte didn't think anything would come from it.

"If it happens, it will be a miracle," she said flatly. "I'm used to my country. I don't have faith. Haiti really needs to remake itself. But I'm very pessimistic."

Gilberte picked the recipients for scholarships at both of her schools. For primary kids, her criterion was poverty. For the college, she chose four students who had been badly injured in the earthquake.

Three of them came to meet me in Gilberte's dusty yard, where a bougainvillea along the property's boundary wall dripped fuchsia-colored petals at our feet. None of the students knew why they had been called there. Gilberte wanted me to break the good news to them in person. As soon as one of the women, Ketcia, heard what I had to say, she put her hands over her face and burst into delighted laughter. Even before the earthquake, she'd been behind on paying her school fees and had taken to arriving at school early each day to sell lunch snacks to her fellow students. Now she was even worse off: the earthquake had destroyed her right hand and her family's rented house. She had decided just that morning to drop out of school because she couldn't afford to pay the tuition.

"This is the best thing I've heard in months," Ketcia said. It meant she could continue her dream of becoming a physiotherapist.

I decided to tell the women about Lovely. After all, she was the reason I was here. I unloaded my anxieties about her future, describing her illness and hunger and how no one could help her with her homework, since neither of her parents could read or write. I worried aloud that education was not enough; she needed so much more to succeed.

"That's my story," said Ketcia. Her parents were also illiterate. She grew up hungry. "Sometimes I had no money to eat. Often, in fact."

The other two women agreed. One of them was the first person in her family to finish high school. Her mother had never attended school, and her dad, who was a plumber, had only made it to grade five. Her stomach was empty the day of the earthquake; she'd eaten nothing. The other had missed a year of schooling and worked as a seamstress when her parents couldn't afford the tuition.

They all agreed fervently that education in itself was all Lovely needed to change her family's future.

"She can be anything she wants," said Ketcia, her face still beaming. "*Même la présidente*. Even the president."

I decided to take Lovely to the dentist. If hunger was the main culprit for her absences from school, pain was a muscular accomplice. She complained regularly about how badly her teeth hurt; peering into her mouth, I could see why. A brown line arched across her upper front four teeth. Crescent-shaped chunks had fallen out of two of them, making them look like they'd been yanked out and stuffed back in upside-down with their roots sticking out. Dark brown holes gaped from two molars in the back of her mouth.

I printed out a photo and canvassed the opinions of dentists, both in Haiti and Canada, about the cause of the problem. Theories ranged from a fever Rosemene might have had while pregnant with Lovely to rot from sugarcane, which was plausible, given Enel's former job.

On my way to the dentist with Lovely, I thought back to Lyla's last checkup. Her dentist's practice focused specifically on kids, and the office felt more like a children's playground than a medical center. One corner of the waiting room had a cave filled with plush cushions and a treasure chest of toys, and each dental chair had a television screen placed seamlessly in the ceiling. Before picking their flavor of laughing gas, each kid got to choose which cartoon he or she wanted to watch during the procedure. At the end, Lyla left with a loot bag of stickers and pens.

Going to the dentist in Haiti was nothing like that.

The dental clinic was just up the street from Lovely's school, set in the Baptist mission headquarters, a series of stone buildings built around a large church. The mission funded many schools around the country, including the one Lovely's cousin went to. Here, it offered a restaurant and bookstore, a dusty museum, a dilapidated zoo, some greenhouses, and a hospital. The dental clinic was on the ground floor of the hospital.

Its waiting room was furnished like a simple church, with white-washed walls and long wooden pews all facing the direction of a white paneled door, on which was tacked a printed list of services ranging from 10 Haitian dollars (US$1.20) for a consultation to 70 Haitian dollars (US$8.40) for fixing a tooth.

The mission subsidized the clinic, but even with those low prices, most people opted for the cheapest solution: pulling out a tooth. I sat in a back pew with Rosemene and Lovely, watching in horror as patient after patient raced out with their hands clasped over their mouths.

The receptionist didn't offer much confidence, either. He was tall and gaunt, with Albert Einstein's wild gray hair and a clear dislike for his job. He didn't greet patients so much as bark at them, revealing a mouth almost entirely devoid of teeth.

I'd come here at 8:30 a.m., when the place was packed, to take a number, and now, five hours later, it was our turn.

We shuffled anxiously through the white door into a room where two dentists worked side by side on their patients. There was a bucket on the floor between them. I stared, dumbfounded, as they both yanked out teeth and threw them in the pail.

The dentist on the left was a large man wearing sunglasses and a green gown that was askew, falling off one shoulder. He ordered Lovely up onto his chair and promptly dug into the back of her mouth with a wooden tongue depressor.

My stomach lurched as I watched her small body coil in pain.

"See this," he said, peering over at us. "This is very bad."

Her cavities were deep. He said he'd seen it "many times before." He declared his theory with authority: they were the result of in utero malnutrition.

"It depends on the health of the mother during pregnancy," he said. "If she didn't eat a lot of vitamins and minerals, this happens."

Her adult teeth would be fine, as long as she brushed regularly. But she would need at least five fillings. Adding in the medication for freezing, which wasn't included on the listed prices, it came to 410 Haitian dollars, or C$51. No one in Lovely's family had ever spent money on a filling; she would be the first.

On our way out the door, Rosemene asked if I would carry Lovely. I picked her up and she snuggled right in immediately, nestling her hot, damp forehead under my chin, just like Lyla did when she was sick or tired.

It was dusk, and Dimitri was driving me back to the Healing Hands guesthouse after another grueling day of back-to-back interviews. I was sitting in the front seat of his car, going over my notes, when my cell phone rang. It wasn't the cheap Haitian phone I'd bought and loaded with minutes to make local calls. It was my Canadian phone, which I used sparingly while traveling to avoid the outrageous roaming charges.

A number flashed on the screen with *Home* above it.

My stomach tightened with anxiety. Any unexpected call from home likely carried bad news.

The sound that greeted me was like a squeaky wheel. It was Lyla. She was sobbing so hard, she could hardly push out the words.

"I . . . don't . . . want . . . you . . . to . . . go . . . to . . . Haiti . . . any . . . more."

Nothing had happened. Lyla just missed me. Over the past two months, I'd come to Haiti twice, each time for ten days.

"Oh, baby," I said soothingly. "I will be home soon, my love. And then I won't come back to Haiti for a while. I'll just be with you."

Slowly she quieted and her little bird voice returned.

"Okay," she said. "Promise?"

Chapter 6

Poto Mitan
(Cornerstone)

My little girl and I were connected again, our bodies clicking together like spoons in a kitchen drawer each night as we lay in her single bed and untangled all the day's events, sorting them into categories of fun, wonder, interesting, and hard/sad.

I had kept my promise and taken a good chunk of August 2010 off work to marinate in family time, mostly at cottages on the shores of Georgian Bay. Now that September was here, I was back working—but not in the newsroom. I wrote my columns on my bed and at home so I could delight in what my children did and said, even from a floor away.

I eavesdropped one afternoon as Lyla put Noah to bed for a nap in her bedroom down the hall. First, she pretended to read him part of *Pippi Longstocking*, the book we'd been chipping through over the past few weeks. Then she tucked him in and told him lovingly that she would be there when he woke up. Listening to her, I intuitively understood why Lovely had been calling for Jonathan those days after the earthquake. They were truly best friends and each other's principal playmates. Up until now, my kids' world was a shared tree fort of daily games and collaborative ideas, which Lyla would soon be leaving to start her own, solitary adventure: Lyla was going to school for the first time.

Her new school was around the corner, a four-minute walk from our front door. Its imposing stone façade looked like a castle behind a moat. The front entrance was so grand, you could imagine knights entering on horseback. Out back, there was a large fenced-in yard with trees, a baseball diamond, and a vegetable patch. Inside, her classroom offered a water table, reading library, and craft area furnished with painting easels and a Play-Doh station. All of this we got for free: I didn't have to pay for a single pencil, let alone tuition.

It came from our collective taxes. I'd been a supporter of Canada's social welfare system before, but my time in Haiti had made me appreciate its genius and generosity in a personal way. Haiti was the perfect libertarian state: it worked for you as long as you had the money to buy water and security and schooling and hospital visits. But if you didn't have the money, there was no safety net to catch you.

Lovely had unwittingly put new lenses on my view of Lyla. Her body, though small and light, seemed sturdy and dense to me now. When she settled into my lap, she felt like a mastiff—all muscle and brawn—compared to Lovely's hollow bird bones. And when she asked me how to spell words, I sounded them out with both pride at her gaining skills and sorrow at how Lovely would never have this kind of support. Her bookcase, already stocked with more books than Lovely would likely own in her life, reminded me each night of the world's unjustness. How could one little girl be nonchalantly given so much, while another was afforded so little?

My time in Haiti had also scratched the veneer of casual assuredness from life's coating. It had made me feel vulnerable even in

Canada, where there were so many protective systems. I now understood how easy it was to lose everything.

The first day of school, I helped Lyla dress in her special outfit, chosen specially for the occasion: white tights decorated with silver butterflies, a fuchsia tutu, a white top, followed by silver Mary Janes. Her short caramel hair was pushed back from her face with a new silver headband.

We skipped hand in hand to the schoolyard and spotted Lyla's teacher, wearing a fluorescent orange crossing-guard vest. Suddenly the line of students was moving. I watched my precious little daughter slip through those giant doors and disappear without even a worried look back or a wave good-bye.

Most of the time, I felt like I had landed on another planet when I arrived in Haiti. But there were fleeting moments when my shoulders relaxed and my eyes stopped darting for signs of wonder or danger, and I could ease into the autopilot that only comes from knowing a place so well, you don't even see it anymore. Going to Giant Supermarket in Pétionville was one of them. If you looked past the armed guards with their knee-high combat boots and antique-looking rifles at the front door, Giant could fit in as a grocery store at just about any suburban shopping mall in North America. Step before the automatic sliding doors at the front entrance, and you were greeted by a blast of cool air from overcharged air conditioners. Behind the deli counter, men with white chefs' hats shaved giant blocks of honey ham or American cheese with gleaming metal slicers, and in neat aisles you could find mixed nuts, cookies with no trans fat, and applesauce with mixed berries, just like I packed for Lyla's school snack in the mornings. Though I find grocery shopping a chore at home, every time I felt the tires of Dimitri's car drop from the grinding dirt and gravel onto the smooth concrete of Giant's underground parking lot, I sighed like they did. This was a place where I didn't need cultural or literal translation. I knew my way around. I fit in here. I was in my element.

The air-conditioning came as a huge relief. It was barely 9:00 a.m. that Saturday, three weeks after Lyla started school, but the city was already stewing outside. The heat dropped off my shoulders and upper lip. We'd had an appointment that morning with the dean at Quisqueya University, but he'd clearly forgotten all about it: when I got him on his cell phone, he'd told me he was away for the weekend. So I'd decided to make an unplanned trip up to see Lovely, who had another dental appointment that day. Ever since I'd discovered she wasn't eating, I'd started a new habit: popping into Giant to buy sandwich supplies for me and the family. Lovely loved salami, it turned out, so I always bought that, along with some baguettes, cheese, and digestive cookies.

The night before I'd left for Haiti, I'd worked through our night-before-I-was-leaving ritual conversation with Lyla, lying in bed beside her.

"I don't want you to go to Haiti," she'd said in her little bird voice. "I don't like it when you go."

I told her the same thing I always did. "I have to go. It's my job. I won't be there for long."

"Why do you have to go there?" she would say next. I reminded her of the earthquake and the people who'd lost their homes. And their schools. And that I was not only writing about them but helping them.

This was all true. But as time went on, I recognized that I was using the *Star*'s unconventional project as a mop to soak up my own guilt from a completely unexpected source: home. I wasn't just going to write stories and advance my own career, which would be unabashedly selfish. I had a nobler purpose: helping people. So that made leaving my children acceptable.

It was a language Lyla could understand.

"Did their schools fall down?" she would ask, loosening her grip on me. In the three weeks since she'd started school, she'd decided she liked it. She'd made a new friend, a little boy named Tyler with whom she held hands. "Are you helping them build new ones?"

I was caught in a constant contradiction. The earthquake had awoken my awareness about how precious time with my children was, because they could be taken from me at any moment. But at the same time, it had presented me with the professional opportunity I'd always wanted, which, by definition, took me away from my children. I felt like I was doing both, neither of them very well.

Back in the car, we drove up out of the city, shedding the heavy heat with every twist in the rising road. We slowly nosed our way into the Fermathe market, with its wooden stalls bunched together on a muddy square. Women lined both sides of the street, sitting behind their straw baskets of cassava and flattened bread. Some sat beneath faded red umbrellas, while others squatted on their haunches in the open. It had started to rain faintly and the women hugged their arms into their sides but stayed resolutely put.

We crept up the road slowly, when suddenly I recognized one of the vendors.

"Stop," I said.

It was Rosita, Rosemene's older sister. At first glance I thought it was Rosemene herself; the two looked strikingly alike, except that Rosita was stockier and less quick to smile.

Rosita was leaning against a pole with a ratty black cardigan pulled over her head. Spotting us, she ran up to the car window. I asked if she would show me what she was selling, so she led me down to her meager basket, filled with garlic and bouillon cubes. Then she all but pushed me back into the car and told Dimitri we should leave.

Dimitri thought she was just being considerate and didn't want me getting soaked in the rain. But I remembered Rosemene's story about the witch at the market who was casting spells on people. Was Rosita pushing us away before we brought any more unwanted attention to her?

We continued down the rocky road and pulled up to what I would always think of as Lovely's place—even though, in fact, she was technically a houseguest. Rosemene greeted us wearing a long red scarf wrapped around her head and the same yellow shirt and jean skirt she'd had on the day I met her in April. She kissed me on both cheeks and asked after my kids.

"*Bebe yo byen?*"

Lovely was quiet and sullen. Snot leaked out of both her nostrils. The whole family was sick again, or maybe they had never really gotten better.

We hurried out of the rain, which was now gaining strength, and into the concrete room, where they were still sleeping. Inside, it was dark. Their single electric bulb hung impotently from the ceiling. It was fed by a wire jacked into the home of a nearby government official; electricity in the country was both notoriously inconsistent and notoriously stolen, by the poor and rich alike. But, government connections notwithstanding, it came to life for only a few hours a day; sometimes it remained dead for the whole week.

As my eyes adjusted to the dark, I noticed the smudged white walls were now mottled with writing in red marker. They were passages from the Bible that Enel had written out, copying each letter carefully, since he couldn't read.

I recognized Psalm 23: "Even though I walk through the valley of the shadow of death, I will fear no evil, for you are with me . . ." It ended more ominously in this version than I remembered: "*J'habiterai dans la maison de l'Eternel jusqu'a a la fin du monde*"—"I shall dwell in the house of the Lord until the end of the world."

Rosemene explained that the quotes were there to bless the family. I thought about Rosita hurrying me out of the market and asked Dimitri to dig more into it. While I unwrapped the cookies for Lovely and Jonathan—who was playing on the floor with just one blue sandal on—Dimitri leaned in towards Rosemene and began a long, whispered conversation. The rain pounded onto the thin tin roof, making such a racket, it was impossible for me to pick up any of their words.

"What is she saying?" I asked again impatiently.

Dimitri flapped his hand at me as if to say, "Calm down. I'll get to you."

When they finally finished, Dimitri turned and fixed his eyes on me.

"Okay," he said. "I told her I wouldn't tell you all this, so don't look surprised or shocked."

One night not long ago, he recounted, Lovely was very sick. She'd been gripped by a fever and her throat had become so swollen, she couldn't swallow. Rosemene rushed to a church to pray for help and met a neighbor there who told her Lovely was the victim of *maji*.

"She told her it had happened because all these white people are coming to their house," Dimitri said.

I knew very little about Vodou, other than it was a religion brought here by slaves from West Africa and that it had an elaborate pantheon of gods who could possess followers during ritual dances. I'd learned there was a dark side to the religion, like in Catholicism, but I was weary of the images of pincushion dolls and zombies from American horror movies.

I did understand how neighbors might be jealous of the attention Lovely's family was getting, though. I imagined all of them watching Dimitri's SUV roll up, bringing me one week and another *Star* reporter the next. Even if we weren't helping the family, the neighbors would assume that we were. The irony of the situation struck me: our help might do more harm than good by drawing envious attention to the family and inspiring attacks they wouldn't have otherwise faced. Was this a parable about aid and good intentions going wrong?

I asked Dimitri what he thought I should do.

"Basically, they don't give a shit what the neighbors think. They are happy you are helping them," he said. They wanted us to stay the course.

As we sat there, more and more people joined us. Lypse, Rosita and Elistin's son, barged into the room, throwing a plastic bag around like it was a ball. Jenanine from next door crept in beside Lovely and the two of them clapped their hands together in a game. Rosita arrived with Elistin, and I noticed Enel sitting shyly by the door. A couple of my colleagues from the *Star* showed up, and I assembled sandwiches from the supplies I had bought that morning and handed them around while the adults briefed me on their work—or lack of it. A pile of our kicked-off shoes had grown by the entrance. Lypse approached them, pulled down his pants, and then peed. He'd been aiming out the door but fallen short, and splashed all the shoes with his urine. The room, which was warm now from the heat of our huddled bodies, erupted in laughter.

Later, after the kids were asleep, Rosemene confided that her business was going terribly. She was down to selling just bleach, washing detergent, and coffee. Her resolve to not eat her supplies had broken in the face of her kids' hunger. She was no longer selling in the market but out of the house, which meant she had even fewer customers. Enel had found another job in construction in a nearby town, but the owner had refused to pay him in full, pocketing one of every four weeks' pay because he said Enel hadn't finished the job. So Enel had quit in protest. In my mind, three weeks seemed better than none, but Rosemene said it was the principle of the thing. The work was hard and he should be paid.

She needed to head out and make money, because the family couldn't survive like this, she acknowledged. It hurt her to see her children hungry.

"The weight is heavy on me," she said. "It's hard for women."

When it was time for me to go, I kissed Rosemene good-bye and made my way back to the car. My colleagues were leaving, too. We decided to convoy out, with their driver leading the way in his golden Nissan Pathfinder. As Dimitri began to reverse, we heard loud shouting from behind us. The Pathfinder had slipped and one half of it hung precariously over the edge of a steep embankment that separated the road from an adjacent farm field. It all happened so quickly, it was as though a giant hand had swooped down and flicked the Pathfinder aside.

Young men appeared instantly, seemingly out of thin air. By the time Dimitri and I leapt out of his car and rushed to the rescue, there were already a dozen of them surrounding the car. *Do they watch the* blans *through the cracks in their walls?* I wondered. *How did they all get here so quickly?* One seemed to have arrived straight from bed, wearing only a pair of shorts pulled just halfway over his buttocks.

"*Gade! Gade!*" they all yelled, as more emerged from nowhere and joined the commotion. They were all vying to lead the rescue operation.

"Look! Look!" shouted one young man with the broad shoulders and wide face of a rugby player. "We have to pull it from the front."

"*Gade! Gade!*" shouted another—this one plump. He'd invited me into his small home once and told me his plans to start a night school for the area. "We have to pull it from behind."

Elistin emerged from his home with a long, thin piece of metal rebar. There were now more than two dozen men swarming the scene. The women were gathered in the distance, standing on the mound of gravel Elistin had bought to eventually use in building his house.

The rugby player twisted one end of the rebar around Dimitri's front axle and the other around that of the tipped Pathfinder, and the men gathered under the hanging wheel to hold the vehicle up. I looked down nervously from the edge of a nearby field of blooming potato plants. I was sure the car was going to roll, and then what would we do?

Dimitri hit the gas. His wheels spun in the mud. But the Pathfinder didn't budge. The rain, which had subsided, started up again.

A sleek, polished SUV pulled up behind us, with a bald white man at the wheel. He was dressed right out of a Patagonia catalogue: hiking boots, shorts with pockets, a crisp short-sleeved collared shirt. He lowered his window and addressed us.

"What will it be, English or French?" he said. Then he drummed his fingers on his forehead. "Right, sometimes one head is better than twenty. Don't worry. Be patient. Give me five minutes."

The night-school entrepreneur approached his window and then shot off up the road past Lovely's home until we couldn't see him anymore.

Dimitri whispered to me, "Can you believe it? He sent that guy to get him a glass of wine."

Sure enough, after the bald man had emerged from his SUV, pulled out a long, flat rope from his trunk, and lay down in the muck of the road to tie the rope to the rear axle of the Pathfinder, the glass of wine appeared and was offered to him. He took a sip and handed the other end of his rope to one of the gathered men, who were no longer shouting. They'd decided to listen to this strange apparition.

When the rope was ready, the crowd of men reassembled around the Pathfinder to lift and push it as the bald man reversed. The aspiring night-school teacher pushed with one hand as the other held a slightly mud-smeared glass of red wine.

The SUV backed up. The men pushed and then jumped out of the way as the tipped Pathfinder swerved, barely missing an electrical pole, and flopped up on the road like a seal emerging from the ocean onto the safety of ice.

"Hooray!" we yelled. Fists pumped into the air. The man exited his car and was received with hugs and lots of backslaps. The *Gade! Gade!* men vanished from the road as quickly as they had appeared. The bald man got back into his SUV, refusing to pose for a photo.

"I'm not supposed to be here," he said. He rolled up his window and disappeared. It all seemed so inexplicably fantastic and bizarre.

As we rode down into the city, I wondered what to take from this colonial moment, other than whiplash. Was this three hundred years of racism at work? Was it classism? The bald man was rich, the others poor.

Another lingering thought chased me down the mountain. Would Rosemene think *maji* had caused the near accident? If she did, what should or could I do about it?

The longer I stayed in Haiti, the more I understood the truth of what Rosemene said: life for women in Haiti was unbearably hard.

As a feminist, I often wrote about women's rights back in Toronto.

I advocated for more money for women's shelters and more attention to domestic violence, the pervasive and pernicious problem of rape, the fact that women still earned 31.5 percent less than men on average, the lack of affordable childcare, and the underrepresentation of women in government and on the boards of *Fortune* 500 companies. Researching these stories, I often felt depressed, like I was fighting the same battle my mother helped fight in the early 1970s. But my time in Haiti opened my eyes to what progress Canadian and American women have made since Betty Friedan published *The Feminine Mystique* and Laura Sabia threatened to lead 2 million women on a march to Ottawa unless the government agreed to host the Royal Commission on the Status of Women.

Sexism still existed in North America, for sure. But it took a more subtle form. In Haiti, it was blistering and blatant. The culture was painfully patriarchal, and it was openly held that the man's role was to work and the woman's was to raise the children and look attractive. If a man had money, he was expected to have a few women on the side and do what my friends called a *pa chat*—cat path—between work and home, visiting his lovers or second wives. A woman was not given the same rights, no matter how rich she was. In fact, up until recently, a man was legally allowed to murder his wife—and her lover—if he caught them in the midst of an affair. If she caught him, her only legal recourse was to fine him—for just US$50.

It wasn't until 1982 that women were deemed adults by Haitian law and gained the right to inherit land themselves or own businesses without their husbands' permission. And only in 2005 were they protected by strong rape laws. Before then, rape was considered a moral crime, and often, if the victim was not a virgin at the time of the assault, the judge delivered a lighter sentence, since her honor had not been breached. It was no surprise that the people making laws in Haiti continued to be almost entirely men. If I thought it was bad that only 26 percent of Canada's politicians were women, in Haiti only 4 percent of the elected parliament was female in 2010, and by 2016 that number would shrink to zero.

Women in Haiti faced huge amounts of sanctioned violence—not just in the form of rape, which was considered an epidemic in the country, but domestic violence. One-third of women reported they were victims, but many of them agreed they deserved to be beaten for things like going out without telling their husbands or misspending money. Girls were more often pulled out of school before boys, or never sent at all if the family was poor. As a result, women were less educated, which meant their chances of landing good jobs—if their husbands let them work—were much lower.

The majority of Haitian women did work, but they did so at the bottom rungs of society. Three of every four people working the "informal" economy were women who had no benefits, no sick days, no security, and very little money. Like Rosemene and Rosita, many were *timachanns*, making US$2 to US$3 a day by selling goods on the side of the road.

When people say Haiti is the poorest country in the western hemisphere, they should say that Haitian women are the poorest.

I thought I understood all of this from reading reports, but it wasn't until I descended into the *bidonvil* of Bobin that I saw what it truly meant.

Bobin was another poor neighborhood of Pétionville, made of cinder-block houses that clung to the side of a valley. Like Vallée de Bourdon, the homes in this *bidonvil* were so densely packed, you couldn't drive to many of them.

Dimitri and I parked at the top of the neighborhood, where we were greeted by a group of men hanging out at a bar drinking *kleren*—sugarcane liquor—near the road. A couple were so drunk, they came out to serenade me with a song. It was midafternoon.

By foot, we set off into the *bidonvil*, stepping between houses and under staircases and at some points walking right down what felt like apartment building hallways—doors on each side, and a roof overhead. As we descended, we passed women carrying avocadoes in baskets and buckets of water on their heads, and others leaning over tubs, scrubbing laundry. The farther down the valley we went, the fewer men I saw, until there were none. This was the domestic realm of women.

We came to a dry streambed choked with giant mounds of rotting garbage that a few massive pigs were nosing through. Hanging over it all was a bunker—a single room made of cinder-block walls, with a tin roof and a tin door held in place by a plastic flip-flop. A woman greeted us carrying a tiny baby. Her pink shirt was askew and done up with just one button, her black skirt smudged with dirt and gaping open at the back. Her hair stuck up in tufts. She wore no shoes, and her feet were filthy. She had six children, including the baby, and all of them hung off her, touching her shoulders and back as she spoke to me. None of them went to school, because she had no money to send them.

What about their fathers? I asked.

They all have the same one, she said. He was very much alive. "Once in a while he comes by," she said. "Whenever he's got something, he gives it to us."

This was not unusual in Haiti. In fact, it was the norm. There is an official system of alimony, but, like most laws in Haiti, it is rarely enforced. Women in Haiti hold all the responsibility and none of the power. In this way I saw how lucky Lovely was. She had a father in her life.

I was in Bobin because of Rea Dol and the women's collective she had started in the area. The members, mostly *timachanns* and single mothers, had built a one-room school atop the house of one of their members. Their children attended it during the day, and in the evenings the women themselves went there for lessons in reading, writing, and basic math.

When I arrived, a dozen of the adult students were waiting for me. One of them stood up and explained how, as a child, she had never been permitted to go to school.

"My father sent my brothers to school," she said. "But he didn't want to waste money on sending a girl to school because I might get pregnant."

She pulled out a book and showed me how she could now make

out the letters on the page. Then she went to the chalkboard and wrote out a line in Kreyòl.

"I can sign my name now," she said. "I'm proud of that." She wanted to learn to read well enough that she could help her three children with their schoolwork. "What my dad didn't do for me, I'd like to do for my children."

Rea sat in the middle of the growing group, laughing at their stories and jumping in with her own. Her partner had left her and their three children for another woman and never so much as looked back. That was the reason she turned to community activism to help other women in her situation.

As we sat there, more women filed into the room until they were shoulder to shoulder. I looked at the reading posters tacked to the yellow-and-blue walls, listing the names of fruit and colors, and realized they were for these women as much as they were for children. Then they all stood up and launched into a song.

"*Solidarity—that's how we develop ourselves,*" they sang, their voices rising and falling in harmony. "*Solidarity—it's how we combat misery.*"

I was incredibly moved, looking around the room at the forty or so women who swayed and clapped in song together. I had intended to fund ten of the night students here. But when Rea told me the salaries of the five teachers who cycled in to teach all 120 women was just US$3,200, I decided to fund their salaries for a year. To help a whole community of women better themselves, and in turn help their children, would cost less than scholarships for three university students. I was confident that readers who had sent me money to put toward school tuitions would agree that this was a good investment.

The issue of rape had become big news in Port-au-Prince—at least among international journalists, aid groups, and human rights organizations.

In the days after the earthquake, many women reported being raped by armed men in the rubble of their homes. Some blamed the escaped convicts from the city's main penitentiary. But the reports continued for months, with women telling horrific stories of masked men cutting through the canvas tents and raping them in front of their children or dragging them into ruined, abandoned buildings to attack them. A midwife working at Médecins Sans Frontières told me they were treating six to twelve terribly injured women a day.

Among Haitian feminist organizations, the stories were a political point of contention. Some of the long-established groups said the problem was overblown by women aiming for attention and aid. The leading candidate in the ongoing presidential campaign, a former first lady named Mirlande Manigat, said she thought the accounts were exaggerated.

The idea that women would lie about rape triggered myths I had carried with me from Canada. I knew this pernicious argument and had seen how it was used to dismiss and silence women back home. It infuriated me. Given how patriarchal Haitian society was to begin with, I didn't understand why women's groups and politicians wouldn't support the victims and see their plight as one that could advance the entire feminist cause.

What I was learning, however, was that the underlying issue was class, and that class in Haiti trumps everything. The women from those long-established feminist organizations—not to mention a former first lady—were from the country's elite. They had property, education, and careers. It was the poor women living in the squalid camps who said they were being raped—just as they had been raped in the slums after Haiti's two political coups.

After the second coup in 2004, a group of rape survivors formed a support organization and called themselves the Commission of Women Victims for Victims—Komisyon Fanm Viktim pou Viktim (KOFAVIV). Their members had been trying to help victims go to hospitals and police stations to report the attacks, although they said in most cases the police didn't take their complaints seriously. In the first five months after the earthquake, they'd counted 250 cases of rape—most by groups of armed men.

One of the recent members of KOFAVIV was a woman named Marie-Carline Marcellus. She lived on the edge of the giant Champs de Mars camp in a shack made of pieces of corrugated metal. Normally she pulled her chair outside to sit, but with all the rain, a muddy moat had formed at her shack's entrance, so we decided to talk inside. A sheet stretched across the shack on a wire, dividing the bed from what you could generously call the living room, which held a metal table, some chairs, and a shelf set on the dirt. The room's only adornment was a pair of polished brown brogues nailed neatly side by side to the tin wall above the bed. Marie-Carline explained that they were all she had left of her husband, who had been crushed to death in their home during the earthquake.

"I loved my husband a lot," she said. "When he was alive, I wasn't suffering."

Marie-Carline's story was similar to the stories told by many of the other victims I'd met at KOFAVIV. She'd been raped twice, the first time two days after the earthquake when she'd ventured back to the rubble of her home to look for things to salvage. Four men armed with guns grabbed her and took her back to a tent, where they beat and raped her.

"People knew it was happening but they couldn't do anything," she told me, mopping her face on the hanging sheet.

When she reported the rapes at the police station, the officers dismissed her. "They said, 'With an ass like that, it's normal to get raped,'" she said.

In May she'd been raped in a nearby Porta-Potty by two men carrying ice picks. Again she'd waved down a police car, but the officer told her he couldn't do anything unless she could identify the rapists.

So here she was, sitting in the mud, with no hope of justice.

"Haiti's women," she said mournfully. "We have the worst lives."

After much political pressure by KOFAVIV, the UN and police began to patrol a handful of the hundreds of camps in the city. KOFAVIV workers distributed whistles that women could blow when they sensed an attack was imminent—but that required people to come to the rescue and put themselves in harm's way. It was a response, at least, but a feeble one.

The air in Marie-Carline's shed was oppressively hot and damp. Sweat rolled down my calves and beaded along my upper lip. In the middle of translating, Dimitri asked to be excused for a moment and rushed outside to gasp for fresh air.

"I feel bad asking your questions and listening to these stories," he explained when I joined him. "Because I'm a guy, I feel guilty."

Once we were back in the car, he ransacked the cup holder and glove compartment for change to buy cold water from a street vendor. He chugged it back. "I know I'm supposed to translate what you are saying. I want them to know I'm not asking these questions," he said. "Most of the time you ask questions about people's feelings. Even in our own families in Haiti, nobody talks about their feelings. It's always a hidden thing."

I fell silent. Dimitri's words surprised me. I had never thought about how the job was affecting him personally, and his struggle seemed illuminating. Dimitri was finding it just as hard being my voice as I was not being able to speak for myself. But while I resented the separation, he struggled with the closeness. He came from the country's barricaded, educated class. This was the first time he'd been intimate with his own country's poverty. I found the need for a translator frustrating for the opposite reason: it meant there was always a distancing echo between me and whoever I was speaking to, even Lovely and her family. I had purchased a Kreyòl primer and had been studying it, hoping that one day I could have direct conversations with Haitians. But I understood why Dimitri would rather have the distance. Coming face-to-face with poverty is painful.

We continued on to the quaintly named Ministry of the Feminine Condition and Women's Rights, where I had an interview set up with the minister, Marjory Michel. She wasn't there yet, but her attendant ushered us into a salmon-colored room where an air conditioner worked furiously, spraying out luxuriously frigid air. I had come to expect people to be late for interviews—in part because the streets outside seemed to be in a constant state of *blokis*, but also because of the Caribbean sense of time. "Now," Dimitri had taught me, meant in ten minutes and *"toute à l'heure"* meant twenty.

After a while I stepped outside for a smoke, and the attendant followed me. She was dressed like a busboy, with a black suit jacket and checkered pants. She brought me a chair to sit on and in Kreyòl told me she was living in a tent in the Champs de Mars camp with her son. Her two daughters slept in the car. When I asked why, she held up a finger and slowly sliced the air before her. You can't cut through a car door with a razor blade. It didn't take her long to get to the point: she asked me if I could help her get to Canada. When I said no, she asked for my card anyway, so we could *kenbe kontak*—keep in touch.

I clenched my teeth and refrained from telling her that, really, I didn't even know her name, so why would we stay in touch? She was just being smart—looking for a *blan* to give her some *èd*. But the demands for help, which had made me feel guilty after the earthquake, were now getting on my nerves. They were relentless; not an hour went by, it seemed, without a stranger appearing and asking for money. Even some of the people I was helping were asking for more. I had decided to enroll ten children in the Baptist mission school around the corner from where Lovely was living, in the hopes of spreading the wealth in her family's neighborhood and defraying some of the jealousy directed against them. While filling out the receipts, the principal told me all about his stomach ulcer and medical bills: Maybe I could help him pay for them? I felt like a walking ATM.

When the minister finally arrived, she launched into a stump speech about the rebuilding of a better Haiti.

"It's not just about infrastructure but reconstructing the mentality—a Haiti without prejudice, a Haiti where everyone has the same opportunity, for women and men. A Haiti where girls have access to school and education, where adolescents have hope for a profession. A Haiti where women are autonomous. The autonomy of women—if we want to combat violence against women, they have to be autonomous with power to negotiate their own security," she said passionately.

Perhaps she believed it. But already I was becoming cynical. Her vision was wonderful, just like the education plan. But in practice, the lives of women were not better than before the earthquake. They were undoubtedly worse.

I had enrolled Lovely in school to secure her future. But an education wouldn't protect her from rape, violence, lack of opportunity, and structural misogyny. Without a plan to "build back better" for women, what would her future hold?

Rosemene and Enel agreed to return to the site of their old home in Fort National. Lucas, my *Star* colleague, wanted to take some profile photos of Lovely there, and I wanted to see where Lovely had been buried in rubble.

Fort National was set on a hill in downtown Port-au-Prince overlooking both the broken cathedral and the shack-filled Champs de Mars. When the city was originally constructed, the neighborhood was full of stately homes with stunning views. Those had been replaced with slapdash concrete boxes, most of which fell during the earthquake. The area was among the worst hit in the capital, and it was now known for two things: poverty and gangs.

Rosemene described how the main road cutting through the neighborhood had once been lined with *boutiks*—little shops selling booze and water and phone cards. Now there was nothing but what looked like dusty football fields flashing through the windshield.

Rosemene and Enel both stared wide-eyed out the back windows.

"This is so weird," Rosemene muttered. "I don't recognize anything."

Where was the spot where she used to sell her spaghetti and bouillon cubes? Where was the little medical clinic where she took her kids? Where were the local schools?

All of them were gone—felled into jumbled messes during the

earthquake, then scooped up by the yellow diggers we saw parked around us.

There was a single building left on the road, surrounded by lounging men. We pulled up to it, and Rosemene leaned out the window, asking for directions. One said he would take us there, motioning with his hand. We all scrambled out of the car and began to pick our way down between tin shacks, jumbled piles of broken cinder blocks, drying laundry, and tents.

Women were leaning over tubs of water and little kids flew paper kites from the open spots where homes had once stood. Enel led the way with Lovely on his hip, followed by Rosemene carrying Jonathan. They stopped regularly to glance around in search of something—anything—familiar.

We stepped over piles of garbage and past the concrete walls of small homes that either had been rebuilt or hadn't collapsed in the quake.

The alley spit us out onto a dirt yard dotted with mounds of sand mixed with small chunks of concrete. We now had a clear view of the sunken domes of the presidential palace below and the sparkling ocean behind it. The tin roofs of distant shacks baked in the blazing noon sun. They had turned brown, as though they were rotting.

Enel stopped before a small platform surrounded by three walls. It was no larger than eighteen square meters.

"That's where it happened," he said. He pointed to one side of the platform. "There was the room where the girls used to watch television."

Rosemene agreed. This was it. She picked up a metal ring from the footpath. It was the remains of her *recho*, a type of metal colander Haitians stuff charcoal into and cook over like a barbecue.

"This is the only thing I remember," she said.

Enel put Lovely down to walk around. She was dressed in a white dress and lime-green running shoes. Her hair was done up in twists, each one furnished with a little white plastic ball. She showed no signs of recognizing the place or remembering the ordeal she had suffered here.

Lovely on the afternoon I met her, sitting between two catastrophe missionaries, eating, as usual. *Allan Woods*/Toronto Star

In the days after the earthquake, many people wore masks over their faces or wiped toothpaste under their noses to mask the smell of death. The rubble clogged city streets for years.

Lovely with her family. Left to right: her cousin Sophonie (*front*); her brother, Jonathan (*in lap*); her mother, Rosemene; her cousin Lypse (*in lap*); her uncle, Elistin; Lovely (*in lap*), and her aunt, Rosita.

Lovely singing her young brother, Jonathan, a song about little babies drinking milk.

When Rosemene tried to make the kids smile for the camera, I felt a kinship with her. I often did the same thing with my two children, who were about the same age as Lovely and Jonathan. *Jean*

Hollywood actor Sean Penn and Haiti's president, René Préval, greeting each other at the new planned settlement of Corail-Cesselesse, a collection of tents in the parched desert.

The playgrounds in city parks were all taken over as shelters for families who had lost their homes during the earthquake. After the disaster, people tried their best to carry on with their regular routines despite the devastation.

The most common job for women in Haiti is a market vendor, or *timachann*. They spend long hours in the heat and often make only US$2 a day.

The *tap-taps* are Haiti's buses—pickup trucks with benches down the back and awnings overhead. Many are painted with hopeful mottos like *Jesus watch over us*.

After taking Lovely to the dentist for the first time, I carried her to my car to take her home. *Dimitri Bien-Aimé*

Lovely's class walking through the grounds of the Baptist mission on their way to a dress rehearsal for the school's end-of-year show.

Rosemene dries Lovely after a bath in a cold tub of water that she carried from a neighbor's cistern. It amazed me how much work was involved in basic cooking and cleaning tasks.

Left to right: Sophonie, Lypse, Lovely, and Jenanine sit in their sun-speckled yard on Election Day in 2010.

The view of Port-au-Prince from a rooftop in Pétionville, the city's upper-class suburbs. The natural beauty contrasted with the realities of Lovely's daily life. Here, she plays in the yard of her family's new home on the first anniversary of the earthquake.

Lovely's cousin, Venessaint (right), and his friend and neighbor Lovinsky. It took me some time to understand that Venessaint was a *restavèk*—a child worker—in Lovely's home, although the family treated him well.

Nigel Fisher in the United Nations compound of Port-au-Prince, where he worked his way up to Haiti's UN deputy special representative. He'd spent his life traveling from one disaster and war zone to the next, and he found Haiti among the most challenging. *Lucas Oleniuk/* Toronto Star

Many of the earthquake victims were buried in large pits in the country's traditional paupers' fields, called Titanyen. The crosses were put up on the first anniversary of the earthquake.

Gilberte Salomon surrounded by students from the school she founded, Muspan Montessori (top). Her plan was to fund the school from the profits of her nursing college, Institut Louis Pasteur, which she rebuilt four years after the earthquake.

Every time I arrived at Lovely's home, she crawled under her bed to find her homework or report card. Here, she is showing me for the first time how she can read.

Lovely at her kindergarten graduation, which lasted more than four hours and required two outfit changes. It felt more elaborate than my wedding.

Lalanne (left) lived in the same neighborhood that Lovely was rescued from. When I asked if he knew who rescued her, he answered, "It was me." *Catherine Porter/* Toronto Star

Lovely, her mother, Rosemene, and her father, Enel, returning to their old neighborhood, a slum called Fort National, to see where Lovely had been buried and to thank Lalanne.

Lovely's friend, Jenanine (middle), her cousin Lypse (right), and her brother, Jonathan.

Here I am sitting with Lovely's family in their third home, after the earthquake. The white plastic chairs and table were my Christmas gift to the family, and they were among their only pieces of furniture. *Dimitri Bien-Aimé*

I always pitched new stories to my editors to convince them to send me back to Haiti. Throughout the course of my trips, I interviewed everyone from earthquake victims (top) to Haitian prime minister Laurent Lamothe (right) to Michaëlle Jean, the Haiti-born governor general of Canada (left). *Paul Haslip*

It seemed right to bring my daughter, Lyla, to Haiti. But it was only when we stepped out of the airport and I snapped this photo of her that I realized what I had done: How could I be both a mother and a journalist in Haiti?

Lyla's first meeting with Lovely in the schoolyard was inauspicious. But as soon as we got to Lovely's home, the pair spilled out of the car and raced off together, hand-in-hand. When we left that day, Lyla burst into tears and declared, "Lovely is my best friend."

Lyla and I started a new tradition of going to the beach with Lovely's family. It was the first time that anyone in Lovely's family had swum in the ocean, and they loved it. It seemed the definition of poverty: to live on a tropical island but never get to enjoy the sea.

Five years after the earthquake, Lovely's family continued to grow. When Rosemene gave birth to another son, Zachary, she asked for names from the Bible. When I got to Zachary, she simply said, "Yes, that one."

I agreed to become *marenn*, or godmother, to Lovely's cousin Lala because, after years of visiting and supporting Lovely and her family, it seemed time for me to accept my role in Haiti—not just as a journalist, but as a friend. Left to right: Lypse, Catherine, Elistin, Lala, and Rosita. *Richard Miguel*

My trip back for Lala's baptism was the first that included no deadline anxiety. I wouldn't write another story about Lovely for the newspaper, but I would document her story as part of my own life. We were now family. *Richard Miguel*

Wait a minute, I thought. *Wasn't the television in Gaëlle's house next door?*

Then it dawned on me: Rosemene had told me they'd lived in a four-room house with their extended family. I assumed they had lived in all four rooms. I believed they were in better shape before the earthquake than they were now. Standing there, I saw the truth: they had rented one room of a four-bedroom house; only half of this platform had been theirs, and the whole extended family—nine people—had lived in that one room.

I finally understood how poor the family had been. I thought the tin shed they shared with Rosita and Elistin had been terrible, but it was no different from the home they'd lived in before.

We all stood there stunned: Rosemene remembering what had happened the night of the earthquake, Enel agog at how much had changed, and me realizing the truth.

On the way back up to their home, I picked up lunch for everyone. Rosemene and Enel raced into a market to spend the last monthly installment of my promised US$600 on supplies to restock Rosemene's business.

They spent 550 gourdes (US$13.75) on a box of 240 bouillon cubes and a bag of rice for 850 gourdes (US$21.25). Rosemene explained her market plan to me. She would sell the bouillon cubes, two for 5 gourdes (12.5 cents US). The rice, she'd sell one scoop at a time, earning her another 930 gourdes in total (US$23.25).

Making that amount would likely take two weeks.

I quickly did the math on the back of my notepad: For fifteen days of work, she'd make 130 gourdes of profit—just over US$3 total.

I hadn't been naïve thinking US$600 would fix Rosemene's business. Where I *had* been naïve, though, was thinking her business would support Lovely.

Rosemene had been saving money for Lovely to go to school; I didn't doubt that. But now I knew it would never be enough. Without help, Lovely would be destined to live at the very bottom of Haiti's social ladder—a poor, illiterate woman living in a slum.

A daunting feeling filled me. Unless the government lived up to its promise of free education, there was no way that Lovely would be able to continue going to school after the two years I promised to fund her were up. Rosemene and Enel couldn't afford to pay even the low tuition of the local Baptist mission school, let alone the middle-class school we'd enrolled Lovely in, without aid. My initial plan of helping the family find their financial independence seemed delusionally ignorant. Having seen how they lived before the earthquake, I realized that they were never on their feet in the first place, so how could I think US$600 would get them there?

I'd set a two-year deadline to my help, in the hope of extricating myself cleanly. But how could I follow through in good conscience now that I understood that bargain was cruelly unrealistic? Would I really stop funding Lovely's education if it meant she would stop going to school?

I was beginning to learn the true danger of becoming personally involved in a story as a journalist. You start to care.

Part 2

Chapter 7

Lovely in the Time of Cholera

Dimitri picked me up at the airport in his green Patrol. We had hardly made it out of the airport parking lot before I pointed out a bundle of faded red umbrellas by the side of the dusty road and asked him to pull over.

I hadn't been in Haiti for half an hour and I was desperate for a cigarette. It didn't matter that I was no longer bombarded by scenes of death and anguish out the car window; my pattern was now set: when in Haiti, I smoked. I'd packed my running shoes and started jogging around the verdant grounds of the guesthouse early every morning, doing loops up and down the rocky stairs like a cooped-up hamster. But it was to no avail. I couldn't rewrite my Haiti habits.

Upon arriving, the first stop I made was always at those umbrellas to buy cigarettes and add minutes on my cheap Haitian phone. The umbrellas were from Digicel, the nation's largest cell phone company, and invariably there would be a guy nearby wearing a red Digicel pinny, who would lean into the car window, take my money, and text me minutes from his phone.

After our pit stop, we made our way to a local gas station, where I changed my American cash for gourdes. Since coming to Haiti, I had never been inside a bank. Dimitri had showed me how to exchange money on the street, finding one of the money changers he knew by sight only. They didn't wear pinnies—they just looked like cool layabouts, wearing flashy sunglasses and leaning against the wall of some gas station as if they were waiting for a friend.

"How would you ever know who they were?" I asked Dimitri once.

"In Haiti, you have to know, to know" was Dimitri's perennial answer.

We then nudged our way through afternoon traffic to the guesthouse, where I dumped my bags and climbed back in. We were heading straight up the mountain to see Lovely and, more importantly, her cousin Lina, Elistin's daughter from a previous relationship who had recently moved up to Fermathe from the city below. Lina was tall, like her dad, and had his apple cheeks and almond eyes.

When I'd left the family in October 2010, Lina had been eight months pregnant. She wouldn't disclose much about the father, other than he wasn't in the picture. But she'd been happy. I'd promised Dimitri a half day's pay if he went up and took some photos of the baby for me.

Instead, he'd phoned me the week before, sounding very somber.

"The child died," he said. It was a boy. He'd been only fifteen days old. "They never took him to the hospital."

Now, as we roared past the mansions of Haiti's elite and skirted the edges of cliffs that looked down over an emerald quilt of impossibly steep farmers' fields, Dimitri repeated the story and added the parts he hadn't already related. When he'd spoken to Lina alone, she'd told him that neighbors were saying she was cursed to always bear children who died.

When we arrived, we found Lina curled in a wooden chair in the dirt yard, swaddled in layers of dirt-smudged clothing and sorrow.

She had another black shirt tied around her head like a turban. She lifted her eyes to greet me and then returned her gaze to the ground.

"I just stopped crying this week," she said softly, playing with the thread of her dark sweatshirt.

As I sat with her, the family surrounded us, their voices barreling over one another to fill in the depressing details of the baby's short life.

Lina had hoped to deliver the baby at the Baptist mission hospital, but it was deemed too expensive. Instead, Elistin had hired a hospital nurse to come to the house and help deliver the baby there. The nurse had come and gone quickly, determining that Lina was in early labor and still had many hours to go.

In the end, Lina pushed the baby out on Elistin's bed with guidance from her stepmom and a neighbor. Rosita cut the umbilical cord with one of Elistin's tailoring razors.

He was *fèt ak kwaf*. Born with the caul still over his head. In Haitian folklore, this meant he was destined for a lucky life. The irony was too much.

"He was white, had lots of hair," Lina said, when I asked her to describe him. "He wasn't so fat."

She hadn't even named him.

"I was going to open the Bible and choose a name when we got his birth certificate," she said. "I didn't want to pick a name that was bad luck."

The family agreed that he was healthy that first week. But during his second week he had stopped feeding, turning his face away from Lina's breast. Then he started to wheeze.

Rosita and Rosemene took turns comforting him, feeding him wet crackers and massaging his naked body with the same *maskriti* seed oil they used on Lovely's hair.

The day he died, Lina was sleeping in bed beside him. One of the children who crept in noticed he was no longer breathing.

"I shook him," Lina said. "I called, 'Baby, baby.' There was no response."

Everyone was clearly still in shock. The family sat glumly, except for Lovely, who danced in the yard, oblivious to the family's sorrow.

They all seemed defensive. They were blaming one another for the tragedy.

Rosita said she thought the baby had fallen and that Lina had held him too tightly.

"He did not fall," countered Lina. She believed that someone had cursed her. The day the baby died, she heard a noise on the roof. She thought it was a *lougawou*—a werewolf—sent to kill him. *Lougawous* were demonic shape-shifters, believed to devour people, children particularly. Apart from armed thugs, they were what people in the camps told me they feared most at night.

"Since the first time, they killed my baby. They killed the second one, too. I know people don't like me and my family. I don't know why. They just hate us," Lina said.

A previous pregnancy? This was the first time I'd heard of it. I pieced together scraps of information she provided with gentle coaxing. It seemed she'd had a baby ten years earlier, when she was just sixteen. That little girl had also died. I was stunned. Losing one child was an unspeakable tragedy, but two? It was too much to bear.

I asked Rosita why she hadn't rushed the baby to the hospital for treatment when he started to wheeze and stopped feeding.

"We didn't think of it," she said simply. "We just thought it was the weather. He had a cold."

Elistin offered a different explanation. They still owed money to the nurse. They couldn't afford to foot the hospital bill.

"The baby was missing vitamins. We could see his ribs," he said. "I wanted to take him to the doctor, but the financial pressure . . . I couldn't deal with it."

The mission hospital charged just US$1 a day for a bed, but every laboratory test and prescription was extra, and they quickly added up. In June, the nurses and doctors staying in my guesthouse had pooled US$320 to pay for ten days' worth of treatment for a premature baby in a Pétionville community hospital.

I understood the math. Spending US$320 was more than a year's earnings for Rosemene right now.

But still, anger bubbled up inside me. I'd been helping this family for months now. How, on my watch, did a baby die without ever seeing a doctor?

Their resignation infuriated me. In Canada, there would be an inquest over this child's death. Professionals would be subpoenaed to testify about how our social safety net had failed to catch him, all so that it might be carefully mended and strengthened to support the next child. But here there were no ambulances to dispatch, few doctors to call, little medication to offer, and no social workers to make sure each child was protected—even from his or her parents, if need be.

No building had collapsed or buried this child. He was smothered by poverty, and no international aid workers had rushed in to help. This was considered normal. It was the human picture of those daunting statistics collected by the World Health Organization that showed, every four years, more babies and the mothers delivering them die in Haiti than just about anywhere else in the world.

"I told her not to cry. The baby's dead. There is nothing she can do," Elistin said.

Later that evening, we stopped at the cemetery. Most of the tombstones resembled miniature concrete apartments, all rising shoulder to shoulder. Each held a number of caskets; people often rented the space by the year. Large stone crosses loomed high above them. Elistin had brought the baby here and buried him less than an hour after he'd died. He hadn't paid for a plot. He had just dug a hole, placed the child inside, and prayed.

"I asked God to receive his soul, because it wasn't his fault he died," he said. "It was his mother and father's fault."

I couldn't help but add a few more names to that list: his grandparents; the Haitian government that looked out only for its own interests and not those of its poorest citizens; and foreign donors, who were still not working together to weave a safety net for Haitian children . . .

The next day, in the city below, I dropped into Port-au-Prince's general hospital, as I did every trip.

The security guards waved Dimitri's SUV in and we parked by the ragged garden that was the central point of the hospital's dismal complex. About 40 percent of its buildings had been damaged or completely destroyed during the earthquake, including the outpatient clinic and pediatric ward. The ones left standing looked as though they'd been hauled up from the ocean floor, their once white walls mottled with gray and brown spots and cut by long, curving cracks. Metal bars curled up the side of one building like eyelashes. The brown tents that had clogged the garden and surrounding cobblestone roads immediately after the disaster had dwindled to just a few. The pediatrics ward had moved into four low-slung plywood bunkers near the entry gates.

The smell of urine was overwhelming. A thin river of gray water pulsed down the gutter by the SUV's wheels. It came from half-naked people who were bathing from buckets out in the open. A man pushed his shriveled father, dressed only in underwear, around parked cars in a wheelchair that could have been fished from the trash, its leather seat and backrest replaced by a white plastic chair. The place reminded me of those Renaissance paintings of hell I'd seen in the galleries of Florence and Paris—all wretched naked people fighting with death.

My mental tape loop was dotted with disturbing scenes I'd glimpsed here over the months of visits. On my first trip, I'd stopped at one of the brown tents and looked inside its plastic window to see a skeletal woman completely naked except for bangles on her wrists and rings on each finger, which rested by her groin. Someone had set a green plastic bin on her chest—the kind doctors throw dirty scissors into after cutting a person open. I could barely make out her face behind it, but what I could see was a hole where her eye should have been. Foreign doctors in scrubs raced behind me, but no one stopped. She was discarded, like the mound of garbage in the tent's corner.

On another trip, I'd walked into the very last tent on one of the paths and discovered it was the ward for abandoned children, where Gilberte's second son had come from. There, a newborn baby lay alone in his mottled crib. His head was giant, his legs and arms curled like baby palm fronds. He was so skinny, each of his ribs protruded like the black keys of a piano. The infant diaper covered his entire belly. A nurse brooding in the corner of the tent about not being paid in months told me he had spina bifida.

The worst part about it all was that this was the best care the hospital had offered Haitians in decades. The aid groups that choked its grounds had brought medical supplies that, traditionally, patients had had to buy themselves from pharmacies across the street—if they could afford them. With the aid groups' help, the hospital had opened its first intensive care unit, fully staffed around the clock—a service that was unheard-of before the earthquake.

By now the hospital had received its first three ambulances, so, on paper at least, it could go collect critically ill patients rather than have them arrange their own transportation there on the back of a motorcycle or *tap-tap*. Even if Lina had made it all the way down the mountain to this hospital with her baby, though, there would have been no assurances he would have received the lifesaving treatment he'd clearly needed.

Over the past few months I'd been trying to understand the health care system in Haiti—or the lack of it. The picture that formed closely resembled the country's education system. The constitution committed the state to run hospitals across the country for their citizens' health, but in practice they were so poorly resourced that patients were forced to pay, which meant many didn't step through the doors in the first place. Just like teachers, there were few trained doctors, as they typically went into private practice or left the country for jobs in Canada, the United States, or France, where they could earn at least thirty times as much as they did in Haiti. And, just like in education, the rich paid for good treatment, while the poor were left to beg for terrible care.

The problem wasn't lack of resources. The government had a meager budget to put toward health care itself, but international donors had funneled hundreds of millions of dollars into health care projects in the country long before the earthquake. The issue was the coordination of those resources.

The hope was that the earthquake would change all that. The Haitian government had drafted a plan to piece the tattered system into a whole, providing free coverage first to the country's most vulnerable, and eventually expanding to everyone.

It had been done before—not just in other countries, like Bolivia, but right here in Haiti. A nonprofit called Zanmi Lasante, or Partners in Health (PIH), had built eleven hospitals, each smaller than the general hospital, of course. But they offered free care, and the quality was reportedly quite good.

Dimitri and I set out to visit one in Lascahobas, a small town near the Dominican border that seemed like a dusty frontier town from a Western movie: saloon-like stores lined the main street. At the end of the road was the hospital, which seemed like a mirage. Its buildings were white seashells set in a pond of green—manicured lawns and green trees. We got out of the car and walked under a trellis heavy with white flowers. There were ponds filled with goldfish, surrounded by banana trees and glorious orange birds of paradise in full bloom.

Inside, the wards were simple but clean, with beds in rows filled with patients suffering from heart disease and malaria. There was a large functioning laboratory, solar panels to provide some of the hospital's electricity, an ambulance to take emergency patients to a larger PIH hospital an hour away, and a large, stocked pharmacy.

The care wasn't just basic, either. On my tour, doctors introduced me to a ten-year-old girl who was sliding her injured left foot up and down the hall, practicing the walk her physiotherapist had taught her. She had arrived from Port-au-Prince six months before with what doctors thought was typhoid fever. Five days later she slipped into a coma and stayed there for two whole months. It turned out she had tuberculous meningitis, a disease that requires four courses of drugs over months.

All of the hospital services were provided to some 250 patients a day for free. Officially, the hospital charged a nominal 25 gourdes (62 cents US) admission fee, but the fee was waived for pregnant women, children, HIV and tuberculosis patients, and anyone who couldn't afford it, which essentially meant everyone.

I decided that if I were ever to fall sick in Haiti, I'd beg Dimitri to bring me here. It was the only place I'd seen in Haiti that projected kindness, inspired hope, and offered first-rate service. It felt like a beacon of possibility.

The hospital had been built on donated land, which was PIH's model. The government paid the staff's base salary, which the NGO topped up. It seemed to be the template for the government plan: NGOs stepping in where the government could not, but following the government's direction and not the other way around.

"If I wasn't hopeful, I wouldn't still be here," PIH's country director said. "There is a Haitian proverb: *'Depi tet pa koupe, w toujou genyen espwa mete chapo.'* As long as your head is not cut off, you have the hope of putting on a hat."

Instead of focusing on all that was wrong here, the director pointed to what was *not* wrong. It was refreshing to hear such optimism for once.

"We haven't seen any major outbreaks of anything, which is good. It's at least something," she continued. And then, as if to convince herself, she repeated it: "There hasn't been a major disease outbreak."

Six days later, on October 12, 2010, a twenty-eight-year-old man developed acute watery diarrhea after drinking from a tributary to the Artibonite River. He died less than twenty-four hours later. Two people who had prepared his body for the funeral developed the same severe watery diarrhea. On October 17, more sick people arrived at the small Hôpital de Mirebalais, not far from where backhoes were clearing the corn and rice fields to make way for Partners in Health's new flagship hospital.

They were the first cases of cholera seen by doctors in Haiti in almost a century.

When I next traveled to Port-au-Prince in November 2010, the cholera outbreak was in full bloom. In just a month it had already killed more than 1,100 people and sent almost 20,000 to the hospital—mostly people from the central plateau near Mirebalais, but the outbreak had already spread as far south as Jérémie and north to Cap-Haïtien.

My second night back in Haiti, I reconnected with Nigel Fisher, the UN deputy special representative, for dinner. He was crisp and charming as ever. But he was less optimistic. An edge of irritation had crept into his voice. The week before, he'd launched the United Nations strategy to combat cholera in Haiti, which called for more of everything, from water purification tablets and rehydration salts to doctors and nurses trained in cholera treatment stationed across the country. It came with a US$164 million budget. So far, only 10 percent of that had arrived from donors.

Accusations—which proved to be true—were swirling that the UN peacekeepers from Nepal had inadvertently infected the country with the disease that was endemic in their country through a leaky septic system at their base near Mirebalais. In Nigel's view, however, an emergency was not the time to cast blame. He feared this would mean hundreds of thousands of people would be infected over the next few months, and that the death toll could reach 10,000.

Nigel had been meeting with the heads of large aid organizations to ask them to commit some resources to combating cholera, so far without success.

"I don't know where the money has gone. I've been singularly unsuccessful at ascertaining how much they have left, what they are planning to do with it," he said. "I know many have got a wad of cash, but I don't know what they are spending it on."

Of all countries to get a waterborne disease, Haiti was the perfect host—and, again, its vulnerability had nothing to do with the earthquake. Most people in the country did not have access to clean water. In the countryside, many drank directly from streams and rivers, and if the waterways became contaminated—as the Artibonite had become—then those people would inevitably become sick. Most city dwellers bought their water, either by the tanker (the rich) or the bucket (the poor). But there was also an ancient underground clay pipe system in downtown Port-au-Prince dating from Napoleon's era, which the government's water authority purified with chlorine. If it got infected, many in the city would fall ill.

As for the sewage system, there was none. The country did not have a single sewage treatment plant. Half of the population practiced what UNICEF called "open defecation." The rest either owned septic tanks if they were rich or dug holes that they paid men called *bayakous* to empty at night. The *bayakous* typically dumped the sewage into the ravines, so during the rainy season the huge slums along the city's waterfront—like Cité Soleil—were flooded, spreading the waste from latrines everywhere.

It was easy to see why government and health workers feared the arrival of cholera to the city. The camps were protected, since they were still equipped with Porta-Potties and water stations. It was the slums that presented the nightmare scenario and, sure enough, when cholera surfaced first in Port-au-Prince, it was in a part of Cité Soleil called Wharf Jérémie.

The disease spread quickly. In one day 85 deaths were recorded in Port-au-Prince. The next: 146.

I saw my first cases at a treatment center in Cité Soleil. I will never forget it: patients lay on wooden cots with their pants pulled down. Their bums had been placed over holes in the beds and liquid poured from them into buckets below.

Experts said cholera could kill someone within four hours, and I could see why: the dehydration was so rapid that it could cause a heart attack or renal failure. But as quickly as cholera could kill someone, it was also mercifully easy to treat. No chemotherapy or blood transfusions were required. All that a patient needed was rehydration with clean water, salt, and a little sugar; even severe cases only needed a simple rehydration IV and some antibiotics. The fact that something so treatable had killed so many people so quickly underscored the feebleness of the country's health care system.

Fear was palpable in the city. Walls that once were plastered with political graffiti had turned their sights to the disease. *Aba UN Kolera*

Kaka—Down with the UN That Brought Cholera—was a popular tag. Locals attacked the new treatment centers opening in their neighborhoods for fear they would bring the disease to them. Mobs stoned bodies left in the streets and blocked city workers who tried to bring them to cemeteries. The government had recently hired a couple of crews in the city to collect bodies from the streets and swiftly remove them before they contaminated others, and those workers were set upon, too.

Early one morning I met with one of the collection teams, made up of a dozen young men, and trailed them for the day. When a call came in about a body, they climbed into a van, a couple of trucks, and a *tap-tap* and raced off. Dimitri and I followed them in his SUV, charging up a road into the poor district of Carrefour-Feuilles. The convoy came to a sudden stop, and we watched the men get dressed into poor men's hazmat suits: yellow rain jackets, large black rubber boots, dishwashing gloves, surgical masks, and chemistry lab goggles. Then they donned the hard plastic backpacks that gardeners use, usually brimming with insecticide, that came with long tubes and nozzles. Theirs sprayed just chlorinated water.

Laid out on the street beside a small lottery stand was a fifty-seven-year-old man dressed in a fresh brown shirt and dress pants. His feet were bare and his eyes were open and glassy. His daughter appeared from a crowd in the distance and pleaded with the crew, telling them her father had died that morning of a heart attack on a *tap-tap* en route to the hospital. They told her to back away and began to spray the ground around his body. Then they showered her father's corpse. Clearly no one believed her: If he had died of a heart attack, why had she left him on the road? Why was he not laid out at home?

I watched as the workers performed their dehumanizing ritual. One worker rolled the man's head to one side and then the other, stuffing his ears with chlorine-soaked cotton balls. Then he did the same to his eyes and nose and finally the dead man's open mouth.

The workers brought out blue flagging tape and bound his legs. They crossed his arms and lifted him awkwardly into one white body bag, and then another, for safe measure. That night they threw his body into a mass pit in the same area where earthquake victims had been dumped just ten months before.

It all was so gruesome and grim. Thank goodness the disease had not made its way up the mountain to Fermathe, where Lovely lived. How could this little country bear so much suffering?

On this trip, for the first time, I packed an extra bag full of *rad kenedi*, one of the names locals used for the secondhand clothes hung up for sale on walls around the city, because the first such shipments had arrived during US president John F. Kennedy's administration.

For months I'd been collecting cute outfits that Lyla and Noah had grown out of and, instead of dropping them off at a neighbor's home, put them in storage bins in the basement. Friends and colleagues added dresses and shoes they no longer wore, which I tucked aside for Rosemene and Rosita. A couple of days before leaving home, I'd done a quick shopping trip, buying golf shirts for Elistin and Enel, as well as some Tylenol, toothpaste, and toothbrushes for all the kids.

Part of it was just practical: I was flying to Haiti; I had all these things and no longer needed them, and they did. So why wouldn't I bring them? But part of me wanted to play the role of Santa Claus. I enjoyed giving Lovely and her family small gifts that brought them joy.

Lyla, despite her continued anxiety and sadness about my trips to Haiti, had slipped a Dora the Explorer doll and a small pink chicken in my bag the night before I left. She also added a few of the colorful rubber bracelets she loved to wear and said they were all presents for Lovely. Even though they had never met, Lyla was building a relationship with the other little girl in my life.

Once in Haiti, I carefully laid out all the clothing into piles on my bed: Lyla's size-three dresses, shirts, and pants for Lovely; Noah's size-two clothing for Jonathan and Lypse; a size-four dress for Jenanine; the small women's dresses for Rosemene and Rosita.

When Dimitri arrived to pick me up, he lifted up one of the women's dresses, held it before him, and laughed. "That is way too big for Rosemene," he said. He picked up a skirt and dress I had set aside for nine-year-old Sophonie. "This will fit Rosemene," he said. "And this could be a nice skirt for Rosita."

He picked up two of Noah's cast-off sweatshirts, one of them emblazoned with a Canadian maple leaf. They were both size two. "These will fit Jenanine," he said.

I looked at him, aghast.

"Those no longer fit my two-year-old son," I said indignantly. "Jenanine is four."

"*Catherine*," he said. "Your son is healthy. These kids are skinny. They are not normal sizes."

When Lovely returned from school later that day, she raced into her family's room to try on the clothes I had brought.

I could hear Lovely giggling. When she emerged, Lyla's pink dress hung almost to her ankles and gaped open at the back of her neck. Dimitri had been right: the clothes were massive on her. But she loved them. She paraded up and down the yard like a model, putting her hands to her hips and shifting them back and forth as she walked.

"*Comme ça.* Like this," she said, pursing her lips. Her visits to the dentist had been a success. Her teeth were no longer causing her chronic pain.

It was a glorious afternoon. The light in the yard was speckled, casting a soft glow over everyone's faces. I sipped a coffee Rosita had brewed for me using a filter stitched from the sleeve of one of her husband's old dress shirts, and watched Lovely doing her supermodel walks. I had a strange sense of being in two places at once. It was like an image of my daughter cast from the projector of my mind and transposed over Lovely, and I could see what she had been doing the last time I remembered her wearing those clothes. Bringing them to Lovely had seemed like a practical gift, but once they were on her, they felt freshly intimate. Just as Lyla was beginning to share her world with Lovely, it seemed that Lovely was inadvertently joining Lyla's.

While we sat talking, Enel's cell phone rang. It was Michel Martelly, the bawdy musician known as Sweet Micky who wore diapers onstage as a stunt and who was now running for president. That is, it was a prerecorded message by Martelly telling Enel that if he wanted the price of rice to go down, he should vote for the bald guy with the bull insignia on the ballot. Sweet Micky's party's name was Repons Peyizan (Peasant Response), and the bull was its symbol. Since there are so many parties running in every Haitian election and so many Haitians are illiterate, it's important that parties have strong symbols voters can recognize on a ballot.

"I don't know who to vote for," Enel said. "I only know two candidates." The last time he had voted for Préval and been disappointed.

"Even if I had an electoral card, I wouldn't vote," said Rosemene, who was still bending over the laundry tub. "They have all lied to us. This government, every government. They put money in their own pockets and not in ours. Food is *byen chè*. School is *byen chè*. I don't trust any of them."

The family's radio was broken, so they hadn't listened to any election broadcasts. But the *teledjòl*—Kreyòl for "mouth television," or the rumor mill—was working just fine. Since so many Haitians couldn't read and didn't have electricity for television or radio, word of mouth was often the only way they got their news. Given their penchant for answering their phones at any time of day or night, the *teledjòl* was incredibly effective. It had brought dirty rumors about another of the presidential candidates having many illegitimate children.

"*Kraze fwaye*. He's a homewrecker," said Elistin, arriving from a neighbor's stoop where he was sewing children's school uniforms on a borrowed machine. "How can you trust a guy like that?"

He was the only one in the family with an electoral card for this election, which would permit him to vote. But he was nervous about the election. The *teledjòl* had also brought news of recent deadly riots against the United Nations Stabilisation Mission in Haiti (Mission des

Nations Unies pour la Stabilisation en Haïti, known by its acronym, MINUSTAH) in the northern city of Cap-Haïtien. Elistin wondered if the riots might spread here.

"Do you know the story of Ruelle Vaillant?" he asked me. "Don't you think that could happen again?"

The story of Ruelle Vaillant would scare anyone from voting. It is the name of a street in downtown Port-au-Prince where, in 1987, there was a polling station inside a school. That year was the first time Haiti had seen democratic elections after three decades of dictatorship. While people lined up downtown to vote, the deposed dictator's hired thugs—known as Tonton Macoutes—marched through the streets with their guns. They opened fire on the people waiting to vote on Ruelle Vaillant and killed twenty-nine.

Politics in Haiti has always been a dangerous sport.

Still, I was planning to join Elistin for the morning when he voted. That thought reassured him. Maybe he wouldn't be shot if he was there with a *blan*. He told me to come early the morning of the election so he could vote and then go to church. As I said my good-bye, Lovely reached for my hand and walked me down the path to where Dimitri had parked his car.

When we got there, she wanted to come with me.

"Are we going to the hospital?" she asked. "I like the hospital."

I did visit the local Baptist mission hospital a few days later, but it was on my own. There was an ancient X-ray machine, two operating rooms, a laboratory, and a small pediatric ward. Like the dental clinic, the waiting rooms were all lined with long wooden church pews, so varnished that they gleamed, adding a dignity and saintly calm to the place.

Some of the programs and staff here were paid by the government, and the costs in the general ward were very low. But its surgeons and specialists worked as independent contractors and had to be paid in full by patients, and that was expensive.

The administrator led me to the accounting office, where I filled out some rudimentary paperwork for Lovely's family, slowly printing out the names of each member on a page to ensure that all of them would be able to get free service here. Then I counted out US$1,000. I figured, given that a family visit we'd made here together in June had cost US$26, this might cover a few years of basic health care and medication. If they had an emergency, they would run through it much quicker—but that was the point. I wanted to prevent any further pointless deaths in the family if I could.

The rest of the money I'd spent on the family, to my mind, had fallen into a long-term development plan. Even though Rosemene's business had not taken off as I had hoped, the idea behind giving her monthly grants was still to boost her back to being self-sufficient like she was before the earthquake. Paying for two years of Lovely's, Sophonie's, and Jenanine's educations similarly seemed like an investment toward their family's eventual escape from poverty.

In contrast, this medical payment was short-term aid, plain and simple. There was nothing sustainable about it. Once the family ran through the account, they'd likely go back to paying out of pocket when they could and going without health care the rest of the time—unless the government came through with its health care plan to provide free medical service to the population, starting with young children and pregnant women. Even that wonderful improvement would be partial.

But how could I not create some health insurance for them? I believed health care was a human right. Having grown up in Canada, I had never had to pay for a planned visit to my family doctor or a rushed one to the hospital. It all came out of our collective taxes. It seemed criminal to force people away from treatment because they were poor, particularly during a cholera outbreak.

Besides, I saw the difference a few visits to the dentist had made for Lovely. What was the point of sending a little girl to school if she was feverous and moaning with pain? How would she learn?

I now knew the stakes were much larger than a toothache. To haul herself and her family out of poverty, Lovely had to do more than learn. She had to stay alive.

Chapter 8

Whoever Is in Charge?

It was hard to believe the country was running an election amidst the rubble and cholera. But in late November 2010, it was. The mantra at the time was stability. International donors said an election was important for rebuilding, and President Préval insisted it was important for the country's young democracy.

Reporters were issued special ID cards by the electoral commission so that we could get into the polling places and, in theory, get through the roadblocks that would be everywhere to contain any violence. There were no assurances, of course. Every rule was flexible here, particularly in its application. I thought it best to sleep somewhere in Fermathe near Lovely's house so that I could be sure to meet Elistin early on the morning of the election.

The two-lane highway I'd become so familiar with looked entirely different at night. It was empty—not a single car, person, or police checkpoint. Most of the lampposts that dotted the edges of the road were unlit, so it was very dark. The graceful trees and earthy cliffs looked ominous under the stark glare of our headlights, and the potholes that hopscotched the road appeared enormous. Dimitri gunned the engine and took the turns so quickly, I gripped my window handle, worried we'd fly off the road.

Dimitri wasn't speeding for the sake of it: he was trying to outrace any kidnappers he worried might be waiting to ambush approaching cars. Reports of kidnapping were routine in Haiti, particularly around Christmas, when many parents lined up at Western Union depots to receive transfers from family members in Canada or the United States for gifts and their children's school fees. But the number of incidents had become alarming in recent weeks, and they were especially bad in wealthy enclaves such as the one we were roaring through on our way up toward Lovely's family. The *teledjòl* buzzed with suspicions that ransoms were funding various political campaigns.

I'd heard enough personal stories about kidnapping, so I didn't second-guess Dimitri's fear. At the end of one interview about the country's health system, a cardiologist told me how, during the peak of the kidnappings just four years ago, armed men had walked into his waiting room, robbed all his patients, and then taken him. What frightened me the most was the gratuitous violence he described. They duct-taped him to a chair and tortured him, breaking his cheekbone and teeth, burning his skin with molten plastic, and cutting his legs. He was sure they would kill him. But after his family paid a ransom, they left him bound and blindfolded in a parked *tap-tap* and he stumbled to a nearby house. Now he was back in the same office, talking to me. Why had he returned? Because he loved his country and was a matter-of-fact fatalist. He would die when he was meant to die, he said. He wasn't frightened, but his story scared the hell out of me.

We found the farmhouse where we'd be staying, and thankfully the gate was open. Our room was musty, with one single bed in the middle of it and a mattress laid out on the floor. I fell asleep to the sound of Dimitri talking on the phone to his wife in New Jersey.

It was still pitch-black outside when we set out the next day at

4:00 a.m. Elistin greeted us at his house in his nightcap and pajamas; he was brushing his teeth. Of course, in Caribbean time, 4:00 a.m. didn't mean 4:00 a.m., so we waited for him to bathe from a bucket. It was incredibly quiet, with only the faint sound of a neighbor's radio breaking the stillness. The sky above us sparkled with stars and a crescent moon casting the only light. It was cold—just 11 degrees Celsius, according to my phone. Dimitri and I jogged in place for warmth.

When Elistin was ready to go, I set out with him on foot up the road, while Dimitri waited behind with the car. The lights of Port-au-Prince sparkled like phosphorescence in the distance below.

The countryside, and the sun, were awakening.

"*Sa k pase?*"—"What's going on?" Elistin said, greeting neighbors on the road. "*Bonjou.*"—"Hello."

We reached the Fermathe market along with the first *timachanns*, pulling their baskets of parsley from their heads and setting up their stands. One swept garbage to the side of the road with an ancient witch's broom.

The voting station was inside the local high school, just down the road from Lovely's school, where all the *goute* supplies were usually lined up. The grounds were erupting with noise as more than one hundred scrutineers rushed around like a swarm of agitated bees, shouting into their phones and loudly demanding they be allowed into the polling rooms.

Prospective voters had already formed into a tight line, their bodies touching, and we pinched in. Up front, a man held a radio to his ear, and we all leaned in to hear the news about violence breaking out in the central part of the country.

A sugarcane seller set up shop from a wheelbarrow. A vendor arrived with heaping bowls of fried pork and *pate kòde*, deep-fried patties filled with salted herring, and set up her table before us.

Two hours after the polls officially opened, the gate to the school was yanked aside and we rushed inside for what felt like a game of capture the flag.

There were polling booths set up in eighteen classrooms.

I ran after Elistin as he rushed up the stairs. He held up his ID card to an election worker in the first room.

"Which office is it?" he asked. I noticed the door was marked *A to C* and figured Elistin just had to find the door with the letter E on it, for his last name. But he didn't know that, so we raced back downstairs, heading to another room.

He wasn't the only one confusedly running around. Everyone seemed to be. An eye doctor we'd met in line said she'd been to every room, and her name was simply not on the list.

We raced around the back of the school, up a different set of stairs, and then back down.

"Have you found your room?" the farmer ahead of us in line asked, once we landed upstairs for the second time.

"No!" Elistin shouted.

Such delicious disorganization. It's moments like this, I thought, that some upper-class Haitians long for once they've moved into the safe, efficient world of North America. "When I wake up in Haiti, life pinches me," one had told me the other day. "A trip to the store requires some problem-solving."

Elistin eventually found the classroom with the letter *E* on the door. The desks were in a large jumbled barricade against one wall, and a dozen scrutineers crowded the edges to watch.

The ballots were the size of posters, filled with the photo, number, symbol, and name of each candidate. Elistin was handed three—one for deputies, one for senators, and the last for presidential candidates. He had arrived with only a plan to vote for Mirlande Manigat for president; he'd told me he thought it was time for the steady hand of a woman to steer the country. The farmer friend in line had instructed him to vote for senator number 11 and deputy number 41, which he dutifully did.

Then I watched as his giant ballots were folded and stuffed into three see-through boxes. An election official stamped Elistin's right thumb with indelible purple marker so he couldn't vote again, and it was all over.

Finally, we could get into Dimitri's car and drive back to Lovely. But as we passed through the market, Dimitri's right wheel started to make a too-familiar squeaking noise. Breakdowns, along with cigarettes and the granola bars I continued to pack for lunch to save time, were becoming a regular staple of my daily Haitian life.

When we stepped into Elistin's yard, it was speckled with light filtering through the trees. The family was all up and Lovely was waiting for me. She wanted to draw pictures of cows and robots in my reporter's notebooks.

I'd covered many elections as a reporter, mostly when I worked at Toronto City Hall. At the *Star*, during provincial and federal elections, every reporter is assigned an electoral district to follow both in the runup to and on election night, so I'd also dipped my feet in federal and provincial races.

Recently there had been a heated race for the mayorship of Toronto. One of the candidates was a loud, populist councilor named Rob Ford, who would later admit to doing crack cocaine on the job, but only after vilifying the reporters who uncovered it. His positions were as unorthodox as his lifestyle. He took pride in not researching topics and shooting from the hip. I went to four debates in ten days in between trips to Haiti and shook my head when I heard him declare his strategy for addressing climate change: get rid of speed bumps so cars wouldn't slow down and spew extra exhaust from their tailpipes.

So I had recent experience covering nutty elections. But the election in Haiti took things to a whole new level. For president alone, there were 19 candidates on the ballot, whittled down from an initial 34 who had registered. Then add in nearly 900 candidates running for 109 deputy and senate seats—the numbers and the accompanying buzz were dizzying. Port-au-Prince was plastered with campaign posters. The graffiti on walls denouncing the UN and cholera were replaced with politicians' names and their slogans. *Tap-taps* were converted into campaign vehicles equipped with loudspeakers repeating theme songs and political messages.

In light of the country's brokenness, mounting cholera deaths, and poverty, the money spent on the election seemed grotesque. Dimitri and I drove to Carrefour, a sprawling suburb of Port-au-Prince, down a highway lined with tents and shacks, to see a campaign concert for President Préval's chosen successor, Jude Célestin. A stage had been built right on the road, and as the crowds arrived, a plane circled overhead, dropping campaign flyers that scattered around us like confetti. Candidates were darting across the country in rented helicopters. When Préval's party couldn't find SUVs for their campaign team because aid groups had sapped the country's rental agencies dry, they purchased the vehicles outright.

Each candidate needed to spend US$10 million to US$20 million to run a serious campaign, experts said—and the *teledjòl* whispered that much of that was for graft.

I dug up some evidence of that myself. Down by the broken palace, I met a man hawking paintings to aid workers or the rare tourist who came by. He had a membership card for Préval's Inite Party and told me he'd received about US$150 over the past few months from them. He smiled when he told me who he planned on voting for: Sweet Micky. He took me through a throng of shacks to his own home but admitted he was not a true earthquake victim: his house in Cité Soleil was still standing, but he hoped to get a second one from some unsuspecting aid group. He was a make-believe refugee and a make-believe Célestin supporter.

As Election Day approached, more and more candidates were loudly complaining the vote was rigged by Préval's ruling Inite Party. By noon of voting day, as I sat drawing robots with Lovely, the complaints reached a fever pitch. Twelve of the nineteen presidential candidates assembled on a stage to denounce the election as a "massive fraud." They demanded the election be canceled and called for Haitians to take to the streets in peaceful protest.

The traditional form of protest in Haiti is to shut down roads with rocks and blazing car tires. By early evening, intersections around Port-au-Prince were smoking. One exception was Route Delmas, which linked downtown Port-au-Prince to Pétionville. There, tens of thousands of people thronged, singing and dancing around a SUV that held the bald candidate Sweet Micky on its roof, alongside Haitian American hip-hop artist Wyclef Jean and beloved Vodou musician Richard Morse.

The crowd was boisterous and happy, chanting "Jude gave us money, but we voted for Micky."

Dimitri and I descended the mountain at the same alarming speed we'd traveled at the night before. But this time it wasn't fear fueling us. It was a hunger to dive into Election Day action. Again the road was eerily empty. Not only was there no traffic, there were none of the traffic stops we expected. Later, when stuck in another interminable *blokis*, I would often think back to that day with longing.

As we roared toward the city, I punched the radio on the dashboard to listen to Kreyòl reports, which Dimitri translated into English. There had been a handful of arrests for fraud. There were charges of ballot stuffing, and in Cité Soleil polling stations had been disrupted by gangs. Mostly, though, voters were just frustrated they couldn't find their names on lists.

That was inevitable. The country was not ready for an election: almost half of the country's voting places had been destroyed in the earthquake; hundreds of thousands of ID cards had been lost in the rubble, and many hadn't been reissued. On top of that, voters were scattered in large camps throughout the city, some far from their original neighborhood where they were forced to vote.

Despite the setbacks, the members of the election commission— widely seen as Préval supporters—held a press conference of their own that afternoon and announced that the elections had been fair.

That was the consensus of most of the international community, too. A team of observers with the Organization of American States and the Caribbean regional bloc said the vote could stand.

I called Nigel on the phone, and he agreed that the elections were considered viable. The noon press conference of those twelve candidates denouncing the process had not been a spontaneous response to cases of fraud they'd seen that day, he said. It was seen as a premeditated move.

Later, things got even more incredible when Préval claimed the United Nations had told him they were taking him out of the country because of "political problems." The head of the UN said this wasn't true.

It was hard to know who to believe. Corruption was rampant in Haiti, but the government wasn't the only culprit. Since kidnapped Africans had cast off Napoleon's troops and declared Haiti the world's first black republic in 1804, the country had been a victim of every type of foreign meddling imaginable: blockades, occupations, embargoes, foreign-funded coups. When France agreed to recognize Haiti as an independent country, the French insisted on being paid for their losses. In 1825, Haiti's president signed a restitution agreement for 150 million francs, even borrowing from French banks to pay the first installment. Ninety years later, some 80 percent of Haiti's national budget was still going toward paying back France and French banks.

It was no wonder the country was so poor.

The official results from the presidential election were released by the election commission in early December, a week after the voting. They gave the lead to former first lady Mirlande Manigat with 31 percent of the vote, which, under Haitian law, was not enough to secure her the presidency. It put Préval's pick Célestin in second with 22.48 percent. And not even a full percentage point behind him was Sweet Micky Martelly.

That meant that Manigat and Célestin would advance to a second round of voting in January, but Sweet Micky would not.

The announcement lit up the streets. Protesters blocked roads— including the one that led up to Lovely's home—by pulling the burning carcasses of cars and garbage containers across them. They lit

Jude Célestin's campaign office on fire. The bullets Elistin worried about were fired. The city was shut down: international flights were canceled, embassies closed, and supermarkets shuttered.

The response from the international community was mixed. Canada's foreign affairs minister urged "all political actors to address irregularities in accordance with Haitian electoral law." The American embassy in Port-au-Prince was more pointed, issuing a statement that questioned the results. And a Republican senator voiced a clear threat: the United States and other countries would withhold US$11 billion in promised aid if the country didn't come through with a clean winner.

Just who that winner might be wasn't clear. Some countries backed the original vote results, while others didn't find the "irregularities" serious enough to void the vote.

What was made very clear, however, was that, whoever was in charge, it was not the Haitian government. After extreme pressure from international donors and a visit from Hillary Clinton, the Haitian election council finally announced the March runoff would be between Manigat and Sweet Micky, not Célestin. In the meantime, an Air France plane arrived in the country, carrying on it an important piece of Haiti's past.

While all of this was going on, I was back home in Toronto, in bed. At first I thought I had vertigo from all the traveling I had done over the past year: seven trips in ten months. But then I visited the doctor, who told me that while I might have felt I was dizzy from the continual culture shock, there was in fact a medical explanation: an inner-ear infection. My immune system was shot from adrenaline and overwork.

The city outside my little house was blanketed in a fresh layer of snow and wrapped in twinkly lights. But I was not in a Christmas state of mind.

I had no gifts hidden around my house and, after walking through the city's biggest mall once and emerging empty-handed, I couldn't bear to return. Every item was translated into guilt: those boots were a year's tuition to school; that lipstick was Lovely's snacks for a week. I couldn't figure out how to write a Christmas letter without sounding maudlin, so I didn't bother. I couldn't even send just a family photo: after digging through my pictures from the year, I realized we had never taken one.

In the days right before Christmas, three unexpected gifts arrived on my desk in the newsroom. They were powerful pick-me-ups.

The first was an email from a Spanish catastrophe missionary who had flown into Haiti after the earthquake to volunteer his logistics expertise with the Red Cross. The Western Union beside the makeshift medical clinic in the Sonapi industrial district was the only place he could connect to the Internet, so he had often sat there with his laptop. Lovely had visited him regularly. He had left in February without saying good-bye and been heartbroken ever since. He had found my articles online and been overjoyed to learn Lovely was doing well.

"Something of my life has been left with that child," he wrote.

The second gift came in an envelope. Inside it I found a typed letter on yellow paper from a couple of readers I did not know. They lived in a small French-speaking town about four hours from Toronto, and they had decided, in lieu of Christmas gifts, they wanted their family and friends to send me money for Haiti. They signed off with "Joyeux Noël, Catherine" and included a check for C$2,000.

The day before my family's Christmas celebration started, the last present arrived. It was an email from a young political science student, one of the catastrophe missionaries I had met briefly during my first trip to Haiti. He was troubled by the four months he'd spent in Haiti, wondering if he had done any good at all. He was haunted by a severely handicapped boy whom he'd cared for at the clinic, feeding him, bathing him, singing him to sleep. When the clinic was forced to close, the boy and his family had no place to go, so the student had left them in a field near their shattered home.

Lovely was one of two rare success stories that buoyed him. The other was an orphaned boy named Carlos for whom the student helped find a sponsor and settle into a new home. He wondered if he had gravitated to Lovely's story because he himself was an orphan, adopted from South Korea by an American couple.

"When I think about that I'm reminded, if only for a moment, that we might all be connected, that we're in this together, and that we need to help each other whenever we can," he wrote.

Halfway through reading his email, the hair on the back of my neck rose: the sponsor whom this student had found for Carlos was Duncan Dee, the chief operating officer of Air Canada, who had flown me down to Haiti that first trip and inadvertently connected me with Lovely.

He was right: we are all interconnected, and we all are in this together. By the end of the email, tears were rolling down my chin and splashing onto my neck. A sense of awe and gratitude filled me. The universe seemed to be sending me a not-so-subtle message: it wasn't an accident I landed in Haiti and that Lovely was my first story.

I returned to Haiti a couple of weeks later for the earthquake's anniversary.

It was early in the morning—just 7:00 a.m., before the Caribbean sun had enough time to rub some warmth into the shoulders of the mountaintops.

Lovely was dressed in one of Noah's old red Gap shirts, with a baby-blue kerchief tied over her head. She sat in a strip of sunlight beside a fire pit, where a large pot of water was coming to a boil for the family's morning coffee. She was playing with the Dora doll Lyla had sent down and singing a hymn absentmindedly.

What a God, marvelous. What has he done, marvelous. Look at God, marvelous. Alelouya. Alelouya."

Shivering, I looked around the family's new rental home. It was perched like an eagle's nest under towering pine trees at the top of a craggy hill. It seemed like a perfect vacation retreat from the heat of the city, and I could see the idea behind the house was grand, with Grecian arches and an actual indoor kitchen and bathroom. But whoever had built it had either run out of money or hired a lousy construction crew. It was so poorly put together, it seemed like it was made of cards, with walls literally leaning in place and holes gapping through the tin ceiling, which was held down with rocks. There was no electricity or water; the sink and toilet didn't work, so the family was begging for water from neighbors and doing their business behind a nearby wall.

Inside, there was not a single piece of furniture. The family had laid out a tarp on the bedroom floor to sleep on, and in the corner they had fashioned a small table from a broken stereo speaker for their comb and toothbrushes.

It hardly seemed an improvement to me, but Rosemene was very happy with it. It was safer than a house in the city. And they were glad to be in their own place and not burdening her sister anymore. She also liked their neighbor, an old woman who came over in the mornings to chat with her.

When the coffee was ready, she sent a young boy with a metal cup for the woman.

The boy was her nine-year-old cousin from the countryside named Venessaint. I had first met him in November, but I hadn't realized he was there to stay. Rosemene told me he had come to help with the children so she and Enel could leave for work each day.

Venessaint was small, with a closely shorn head. The clothes he was wearing were filthy and at least four sizes too small: his pants fit like culottes, and the sleeves of the smudged rugby shirt reached just past his elbows. He was wearing red adult-sized sandals that overwhelmed his feet.

I watched as he tended to the fire, feeding it more wood to warm Lovely's bathwater. Suddenly it dawned on me: Venessaint was a *restavèk*.

"Have you ever gone to school?" I asked him.

"*Non,*" he answered in a husky voice. He had a stutter.

How could this be? *Restavèks* were renowned in Haiti as child slaves. If Lovely's family was considered well-off enough to afford a domestic helper, how poor must their cousins in the countryside be? Was it possible that Rosemene and Enel were mistreating this kid? I just couldn't believe that.

Venessaint brought me a sugary cup of coffee, which I gratefully cupped in my cold hands and sipped while Rosemene oiled and braided Lovely's hair, adding red flower clips at the end of each one. Like the entire country, Rosemene was thinking about the earthquake. But instead of mourning, she was full of gratitude.

"I always think to say thanks to God. If Lovely had died, it would be one year today," she said. "God gave me a gift, while so many other people died."

Lovely was bathed with warm water in the bathroom, then poured into a white dress. Rosemene wore white from head to toe, too, as did Enel. The plan for the day was to go to a *jèn*—a prayer session.

"Make some food for yourself but wash the dishes," Rosemene called to Venessaint as we gingerly made our way down the path to the car.

The *jèn* was not in a church as I expected. It was under a blue tarp, held up with crude wooden posts and stretched like a roof across the dirt yard of a house in the center of Fermathe. A couple of wooden benches extended like pews on both sides, and we took a seat in the back. There were only a handful of women there when we arrived, most of them dressed in white and holding babies, but soon the tent filled to capacity.

The congregants sang hymns together and then each took a turn to pray loudly as the man directing the service clanged two cymbals together in his hands. The prayers rushed out of people, so fervent and unabashed they seemed to be speaking in tongues. They raised their hands in the air and waved as they spoke. When it was Rosemene's turn, she thanked *Seyè*—the Lord—for giving her another twelve months with Lovely.

I sat back, suddenly hyperaware of my awkward foreignness. My blotchy white skin felt glaring, my purple T-shirt and green skirt garish. My silence and stillness was deafening. I felt so out of place not only because of my culture but also because of my tenuous connection to faith. Even though I had started showing up at church from time to time, I still wasn't sure I believed in God. If I granted there was a higher power, it was not one that controlled such choices of life or death. It wasn't God's fault, for instance, that Lina's baby had died. And if it was God's decision to spare Lovely, why did he kill so many other children? I believed it was up to us to make the most out of our lives.

As if she could sense my conflict, Rosemene suddenly stood up and handed Lovely over to me. The tent had heated up, and Lovely was sweaty. She lay her head lightly on my chest, and I rocked her from side to side as I had done with my own children when they were babies. She soon fell asleep.

Looking down at Lovely, I thought about how the whole world had come crashing in over her head and how, despite it all, she had survived. I thought about how many people were trying to piece their world back together again, but still, after a year, Haiti seemed in a more precarious situation than before. I thought about my own naïve and presumptuous expectations of Rosemene.

Among the babbling and singing and rocking, a realization came to me: I might not believe in an all-powerful God, but I was not in control. I could help Lovely's family, but I couldn't fix all their problems. Even with the support of readers and the *Star*, I was just one small person. I had to reset my expectations, of them and myself. I needed to look at the help we were offering as just that: help, and not development funding. I shouldn't expect a return on my investment in terms of their self-reliance. Just like Michele, the Montreal nurse I had met my first day in Haiti, this was my "cry of the heart."

I made two decisions that day.

The first was that I would fund Gilberte Salomon's school for one year starting that September. I would have to raise US$26,000—enough to cover all fourteen staff salaries and a little extra as a cushion—for all 350 students to go there for free. This time, though, I would do it privately in my spare time. I would not write about it in the newspaper. I felt that, with my friends and connections, as well as some speaking engagements I was doing, I could raise the money myself. It was probably what I should have done from the very beginning: funded an institution instead of a family.

My second decision was to enroll Venessaint in school.

Rosemene loved the idea when I talked about it with her later. "Venessaint is like our child," she said. "We are like his parents."

I left Dimitri with enough money to pay Venessaint's tuition and buy some furniture for the family's new place.

After I'd returned to Canada, Dimitri called me with his report. Venessaint was taking grade one classes with a private tutor. And Dimitri had bought a small plastic table and four plastic chairs for the family. Rosemene was ecstatic with the gift.

"I'm so sad you couldn't see how happy she was to have those chairs," Dimitri said over the phone. "I thought she was going to cry."

The image filled me with joy. It was the best Christmas gift I had ever given.

Chapter 9

Catastrophic Aid

The newspaper's "Lovely Project" officially ended with the anniversary of the earthquake. The end of the year is a natural time for newspapers to finish series, and this one had run its course. We had published dozens of stories; paid for around 180 Haitians, young and old, to go to school; and helped Lovely's family in a myriad of ways. It was time for the newsroom to turn its energy to the next big idea.

I was disappointed. But, given the amount of money the paper had spent sending correspondents to Haiti over the months, I couldn't blame my bosses.

It meant I wouldn't see Lovely every other month, as a matter of course. But it didn't mean I wouldn't see her at all. Instead, I'd have to convince my editors each time that a trip to Haiti was worthwhile—by pitching story ideas and drafting out budgets, as I had done for foreign trips before. I was sure I could do that, between writing columns and large features.

I framed one of Lucas's photos of Lovely and put it on my bedside table so that she was the last thing I saw each night and the first thing I saw each morning. It was like she was waiting for me.

I also quietly worked on my plan to raise the US$26,000 for Muspan Montessori, Gilberte's school. One of the biggest difficulties, as far as I could see, was that I wasn't running a registered nonprofit charity, so friends and family I leaned on couldn't get a tax receipt for any donations they might make. I poked around on the Internet a bit and talked to some people with charities of their own, but what I learned sent me into a quick retreat. The last thing I wanted to do was create a heavy bureaucracy that would suck up my time and energy, particularly since I'd committed just for one year.

Ryan Sawatzky came to the rescue. The *bon bagay* Rea Dol had told me about drove down to Toronto to meet me one frigid day in early 2011. Ryan was still designing theme parks with his father for a living, but he admitted that running the Sawatzky Family Foundation took up most of his time. Since the earthquake, he had broadened the foundation's mandate to cover not just the costs of running Rea's school but also the tuition for one hundred kids at another little school near Rea's house. He figured stretching his umbrella over Muspan wouldn't be much more work, since I would be the one raising the money. Once Rea met with Gilberte in Port-au-Prince, and they both agreed to the idea, it would be a go.

This was incredible news. It meant not only that donors would get tax receipts but that their money would go straight to the foundation. No more personal checks to me, which was a relief. I still felt uncomfortable handling strangers' money. It also meant that I didn't have to deliver the cash personally: Ryan would include it in his regular transfers to Rea each month. This added a layer of impersonal administrative padding, which I was grateful for, as well as an element of oversight. All Gilberte had to do was arrive monthly at Rea's office to collect the money and sign a receipt for it, leaving a clear paper trail.

By the time I was packing my duffel bag with presents and *rad kenedi* for Lovely's family in September 2011, I had managed to raise US$28,000—US$2,000 more than I needed. I should have felt triumphant, embarking on that ninth trip to Haiti. But, as always, I was uneasy.

Lyla was a quivering mess in her little bed, sniffling and sobbing. The night before I left, she hid my shoes behind the couch in an attempt to keep me home. It was her new trick, her logic being that if someone she loved didn't have shoes, they clearly couldn't walk out the door. It felt like a good allegory for all of us.

I was nervous about what would await me in Haiti, too. For one, Dimitri was no longer there. His green card had come through and he'd moved to New Jersey to join his pregnant wife. They were expecting a baby girl in a month's time, and he had landed a job as a security guard.

It was good news for him but terrible news for me and the country. I had lost a trusted friend and dependable fixer, and Haiti had lost another of its rare educated citizens, who now, more than ever, seemed essential for rebuilding the country. He had become part of the country's enormous brain drain.

Haiti remained stuck in an emergency. Around 600,000 people were still living in squalid camps that, a year and a half after the earthquake, had long lost most of their support from NGOs. It wasn't hard to see that peoples' living situation in the camps was desperate— no water or food, broken toilets, high crime rates—but they were increasingly being characterized as freeloaders and fakes looking to game the system. The threat of eviction was real and constant. Sympathy had turned to blame.

It didn't help that Haiti's political ghosts had returned. Shortly after the election, Jean-Claude "Baby Doc" Duvalier—the country's former dictator, who'd maintained a lavish lifestyle while the country suffered—stunned passport officials at the airport when he arrived on an Air France flight. He said he had no political ambitions, but still, his arrival brought with it a general nervousness that descended across the country. A couple of months later he was followed by

Jean-Bertrand Aristide, the left-wing priest who had been the country's first democratically elected president in decades and who had been deposed in not just one but two coups. Aristide also said he had no plans to enter politics, but his return further stoked the country's fear.

Sweet Micky, the bawdy musician, had handily won the runoff election in March and been sworn in as the country's new president in May 2011. He quickly announced two big plans. The first was free schooling for more than 100,000 children, funded not by donors but with a new tax on international calls and money transfers. He was sick of the country being an aid case. His slogan was "Haiti is open for business."

His second plan seemed much less ambitious. He wanted to close six camps in the capital, moving 30,000 people from them and into sixteen restored urban neighborhoods. The majority of people in the camps were renters before the earthquake, and they would remain so; each household was offered a US$500 rent subsidy. That didn't pay for much more than a one-room apartment before the earthquake, but since so many places had been destroyed, the ones left standing were twice as costly. The idea of building back better seemed to have been forgotten. Instead, it was returning people to where they were before: the slums.

Among the families evicted was Lovely's. One Sunday, while they were having coffee, the owner arrived—a different man from the one who had rented the place to them and who, they learned, was only a caretaker. The real owner kicked them out. The family found a new place, but I didn't expect it to be any better. Desperation does not make for a good bargaining position.

I had thought that first flight down to Port-au-Prince after the earthquake was special—packed with donations and people wanting to help. But it turned out to be the norm. Every flight from Miami was packed with T-shirt brigades: Americans and Canadians in matching bright-red or lime-green T-shirts with slogans printed across them that invariably included the word "Hope."

The most volunteer groups I ever counted on one plane was seven. Imagine: seven crews of fifteen to twenty people each, all in matching T-shirts. If you stumbled onto the plane by accident, you'd think you'd entered a spring break trip to Daytona Beach, filled with university students.

They were all volunteers, usually going to Haiti for two-week trips to help out at an orphanage, teach English, or build a school.

Many were deeply religious. Their T-shirts included snippets of scripture that I read off their backs while standing in line to board. "God loved the world so much that he gave his one and only son that whoever believes in him may not be lost but have eternal life," read one.

One group, dressed in red T-shirts with the words "Haiti Missions" on them, called their trip a "crusade" and prayed around the luggage carousel. Another was on a mission to travel to every country in the world—all 196—to pray. Haiti marked country number 16. I watched in bemusement as their leader fought with the airport porters over their luggage. When I told him the US$10 the porter was charging was the cost of a sandwich and a drink in the States, he snapped, "That money could go to the orphans."

Even when the T-shirts were conspicuously absent, the flight was jammed with volunteers who had come to help the country in one way or another. On one trip, I was standing in a customs line in the temporary luggage hanger when I struck up a conversation with two young men from small town Ontario who were behind me. There was no air-conditioning in the airport arrivals hall, and all of our brows gleamed with sweat. They told me they had come with their church to rebuild a school, but they couldn't tell me where it was, because they didn't know. In front of me was a young nurse who had come to work in a Christian tent hospital. When I asked her where it was, she answered, "I can't tell you where it is, because the mission really doesn't want any credit for this work." I figured she didn't know where it was, either.

On the surface, all of this compassion and care was wonderful. Extreme poverty anywhere in the world *should* inspire these kinds of responses among those of us who are well-off, as well as donations to charities working on the ground.

But this was my ninth trip. I had started feeling like I was a part of Haiti, so the groups irked me, the same way Haitians got upset at white SUVs roaring by with aid workers. The earthquake had been eighteen months before.

The audacity of it also galled me. After meeting a crew that had come to teach English at a school for two weeks, I tried to imagine my reaction if Lyla returned home from school to say some special Chinese people had dropped in and taught her Mandarin. I would assume they were professional teachers who had been thoroughly vetted by the school. Even parent volunteers required police background checks, and those took no fewer than two months to complete. If I had discovered that those volunteers had not been vetted, or that they weren't professionally trained teachers and that they'd simply showed up at her school unannounced, I would have called the Children's Aid Society. So why did people from North America think the standards should be so different in Haiti? Why did they think that Haitian kids should take whatever was offered for free? Dimitri had said it reinforced a slavery mentality—that any *blan* from the developed world with enough money to come to Haiti clearly had something to teach. More and more, I saw the truth in his words.

Sure, the money they were spending on food and transportation and guesthouses was helping Haiti's struggling economy. But wouldn't it be better if all these volunteers just sent the US$600 it cost for a round-trip ticket down to Haiti to hire locals to do the job they were doing for free? When I asked people in the camps what they most wanted, they invariably answered, "A job." US$600 could cover four months of a minimum-wage, full-time job in Haiti—which in itself was more than double what most people there made. That would offer real hope, in the form of self-reliance and the ability to buy the things they needed and rebuild their lives themselves, without the indignity of waiting for it to arrive on the back of a truck packed with *blan* volunteers.

There were exceptions, of course. In the days following the earthquake, the medical teams and search-and-rescue crews that flocked to the country saved many Haitian lives. So did the untrained catastrophe missionaries who helped in those early hours, handing out water and scooping out food. But these T-shirt brigades were a different matter. As individuals, I couldn't see how their help was harming anybody. The problem was, they weren't coming as individuals. They had been filling planes and descending on Haiti even before the earthquake, to work on their little projects here and there. The emergency was long over now. When was the country going to start its development phase?

I pushed through the piece of corrugated metal into the yard of Lovely's new home to find her crouching in the dirt by the kitchen fire pit, a giant plate of *diri ak sos pwa* on her lap. She set her plate down, sprang up, and ran at me. "Madame Katrin!" she yelled. I loved how sharp my name sounded coming out of Lovely's mouth: "Katrin." It was a pronunciation I heard only in Kreyòl. For any Haitians who spoke French—typically upper-class, educated citizens who I was talking to as a reporter—I was the gentler "Catreen." Two names for two different roles.

While we hugged, Jonathan, Venessaint, and Enel emerged from the house. Lovely tugged me into the new *kay* (house) for a tour. It was a simple box made of white cinder blocks topped with a tin roof. There wasn't a single window, but from the inside it seemed bright and cheerful. Morning sun spilled through a pretty lace curtain that hung in the doorframe and speckled the smooth, polished floor. The four chairs Dimitri had bought sat around a small matching coffee table. There was a single bed in the corner, covered by a white ruffle-trimmed cover.

Lovely danced around the room and then dove under the bed,

her little bum sticking up behind her, to dig out her report card to proudly show me.

She had excelled in her second year of kindergarten. The check marks showed she was generous, orderly, and well-dressed *"toujours"* (always), obedient *"souvent"* (often), and aggressive *"parfois"* (sometimes). *Attagirl*, I thought. *You better be aggressive sometimes*. At the bottom her teacher had written, *"Bon Travail, bonnes vacances* (Good work, happy holidays)."

Enel pulled out two of the plastic chairs into the small, stony yard in front of the door so we could sit and catch up. From our vantage point, I could see the house's other bonus: a couple of rusty eaves that directed rainwater into a reservoir. For the first time, the family could access their own water—for bathing, at least.

A banana tree hung its giant frond down over our heads and trumpet flowers opened their wide white mouths from the bushes around us. It felt like a secret garden.

"We found peace here," Enel said shyly. Lovely climbed up onto my lap as we talked, and I could feel by the heft of her body that she had gained weight.

Things in their life had finally begun to improve. Yes, they'd been evicted, but they'd gotten their money back from the corrupt custodian and used it to rent this home.

Lovely had not needed to go to the doctor in months. The family was eating twice a day, a big meal at 2:00 p.m. and soup at night. Both Enel and Rosemene were working. Right now, Rosemene was down in their old neighborhood, selling lemons and oranges in the market. Up until recently Enel had worked on a construction site, building a wall around a nearby house and making US$7 a day. The job had ended, but he thought it would start up again soon. And Rosemene was also doing a little business out of the house: she'd bought a metal hand mill to grind pistachios and corn kernels for neighbors.

It didn't add up to much, but it was more than they had before and enough even to save some money—not in a bank account, but in the form of a ewe. When they needed to pay next year's rent, Enel said, they would sell it.

I was thrilled. Clearly, my standards for success had dropped. I no longer used Canadian benchmarks when thinking about Lovely's future. Instead, I thought of the pregnant girl in Cité Soleil and the single mother in the trash heap at the bottom of Bobin.

Lovely snatched my pen and scribbled on my notepad.

"I am writing a book here," she told me. "*Gade.* Look what I made. It's beautiful."

It had been seven months since I'd last seen Lovely. I knew from personal experience how long that was in the short life of a child. But she nestled into my lap as though I had never left. In fact, she was more familiar with me than she'd ever been, tracing her little fingers along my arms and neck to gently poke my freckles, then reaching up to rub my cheeks.

Soon her brother was at my side, wearing nothing but a red shirt and demanding to be pulled up onto my lap, too. I felt Jonathan's little bare bum nestle into my thigh and laughed at how intimate and natural it all felt—like these were my own children.

I wanted to go and check in on Elistin and Rosita to see how they were doing. The new house was a short walk down the dirt road and up a farm field away. Lovely led me there. She was wearing the tiniest blue jelly sandals and she shuffled them forward, pretending to be a *machinn*, or car.

"Beep-beep!" she yelled, giggling. "Beep-beep!"

Pride filled my heart, as it did when I'd watched Lyla perform recently in one of her Irish dancing concerts. Lovely was thriving.

The constant rush of volunteers and aid workers flooding Haiti was not a new phenomenon. The numbers were amplified because of the earthquake, but Haiti had long been known as the Republic of NGOs.

No one knew how many of them were operating in the country.

In a speech in 2009, Bill Clinton said that Haiti, with a total of 10,000 NGOs, took the silver medal for the most NGOs per capita after India.

The government's records were well out-of-date, and the bureaucrats had no capacity to monitor or coordinate them, so the NGOs operated on their own, unaccountable to anyone but their donors in far-flung countries. Many were tiny—little church groups that filled the planes from Miami. Others, like World Vision and Save the Children, were so big that they were like governments themselves. They received large parts of their funding from foreign governments, many of which, since the 1990s, had largely stopped channeling aid directly to the Haitian government for fear of corruption and incompetence. Ironically, aid had been a mainstay of Duvalier's regime, which had openly terrorized the population and made few investments in the country, simply pocketing the money.

Haiti was also known internationally as a "failed state." Despite all the NGOs' efforts, the country remained the poorest and least developed in the western hemisphere. The websites of many large NGOs proudly stated they had been in Haiti since the 1970s—more than thirty years. To me, this was a sure sign of their failure. The point of development is to work yourself out of a job.

There was no doubt that the NGOs were helping individual people, but aid by itself had not built the country. The only thing that could do that was the country itself, through a strong government with a coherent plan.

The international body set up to coordinate aid in Haiti had approved many projects that fit the government's plans. But almost half of those approved projects had not been funded. Donors were back to earmarking their own pet projects.

Nigel was increasingly frustrated. I met him in his office in the middle of the barricaded United Nations compound. We sat on blue leather couches across from one another, the air-conditioning blasting. He complained that he found himself stuck in meeting after meeting with an endless parade of visitors and evaluators.

"It's so hard to get things done here," he moaned. "It's a curse that

Haiti is so close to North America. We have so many specialists. It goes on day after day."

The exact number of international NGOs in the country eluded even him. Only four hundred to five hundred NGOs had registered with the government—mostly the large and medium-sized international organizations, he said. But there were so many small groups that arrived to work on projects and the government complained to him there was no way to ensure their plans fit into the country's larger vision.

"In Haiti in particular, NGOs have so much money. To whom are they accountable?" he said. "I fund-raised for an NGO for five years. It's a business. You have thousands of actors; it's not an effective system. It's out of control. The whole humanitarian enterprise needs to understand how a local economy works when a disaster happens instead of just bringing in aid."

Nigel had worked as a humanitarian for more than three decades in some of the most dangerous and difficult places in the world. After only a year and a half in Haiti, he'd concluded one thing: "The aid industry is broken."

The irony, of course, was I was increasingly part of that broken aid industry. Whenever I arrived at the airport, my bags were stuffed with donations—just like the volunteer T-shirt brigades I mocked. How was I any different from any of them—the two-week voluntourists, the small church groups, the giant aid organizations, or the foreign donors who funded what they wanted? I told myself my actions were far more personal than the T-shirt brigades—and far less grand than the big aid organizations. My projects fell somewhere in between. And I was relieved to find they were working well.

I dropped in to Gilberte's house to find the yard out front buzzing with workmen hammering together simple wooden benches and painting green chalkboards in preparation for the school year. Gilberte's staff greeted me from a table placed by the house entrance where they were registering students.

Gilberte met me in her sitting room, dressed as always in a simple blouse, long skirt, and straw hat. Compared to our last visit, she was erupting with energy and enthusiasm.

She showed me the posters she'd printed, advertising Muspan and the Canadian funders who were sponsoring it. She expected 350 students this year. She'd enrolled the school in the government food program, which offered hot lunches to students for just 20 cents US a day. And she'd used the start-up money to replace the school's tarps with rudimentary cinder-block walls, plywood, and tin sheets. The last two she'd bought from a black-market vendor who was selling the components of T-shelters meant to house earthquake-affected families.

"We asked different NGOs for T-shelters, and they said, 'No, they are not for schools.' Other people heard I'd been refused, and they approached me. It's robbery," Gilberte said, leaning toward me. Her mouth stretched into a wide smile that revealed her gap teeth. "It would have cost so much more at a store."

She agreed it was a sign of corruption, but she was a realist. Corruption in Haiti was a curse, but she wasn't above its petty forms if it propelled her cause. The building was far from a permanent structure, but she was feeling very optimistic.

"Your help has rebuilt my morale," she said.

Up in Fermathe, all the kids in Lovely's family were now enrolled in school, except for Lypse—Elistin and Rosita's three-year-old son.

I arrived one morning at their home to find Lypse dressed in a new pair of pants and a shirt that Elistin had made on the sewing machine. Four hands touched him: Rosita rubbing cream on his face, and Elistin brushing his short hair.

I'd never discussed paying for Lypse's tuition with his parents. They just assumed I would, since I was already paying for the other kids'. And, really, what would I have said? With help from friends, I was now paying for every other kid in the family, including Venessaint, who was starting grade two. How could I justify to them excluding Lypse?

When Lypse was ready, we set off down the dirt road proudly, as though we were part of a parade. I had assumed we were heading to the Baptist mission school, where Sophonie would be starting grade four. But instead of turning left at the crossroads, we continued straight toward the little dilapidated church that clung to the edge of the road. A sign leaned against the wall out front: *École Univers Fraternel, inscriptions open every day, kindergarten to Grade 6. Required: Birth Certificate and report card from last school.*

The school was located in the basement of the church, which we accessed around the side. The stairs down were so badly broken that we had to jump over them to reach the landing.

Inside, the rooms appeared like caves: dark, separated by half-finished cinder-block walls, with wires sticking out from holes in the ceiling. There were doors, but all of them were torn in half as though a bear had barreled in at night and clawed its way through.

We found the administrator in a closet-sized room, working on a silver laptop on a desk. His feet were resting in a puddle of water. He handed us a flyer from a stack on the desk that outlined the school fees: US$250 a year. He assured me that he followed the state curriculum, but no matter how many times I addressed him in French, he answered in Kreyòl. For me, that was a clear sign he likely hadn't finished high school, which was taught largely in French.

I asked Elistin to talk outside.

"The school isn't good," I whispered when we were alone. "It's not safe. If there is another earthquake, *li pral kraze nèt*. It will totally break. And Lypse will die here."

Elistin calmly listened to what I was saying. "I am comfortable with the school," he said.

"I'm sorry," I responded. "You should *not* be comfortable with your child going to this school."

It was the first time I had put down my foot with anyone in the family. Up until that moment, I had been the opposite of a classic aid worker: I hadn't taken charge at all. I hadn't picked the kids' schools or told Rosemene how to spend the money I'd given her to rebuild her business. I hadn't offered an opinion, even—because, frankly, I hadn't thought it was my place as an outsider.

But now I understood that respect comes only with mutual trust and understanding, and there was nothing mutual in our relationship. It was all one-sided—me offering them money, them taking it. I didn't want to be a benevolent parent, watching silently from the sidelines, nor did I want to simply be a walking bank account. I still struggled with that feeling in Haiti, and it was particularly acute around Lovely's family. To me, they'd become much more than a story, but in my weaker moments I worried that they saw me as a less-than-human piggy bank. They rarely asked about my life back in Canada, my family, my job. That was not surprising, because they couldn't imagine the right questions to ask, and they were so used to answering my queries. But it still smarted a bit. I decided that if I respected them, I'd challenge them on things and debate their decisions with them. That's what I did with my family and friends and colleagues back home. That was the sign of truly treating someone as an equal.

I couldn't in good conscience allow Lypse to descend into this wet crypt every day. Not without protesting, at least.

We moved to the road, out of the principal's earshot. Rosita, Lypse, and Sophonie joined us. The sun beat down on our necks. I turned to Elistin.

"You are Lypse's father," I said. "You can send him to any school you want. But not with my money."

Elistin leaned back and smiled. Rosita, standing beside him, beamed at me. My outburst either shocked them and they were masking their reaction, or they enjoyed seeing me get passionate. In any event, they agreed they would enroll Lypse in the Baptist mission school that Sophonie was already attending.

We toured the mission school, and I asked Elistin if he liked it.

"There is no problem," he said.

"That wasn't my question. Do you like it?"

"Yes," he said.

"Are you sure you want Lypse to go here? Is there another school we should check out?"

"No," he said. "Lypse will go there."

There is a Kreyòl expression: "An egg today is better than a chicken tomorrow." Perhaps Elistin thought it was better to get me to pay then and there, rather than risk that I wouldn't send the money after I'd left the country.

But after I'd registered both Sophonie and Lypse and we'd returned home, Elistin and Rosita seemed genuinely happy, retelling the story of my reaction to the school for Rosemene and Enel's enjoyment, and laughing at how the principal was standing in water.

It was a moment when I had shown my real self, and I realized I needed to do that more. If I wanted a relationship with Lovely's family that wasn't just transactional but personal, I needed to share more of myself: my thoughts, my reactions, my own life. Listening to them laugh, I thought, perhaps, that they recognized our relationship was changing and that they welcomed it, too.

While we sat around the sun-dappled courtyard, the kids took turns climbing up onto my lap and I bounced them up and down and rocked them side to side, pretending to be the frame of a car. It was the same game I played with Lyla and Noah, except they always wanted to ride a horse. In rural Haiti, a *machinn* ride was not boring. It was a luxurious thrill. So I purred and bounced and turned the imaginary wheel while they squealed with laughter.

When I announced it was time for me to go, both children threw tantrums. Jonathan wailed loudly. Lovely raced after me and clambered onto my lap in the front seat of my driver's *machinn*.

"*Kite m!*"—"Leave me!" she yelled at Rosemene, who'd come after her. It was her version of Lyla's hidden shoes. Rosemene scooped up Lovely so we could pull away. As I waved good-bye, Lovely kicked and screamed in her mother's arms.

Before I left, the tantrums had exacted one more promise from me: I would return for Lovely's graduation from kindergarten next June.

Chapter 10

Chèche Lavi

(Trying to Make a Living)

June 2012 arrived like a bicycle without brakes, and suddenly I was speeding into Port-au-Prince for Lovely's graduation.

The morning after I arrived, I met Enel by the park in Pétionville. He'd been working in the city, selling pop and living with his relatives during the week, only making the trip to Fermathe on Sundays to bring money home. He was joined by two of Lovely's aunts and one uncle. We stopped at a bakery for beef patties, some pops, and a large vanilla cake, and then we all squeezed into the car to slowly climb up the mountain.

Rosemene greeted me warmly with two kisses and a hug. "You are Lovely's mom," she said. "If you weren't here, I wouldn't feel good."

And then there was Lovely: she had a white towel wrapped around her head and a white baby doll in her hands. She seemed taller and more poised. She retrieved a school notebook and showed me what she had learned since I'd last been there, nine months before.

Rosemene's comment echoed in my head. It was meant in kindness, but it rattled me. I obviously wasn't Lovely's mom. But I also was no longer just an impartial journalist who'd come to document her story. So what was I?

I pushed the battling thoughts away and sat down on the stone floor beside her to watch in wonder as she sounded out the combinations of letters printed on a page of homework. She was the first person in her immediate family who could read. It was a huge accomplishment and a leap up the development chart. Already Lovely could enter worlds closed to her parents.

One of Lovely's aunts took her into the yard and bathed her in a plastic laundry tub brimming with cold water. Then two of them groomed her, rubbing oil onto her arms and cream on her face. Finally, they slipped her into her school uniform. It all took more than an hour—more time than I spent dressing for my wedding. This was clearly a special day.

The graduation was held in the large stone church set in the middle of the Baptist mission campus. The place was packed by the time we arrived. Fans spun slowly above the heads of family members cramming the white pews, languidly lifting and dropping violet balloons and streamers strung between white pillars. People outside pressed their faces against the large glass windows that spanned the sides, looking in.

The ceremony stretched more than four hours. At one point Lovely and her classmates appeared in beige gowns with matching graduation caps. Hers was too large for her small head and tipped to one side, the tassel hanging by her nose. We watched as she crossed the stage and collected her kindergarten diploma from the principal, who delivered a flowery graduation address.

Lovely sat stone-faced up on the stage, not smiling or paying any attention to the many parents who came forward to take photos. She was bored but not acting up. I couldn't imagine my kids sitting through that many hours in a church—even with music and little skits going on—without having a meltdown.

Afterward we returned to her home for cake and pop, set out under the sunshine on a big table. By now, Lovely had changed into her second graduation outfit: a violet dress with an eggplant-colored ribbon. She posed for photos and became a child again, chasing her brother gleefully around the table as the adults chatted idly. A cow mooed nearby.

I always had to rush off, and today was no different: I had to write the story about Lovely's graduation for the newspaper and file it before deadline. But I recognized, digging into my piece of cake and watching Lovely dance around the table, that this was a good day not just in Haiti but anywhere. And that, despite all that was going wrong in Haiti, some things were going right.

Pink posters with big photos of the president's smiling face were plastered all over the city. One hung from just about every lamppost, whether it offered light or not. They were publicizing the success of Sweet Micky's now year-old free education program, and they were tailored to each area of town; in Pétionville they boasted that 18,685 local children were now going to school gratis. In Delmas—where Gilberte's school, Muspan, was located—the number on the posters was 18,778. Then even bigger billboards perched on the side of the main roads proclaimed 903,000 children across the country were now in school for free, thanks to Martelly's "bald head." At the bottom were the words *pwomès se dèt*—the Kreyòl version of "delivering on his promise."

Those numbers seemed suspicious to me. They were too precise, particularly considering that official reports disagreed as to exactly how much money the government had collected. How could the politicians be so vague on funding yet forensically precise when it came to the numbers of students enrolled?

Since I couldn't justify a trip to Haiti with just one story about

Lovely's graduation, I had pitched a few others to my editors, including one that looked into whether Martelly's program was legitimate or not.

I'd scheduled an interview with Sophia Stransky, the newly named president of the Digicel Foundation, the biggest private foundation in the country. The charitable arm of the international mobile telephone company focused on education, building new schools, and training teachers at them.

Digicel's corporate office was a gleaming eleven-story building that looked more like something from Toronto's Bay Street than Port-au-Prince. It was sleek and mirrored, and among the city's few structures built to be earthquake-resistant.

Sophia looked more like a lawyer or a corporate manager— which she had been, before jumping from Digicel's sales team to its charitable wing. She was tall and thin, with blond hair pulled back into a tight bun. Her nails were beautifully manicured, her shoes exquisite, her teeth gleaming; I could not picture her picking her way around the garbage piles and open gutters of the country's *bidonvils* to inaugurate new charitable projects. She greeted me with a firm handshake.

Spanning one wall of her office was a giant map of Haiti dotted with little pins, one for each of the seventy schools the foundation had built, most of them since the earthquake. There were eighty more on the books for the next two years.

Sophia was explaining how the foundation selected which schools to construct when I remembered an email Gilberte had sent me a few months before. In it she had mentioned that Digicel had given her a grant to help her rebuild. I had meant to quiz Gilberte more about it, but with everything else going on I had forgotten.

"Was there any chance a little school called Muspan was among those selected?" I asked Sophia.

"Yes," she said, eyes locking with mine across the table. "We all really admire Madame Salomon. She has such vision."

Since Gilberte's property was so small, her school building would have to be three stories—a floor taller than most Digicel schools. That had added an extra US$120,000 to the cost. So Sophia had set out to look for a partner to carry some of the cost, she explained.

"We found the Stiller Foundation," she said.

The Stiller Foundation, as in Ben Stiller, the Hollywood actor? The guy whose *Zoolander* character made my husband, Graeme, and me howl whenever we thought about the gasoline fight in the movie?

Yes, *that* Ben Stiller.

Sophia was not kidding. Stiller was one of the many celebrities who had descended on Haiti after the earthquake, along with Matt Damon, Shakira, and Sean Penn. His aim was also to rebuild schools, and last winter he'd signed a partnership with Digicel to do just that.

"He met Madame Salomon, too," Sophia said. Supermodel Petra Nemcova's foundation, called Happy Hearts Fund, had also contributed to the construction costs.

The work had already started. Crews had removed the rubble of the old, damaged building and were well on their way to finishing the new one. The completion date was less than two months away—August 1—so Gilberte and her staff would have plenty of time to prepare for the new term.

I left the office in a daze. What were the chances that, of 1,300 broken schools and universities in Haiti, Ben Stiller and I had chosen the same one to help?

The next morning I went straight to Gilberte's. I found her in the courtyard of her temporary college.

The tarps were still up, but the separations between the classrooms were gone. It was now just one giant space filled with benches. And every single bench was crowded with Muspan students in their green tartan uniforms and plastic hair barrettes. In the midst of all of them, like a mother goose, sat Gilberte. She was being interviewed by a film crew working for the Stiller Foundation, and everyone was listening quietly like perfect students.

I snuck behind all the kids and had begun snapping photos of the scene when I heard her pronounce: "I prayed to God after the earthquake, to let me continue his mission. And he sent me a Canadian journalist who, by chance, just arrived."

The gazes of more than two hundred students turned and fell heavily upon me, together with that of the interviewer who craned around and waved hello. I blushed, then waited until the filming was done, watching the crowd of kids mob Gilberte and slowly recede back to their classes.

"When you said you were rebuilding, I didn't realize you were serious!" I exclaimed to her when we were finally alone.

"I am a very dynamic person. I would have built the school anyway, but maybe it would have taken years," she responded. "Why don't you head over and see for yourself?"

By then I'd seen enough construction in Haiti to know the difference between a professional job, with engineers and architects, and the regular homemade ones that dotted the *bidonvils*. Here, the workers were wearing not only hard hats but boots, too. The walls they had already erected were thick and even, with fat pieces of metal rebar poking up from them, crisscrossed with many intersecting metal stirrups—the key, I'd learned, to holding the bars together so the building would sway as a unit during an earthquake and not fall apart.

This clearly wasn't going to be a typical private school in Haiti. It was going to be an institution, with wide halls and big windows, just like most schools in Canada. The only difference was that the playground would be up on the roof, since there was no room for it outside.

Gilberte rolled up in a truck, which she parked beside the construction site, offering her a clear view. She beamed.

She had more good news for me: she was rebuilding Institut Louis Pasteur, her nursing college, on the old site. She had raised the money herself by selling two pieces of land she'd inherited in Les Cayes, a town in the southwest panhandle of the country. The school wouldn't be as big as it had been before, and it would be made partly of wood so that, if another earthquake hit, the students and staff would be in less danger. But she was almost back to where she'd been before the earthquake.

"What did you think of Ben Stiller?" I asked.

"He gave a good first impression," she said. She had never seen any of his films, but, no, he didn't seem funny. He was serious. She'd told him that she hoped to open a Muspan in every province and wanted his help.

"He laughed," she said. But she held out some hope.

All of this was astounding and wonderful. It perfectly captured why I loved coming to Haiti: I never knew what remarkable thing the day had in store for me. I'd stumbled onto dead bodies, women giving birth, and now this—the remarkable rebirth of not just one but two schools.

Before I left, Gilberte grabbed my arm.

"Catreen, I carry you in my heart," she said, looking me in the eye. "If you live for another sixty years, it will be because of what you have done for Muspan."

The recent resettlement programs were slowly changing parts of Port-au-Prince. Many of the enormous tent camps that had spanned parks were gone. For the first time since I'd come to Haiti, I watched kids swing on the monkey bars in Pétionville's Place Saint-Pierre and not live below them. What a glorious sight. It seemed like the moment a hangover lifts and you remember how wonderful regular, everyday life is. The park seemed so much more than an ordinary park now.

Back in January, on the second anniversary of the earthquake, the Canadian government had announced that it would donate just under C$20 million to empty and refurbish the most visible camp in the whole city—the Champs de Mars—where 25,000 people lived.

The Canadian government wanted the park back in decent shape by late July to host the upcoming Carnival of Flowers. Embassy staff admitted that the help wouldn't solve the problem, but it would give them some money to start over with, similar to what I'd originally hoped for Rosemene.

I wanted to see exactly what kind of housing Canadian taxpayers were moving Haitians into.

Just a couple of months before, the Champs de Mars had been crowded with 5,000 shacks. When I arrived, I found only one left. I asked the last resident where his neighbors had gone, and he directed me to Fort National, Lovely's family's old neighborhood.

I knew from previous visits that I needed a bodyguard to go there. After Dimitri left, all my fixers had either burned out, found other jobs, or driven cars that kept breaking down. Out of desperation, I had called the Associated Press bureau chief in Port-au-Prince and asked for any leads. He'd connected me to a man named Richard Miguel, with one warning: "He's a character," he said.

I discovered almost immediately what that meant. Richard was bald and short, with dark bulldog circles under his eyes and a permanent scowl on his face. He spoke English with a New York accent and swore like a New Yorker, too. Driving through Port-au-Prince with him was like taking a gangster's tour of the city. He pointed out street corners where he'd been arrested for robbery and crack houses where he'd passed years in a dazed stupor.

People who recognized Richard on the street usually knew him from time in jail together; he'd cycled in and out of prison in New York for years on convictions of robbery before the system discovered he wasn't an American citizen. Finally he was deported to Haiti, a country he hadn't known since he was four. Soon after arriving, he landed back in jail for the same thing. He'd been clean for seven years now and had settled down with a girlfriend, their young daughter, and honest work. His lingering weakness was gambling. He'd blow a whole week's pay in thirty minutes at the casino, so he was always hustling for more money.

"I have a compulsive, addictive personality," he said. "I like taking risks."

We quickly developed a love-hate relationship. I loved his sharp sense of humor and the way he exploded into laughter at his own inanities. But his not-so-subtle attempts to weasel cash out of me set my teeth on edge. Richard exacerbated my irritation at feeling like an ATM in Haiti.

But the permanent scowl on his face made Richard the perfect companion to take me back into Fort National. The *bidonvil* had not changed much since I'd visited with Lovely and her family two years before. Other than a handful of tin shacks cluttering the edges of the main road, very little rebuilding had taken place.

Most of the homes we passed were dismal cells. On the main street was a little *boutik* selling water and building supplies. Richard knew its owner, a tall, lean man with the serene eyes and defined cheekbones of a Siamese cat. His name was Gueteau Lalanne, but everyone just called him Lalanne.

Trailed by a couple of dogs, he brought us down to his house, a bungalow in the middle of the slum, with three rooms, each covered in ceramic tile—a sign of his success. There was a pigeon coop on the roof, and goats and turkeys in a fenced-in backyard. After we arranged ourselves on the couches in his living room, a small white rabbit hopped by our feet.

I quickly learned that Lalanne wasn't just a shop owner and animal enthusiast. He was also an entrepreneur. On top of the *boutik*, he was the director of security for the Ministry of Social Affairs and Labor and he worked on the side as a mason, building local homes. Oh, and he had built two reservoirs on this property to collect potable water from tankers, which he sold by the bucket to locals.

For him, the Canadian-funded move from the Champs de Mars was a great thing. His businesses were booming and the neighborhood was regaining its old life.

Even two years later, conversations always had a way of veering back to that terrible afternoon, and, sure enough, Lalanne recounted how he'd just returned home from work at the ministry and was up on his roof, feeding cornmeal to his pigeons, when the ground around him heaved. He watched the dust and heard the screams to Jesus rise in waves, and he scrambled downstairs to find his wife and children unharmed.

He'd immediately started to pull his neighbors out of the rubble. That first evening he manically broke concrete with his sledgehammer and sawed through metal rebar to free people. He described himself as a motor running on adrenaline and raw strength.

"I took so many people out. By midnight I couldn't do it anymore. I went back to my house and cried and cried and cried," he said. "But I kept hearing the screams. So I got up and went back out to dig some more."

Soon he was joined by a handful of other men and they worked as an *ekip*—a team. Over the next few weeks they saved twenty-six people. They buried even more, delivering the bodies to the top of the road, where a giant hole was dug for a mass grave.

In the middle of Lalanne's description, I began to wonder about Lovely. I had never searched for her saviors; frankly, I figured if Rosemene and Enel hadn't found them, I wouldn't be able to. But here was a guy who'd saved many people in their neighborhood. Maybe he'd know something.

Had he heard of the little two-year-old girl who had survived six days under rubble somewhere in Fort National? I asked.

"Of course I know Lovely. Everyone knows about her," he responded. "But no one knows what happened to her after she was sent to the hospital."

I was astounded.

Did he know who saved her?

"It was me," he said.

The next morning I drove up to Fermathe to tell Rosemene and Enel the news. I brought photos of Lalanne on my laptop in case they recognized him.

When I arrived, Rosemene was sitting on the floor, combing Lovely's hair into braids. Her hands froze in place as I told her about my conversation with Lalanne. She stood up, walked over to the small bed in the corner, and sat down on its bony edge.

"Did you confirm it? Are you sure it is him?" she asked. I had always thought it was a foreign search-and-rescue team that saved Lovely, but Rosemene told me she had heard through the *teledjòl* it was a local drunk with a thin beard named Chocholi.

"If it was him, I'd like to thank him for saving Lovely," she said.

I decided to do a little more digging. I returned to Fort National a couple of days later and Lalanne took me to his shed, where he kept a cache of masonry tools. They were the same tools the *ekip* would have needed to smash through concrete and cut metal: sledgehammers, crowbars, metal pikes, and metal saws.

I managed to track down many of the people who Lalanne's team had saved. I met the father of one on the main street one morning, looking as bright and promising as a new penny in his crisp uniform, canvas suitcase in hand. He was going to work. But two minutes into our conversation his eyes brimmed with tears. Lalanne had saved his youngest child. "Around 11:00 p.m. he brought her out. I hugged her," the man recalled, his voice cracking. She had died a few hours later.

It became clear Lalanne was telling the truth: he was truly a hero who had saved many people in the area. I grew even more certain when I met the other members of his *ekip* and one of them turned out to be a man named Chocholi who loved his *kleren*. Together, the members of his team recounted how they'd worked three days to locate the little voice that was calling for her brother under levels of concrete. Finally they found her at the back of the third spot they smashed down into.

"The reason the cement roof didn't splatter her was there was a table and the roof fell on the table, leaving her a very small, secluded space," Lalanne said. "She kept asking for water. I threw down some crackers to give her hope." He cut a lot of rebar so Chocholi could get down to Lovely. As soon as they pulled her out, they carried her dust-coated body up to a Red Cross vehicle.

All of that added up. But there were parts of the story that didn't. The biggest one was Lalanne's description of Lovely when she emerged from the rubble in Chocholi's arms. Lalanne said Lovely had looked up at him and said, "Thank you." That did not sound like Lovely when she was well-fed and happy, let alone dehydrated and distraught. The people at the Sonapi clinic had told me it was days before she stopped crying and spoke her first words. Maybe he was confusing her with someone else?

I decided I'd let Rosemene and Enel be the final judges. My plane ticket back home was already booked, but I talked to my editor and she agreed I should fly back a couple of weeks later for a reunion of Lalanne's *ekip* and Lovely.

It was a hot July morning, and Lovely sat in the crowded back seat of the car on her father's lap. Rosemene was there, as were Elistin and Rosita. They all wanted to be part of the moment, in case these turned out to truly be Lovely's saviors.

I led them down to Lalanne's house, where he and his crew were waiting. It was barely 8:30 a.m., and Chocholi already looked glassy-eyed from *kleren*.

We sat down together on couches in the small front room. The tin door to the roof had been moved aside to allow sunlight to spill onto the floor. Lovely climbed onto Rosemene's lap. She was dressed again for church, in a pink floral summer dress, white socks, and her Mary Janes, which were so clean, they gleamed.

An awkward silence followed the introductions. No one knew what to say.

Finally, Chocholi spoke: "It took a great deal of effort to get her out."

Then Lalanne, dressed entirely in army fatigues, piped up: "She's grown a lot. She was shorter. She had dust all over her face. She kept saying 'I'm thirsty, I'm thirsty.'"

Rosemene's voice was husky and soft when she asked Chocholi which hospital he had taken Lovely to. She was testing him.

"I took her to the Champs de Mars," he said, adding that he'd put her into a mobile clinic. He couldn't remember the name.

Lalanne bent his long frame down and nuzzled Lovely's little face.

"Lovely, *ça va?*" he asked. "Do you remember me? My, you've grown. Speak to us, Lovely. Do you remember Chocholi?"

Lovely smiled coyly and pressed her head into her mother's chest.

Lalanne began to hold court. "I spent three days looking for a position to get that girl," he said, standing up and addressing the room. "She was screaming under the cement. I said, 'That's not the voice of an adult. That's a child's voice.' Every place we broke, it wasn't where she was."

From his seat on the couch, Enel quietly asked Chocholi if he stayed with Lovely at the clinic. It seemed like another test.

Chocholi said he returned to Lalanne to work and drink more *kleren*, which Lalanne had on hand for him. "It mostly gives me force," he said. "When I drink *kleren*, heavy stuff becomes light."

I could tell Rosemene and Enel were still not convinced; nor was I. So I asked Lalanne and Chocholi to take us to the site where they had rescued Lovely.

Lalanne led us out his back door, through his crowded pen of turkeys and goats, and out the corrugated metal fence into the heart of the slum. The thin alleys were clogged with garbage: Styrofoam containers, rum bottles, discarded limes—all in blackened mounds. In places, the smell of urine was thick and heavy. We passed a half-naked girl bathing from a bucket and some young boys kicking a tennis ball around the floor of what had once been a house. We climbed a hill, slipped down another thin alley, made a sharp left, and stopped abruptly before a little two-door shed roughly hammered together with scraps of plywood and corrugated tin.

"This is where you lived," Lalanne said, turning. "Do you remember this place?"

Rosemene was holding Lovely in her arms. Her eyes narrowed. She scanned the surrounding homes, now mostly quilts of metal and plywood, searching for something familiar. It seemed we'd been here before, on our previous trip to Fort National to see Lovely's original home, but everything had changed again.

Then a man stepped out of the shack wearing nothing but a red towel around his waist.

"*Bonjou*, friend," he said to Rosemene. "Where are you living now?"

It was her former landlord, who had moved back from the Champs de Mars a few months ago and built this small two-room house.

Curious neighbors poked their heads out their doors to see what the commotion was about. Suddenly, Rosemene was flooded with familiar faces. A smile stretched across her face.

"*Bonjou*, Felicine," she shouted, waving to one woman at her door. "Is Mama Sul still here?"

Just like that, it was clear that Lalanne was telling the truth. Rosemene made the rounds, greeting her old neighbors and putting Lovely down to walk around by herself. I tried to imagine what Lovely's life would be like if she were back in this slum. Both her parents were taking turns to sell their wares downtown, and Rosemene had often spoken about moving back to Port-au-Prince, where it was easier to make money. But, standing there, it seemed like such an oppressive place to live. I hoped they wouldn't make the move. Where Lovely lived now was modest, but it was clean and safe.

Rosemene thanked Lalanne and Chocholi. She was convinced of their legitimacy. As we made our way back to the car, I was relieved to hear that Rosemene shared the same thinking as me. "There is too much garbage, too much pee, too many mosquitoes," she whispered. "I don't like this area anymore."

As we pulled away from the slum, it seemed like a chapter had closed. We knew who had saved Lovely and we knew that her present life was infinitely better than it would have been. Now it was just a matter of finding out what the future would bring.

Part 3

Chapter 11

Lyla and Lovely

The idea of bringing Lyla to Haiti had been fermenting for at least half a year. It seemed only fair that she got to meet the little girl she had been sharing me with. And giving her a glimpse into the place I had disappeared to so often over the past two and a half years might make my future departures easier.

I was interested in what Lyla would make of the place—its chaos and noise, its vibrancy and blistering poverty. It would be the first time she confronted the Third World, and the first time she would be a visible minority—a white person in a black world. She had just started grade one and was only six years old; I wondered how she would handle it.

My husband, Graeme, cautiously supported the idea. He agreed that, in theory, it would be good for Lyla, but worried about what might happen to her. After every trip to Haiti, I had unpacked my stress late at night as we got ready for bed, describing how I'd seen life drain from people in cholera units and corpses literally pile up in the general hospital morgue. How could he willingly send our precious daughter there? It was hard enough for him to see me go repeatedly.

In the end, his trust in me won over and I booked our tickets for a long weekend in October 2012. We would be on the ground in Haiti for just under three days—long enough for an introduction but short enough to skirt danger. In preparation, we visited my travel doctor in downtown Toronto. While Lyla sorted through the stamps on his desk, he rattled off the fruits she should avoid and the importance of handwashing. He jabbed her with a number of inoculations and gave her an oral vaccine for cholera, which I'd thought was unnecessary; after all, she'd be drinking only bottled water there. But Graeme had insisted.

Before the doctor ushered us out, he gave Lyla some parting advice that rang in my head for days.

"Lyla, you are going to a different world," he said. "People don't have shoes there, and if they do, they will be broken." It wasn't the physical illnesses she needed inoculation from, he seemed to be saying, but the existential and emotional ones.

As the trip approached, Graeme drilled two cardinal rules into Lyla's little brain, getting her to repeat them ad nauseam whenever we were all in the car together.

"What won't you do in Haiti, Lyla?" he'd ask, palming the steering wheel and looking at her in the rearview mirror.

"I won't put my fingers in my mouth," she'd repeat from her booster seat in the back. "I won't drink or eat anything unless I ask Mommy first."

"That's right," he said. "Tell me one more time."

"I won't put my fingers in my mouth. I won't drink or eat anything unless I ask Mommy first."

We packed her bag carefully, putting in her colored markers and journal, her favorite book, and a doll. In my bag we loaded presents for Lovely and her family.

Port-au-Prince isn't that far away from Toronto—just a few

minutes past Havana. But there are no direct flights. We endured thirteen hours of travel, two sterile airports, and two frigid planes before we stepped out into the welcoming Caribbean heat.

Just as we pushed our luggage trollies outside, I asked Lyla to stop so I could take a photo of her first moment in Haiti. She pulled her pink sweatshirt off to reveal a gray Minnie Mouse T-shirt with lettering that read *Genuine Love*.

As I looked at her little face through the frame of my phone, it hit me: I hadn't just brought Lyla to Haiti; Lyla was in Haiti with *me*, her mother. How could I be her mom *in Haiti*?

I still wasn't a real person in Haiti, despite my resolve to change that fact. I was an eighteen-hour-a-day work machine. I didn't exercise, I didn't socialize, I didn't break for lunch. And I smoked! How was I going to make it three days in Haiti without smoking?

In all the hours of careful planning and packing, I had focused simply on Lyla and what she might experience on her first trip out of North America. It hadn't dawned on me that I would have to carefully pack some other parts of myself and bring them here—not just the journalist who took notes and interviewed people and stayed up till 2:00 a.m. scratching at issues inside my brain, but the mother who played, read books aloud to her kids, packed lunches, and stroked her daughter's hair as she fell asleep on my lap, which she did on the ride to the guesthouse.

I roused Lyla when we arrived and led her upstairs into the building's turret. The guesthouse dog, a small yellow mutt named Gracie, followed us excitedly and jumped around Lyla's bed begging her to play. While they were getting acquainted, I dove into my normal routine of unpacking and preparing, plugging in my cell phone and computer, and ordering my files and books on a side table.

Just as I had pulled out my digital recorder and headlamp, a strange rasping sound echoed out behind me. I spun around to find Lyla, bent over the sink, drinking from the water faucet.

"Oh my God!" I shrieked. "Remember the rule: you can't drink or eat anything until I tell you it's okay. That water is *not okay*."

Her little face collapsed and she began to cry.

"I'm sorry, Mommy," she said between sobs. "I forgot."

I barely slept, coiling my sheet around my legs and kicking through my mosquito blanket all night. It always took me a while to get accustomed to the night noises of Haiti—the dogs barking, roosters calling, and sounds of gunshots down in the *bidonvil* below us. But it was the noise inside my head that kept me awake that night. I was primed to spring into action the instant Lyla began to explode from both ends. Thanks to Graeme's wisdom, I wasn't worried about cholera. It was giardia that concerned me. I walked through the plan: I would yank up her mosquito net and hustle her to the bathroom. I would leave her on the toilet for two hours, so her system was flushed, before giving her some Ciprofloxacin. I would call Richard and cancel our plans. Instead of visiting Lovely, we would spend three days here, in this little turret, on and beside the toilet, all because of my own distracted mothering.

Lyla had taught me this lesson many times. When I was pregnant with her, I envisioned my life as a motorcycle. I would simply attach a sidecar and do all the things I had always loved, but with her. I wasn't going to be one of those mothers who lost interest in everything but her baby; I'd still go out for dinner with friends, see movies, go for runs pushing her in a jogging stroller.

When she was fourteen days old, Lyla started to scream, and she didn't stop for three months. The doctor said she had "extreme colic." She screamed until her little face went deep purple. Already sleep-deprived, I became frantic, searching for ways to calm her. The only trick I found that worked was to tie her to my body with a long piece of fabric and head outside for a fast walk. The pounding of my heart put her to sleep, and then I would have two hours of quiet. Sometimes I would go to the park and climb on a swing just to keep her from waking up.

There would be no dinners with friends, no movies, no reading books, no sleep, no sidecar. Lyla and I were in a whole new mode of transportation, heading to places I hadn't planned. Strangely, looking back, I enjoyed that time. All those walks through our neighborhood with her tied to me prompted me to start a residents' association later that year around our dining room table. I lost some of the things I loved about my life, but gained new perspectives, thanks to Lyla.

I could see what I'd lose in Haiti, but what new things would Lyla reveal? I wondered.

As dawn leaked through the turret's windows, I watched Lyla sleep on her tummy, completely naked, her little lips puckered. Her groggy morning voice rang out.

"Hi, Gracie," she said, shooting her hand out from under the mosquito net to stroke the dog, who had slept on the floor between our beds. "How are you?"

With that, she was off, pulling a sundress out of her bag and running after Gracie down the stairs and into the garden outside to explore.

I heaved a huge sigh of relief. Montezuma had spared us his revenge. We were very lucky.

In fact, Lyla had second helpings of breakfast and then announced she wanted to swim in the pool, so we both tugged on our bathing suits and jumped into the cold water. I was determined to be attentive to my daughter, and threw coins for her to retrieve from the watery depths until I was so cold I began to shiver.

When we arrived before the maroon gate of Lovely's school, it was recess: Hundreds of kids in red-checkered shirts and red shorts and skirts swirled around the small courtyard. There was no room to play soccer or do handstands, so the kids just ran around in small knots, dodging one another.

Lyla gripped my hand firmly as I scanned faces, looking for Lovely. There she was, over by the pillar, squatting on the ground. Her hard brown eyes twinkled mischievously, and her mouth was knotted to the side. I felt like we were her secret and that she was watching to see what we would do.

I called out to her and she walked slowly toward us, offered up her cheek for me to kiss, then melted back into the crowd. It was not what you'd call an auspicious first meeting between the two girls in my life.

Dozens of other little girls had taken great interest in us, hovering around Lyla in a circle. Their hands darted out to touch her arms and hair. She was an oddity to them—an exotic pet that had been brought in for show-and-tell. I remember Rosemene telling me that I was the first *blan* she has ever known, and about a year after we'd met I'd let her pick through my fine hair, her fingers and eyes burrowing in to quench a curiosity.

Lyla found it intimidating.

"Why are they all staring at me?" she asked.

Jenanine came to Lyla's rescue, taking her hand authoritatively and leading her up the concrete stairs at the corner of the courtyard. I assumed they led to a playground. A few minutes later they were back and Lyla was in tears. She'd tripped and skinned her knee.

"I want to go back to the car," she said.

I convinced her to sit in the back of Lovely's class, just for a few minutes, and then we'd go. When recess was over, we got in line behind Lovely's teacher Madame Violet, a kind-faced woman with glasses, who led us up the concrete steps. Instead of a playground, we were greeted by a small construction zone on the second story: stacks of cinder blocks and long wooden beams leaning against an unfinished wall. At the back were two classrooms.

Lovely's small classroom was crammed with desks of different shapes and colors, so close together that there was barely room to move between them. Lovely sat down at a desk in the front row, sharing a single bench with five other girls. Lyla and I squeezed into chairs in the back and Madame Violet launched into her lesson from the front of the room. She was teaching the children how to make polite introductions in French.

As she called on students to stand in twos and role-play, I counted heads and recounted them, to be sure. There were forty-two kids in

Lovely's class—double the number in Lyla's back home. How could a teacher command that many five-year-olds?

The answer was soon obvious: she didn't. Little boys promptly fell asleep in the row ahead of us, their heads side by side on the table. Nearby, I watched two girls share a lollipop, hiding it behind the backpacks propped up on their desks like a screen.

A little troublemaker near me hit the boy beside her with her ruler until it broke. Backpacks were hurled, children were pushed, and the classroom door repeatedly burst open as Madame Violet's three-year-old niece wandered in and out. It didn't help that the wall separating the class from the one next door was plywood and offered no soundproofing, so the chaos of that class washed into the room.

"This the loudest class I've ever been in," said Lyla, looking up from her journal, in which she'd been drawing a picture.

I assumed the noise would die down, but it didn't. After an hour Madame Violet got the children to repeat a list of random words written on the blackboard, under the title "Dictation":

Le bebe. Tire. Le moto. Vole. Vomi.

The children screamed them out in unison until my head began to throb. How Lovely had learned to read in this environment was a testament to her iron will.

I had assumed this school was good because middle-class parents sent their kids here and the teachers could speak fluent French. It took a trip with my daughter to understand this formula was too simplistic. That day, it seemed like expensive babysitting.

I had to get out of there. I stood up, thanked Madame Violet, and left with Lyla. Lovely grabbed her bag and followed us.

The instant we arrived in the parking spot before Lovely's one-room house, Lovely grabbed Lyla's hand and the pair disappeared behind the banana trees. I pushed through the gate and reconnected with Rosemene while Lyla and Lovely darted in and out of the room, racing after each other. I zipped open the duffel bag of *rad kenedi* and toys Lyla and I had packed, and Lovely immediately grabbed Lyla's doll. She and Lyla took turns brushing its white hair.

A while later, Lyla kicked off her shoes and climbed up on top of the room's single bed, asking for her sketch pad and markers. Lovely followed her, and they began to draw on the same page, their two heads pressed together.

"*Bonne fête, Lovely,*" sang Lyla.

"*Bonne fête, La-La,*" Lovely sang back.

I was amazed. I had expected the two of them to be awkward with one another at first, like strangers on a blind date. Their inauspicious first meeting at the school had seemed to confirm that: the two parts of my life were like mismatched pieces of a puzzle. They would take some forceful jamming to fit together. Yet, here they were, instant friends without any input from me.

"How do you say, 'Let's play tag'?" Lyla asked. Richard translated, and Lyla raced after Lovely. When she caught her, they collapsed in a giggling heap on the ground like puppies.

Mostly they spoke to one another without any translation. Lovely spoke to Lyla in Kreyòl and Lyla responded in pidgin French, making up words as she went and using a lot of exaggerated hand gestures. She talked in a baby voice, as though she had become suddenly younger than her six-year-old self.

It reminded me of the summer my husband and I spent in northern India, before we were married. We lived with separate families in a small village on a glacier-fed stream, surrounded by desert mountains, where we learned how to harvest barley. It was there that I saw how, without language, your personality changes. In English, I have an off-the-wall sense of humor. But clearly, my basic Ladakhi skills couldn't convey sarcasm or irony. So I used physical humor, of the Laurel-and-Hardy kind: pretending to trip through the door, or poke my eye out with the handle of a broom. It was strange and liberating, like I was trying on a new persona.

Lovely led Lyla up a field edged with blooming peas, their delicate white and purple flowers glimmering in the hot afternoon light. Two cows were tethered to trees, and I watched Lyla walk around them as if they were parked cars. She leapt over their giant fresh patties, utterly at home.

I noticed for the first time that although Lyla was just one year older, she was a full head taller than Lovely was. No wonder her hand-me-down clothes were years too big for Lovely.

Halfway up the path, Lypse and Sophonie appeared, still dressed in their blue uniforms from the Baptist mission school. Word had gotten to them that the *blans* were here. They reached for Lyla's hands, and Lovely yelled at them to back off. Lyla was her friend and she was holding her hand!

Elistin's home was just as I had left it last, except coils of rebar and gravel mounds dotted the edges of the dirt yard. A big, solid, rectangular house—the size of my own in Toronto—had sprouted in the small farm field below. By Haitian standards, it was enormous: three or four rooms had gone up in the past two months since I was last there. That meant the owner was either upper-class Haitian or part of the diaspora, with a full bank account in Canada or the United States that permitted a big construction push.

Most Haitians built their homes little by little as they came into money. Elistin had been tucking bills into a wooden lockbox for fourteen years to buy cement, rebar, and gravel for the two-room house he was building just down the hill. So far, all he had finished was the foundation and one wall. It had been so many years, weeds were growing between the cement blocks.

He'd even presented me with a handwritten budget of necessary supplies and their corresponding estimated costs, looking for some *èd*. But it had seemed a shaky investment, since Elistin didn't own the land he was building on. While he said his landlady had agreed to let him build a small house there, he didn't have it in writing.

So, for now, Elistin's house remained a dream and a playground for the kids, who led Lyla there to explore it. Meanwhile, Elistin and Rosita pulled their wooden chairs into the yard for us to sit and catch up. After about twenty minutes I went to check on Lyla. I found her and Lovely squatting next to the wall. They were peeing. I watched Lyla help Lovely pull up her underwear.

My daughter had fallen in love with Haiti at first sight, which I didn't think was possible. It's a country that has to grow on you. It's like a puzzle you can't put down. But Lyla had responded with her heart, not her head, just as I had done almost three years ago, before the silty layers of cynicism had begun to fossilize those feelings.

I also gathered that Lyla felt so comfortable here because *I* was so comfortable. Over the past two and a half years, Haiti had become my second home. Lyla had listened to my stories at the dinner table, looked through my photos, and discussed Haiti while curled in her bed at night. She and Lovely might have just met, but Lovely had been part of Lyla's life for a long time.

Once the sun turned honey gold, I announced it was time to go, and Lyla said her good-byes to all the kids with hugs. We made our way gingerly down the rocky path and around the cows, with both girls holding my hands.

Lyla and I waved good-bye as we climbed into the back seat of the car. We bumped past the lonely cemetery where Lina's baby was buried, past the Baptist mission school, and onto the main road. Port-au-Prince came into view down below us, blanketed in a haze of dust and humidity. Suddenly, Lyla burst into tears beside me.

"I don't want to go," she said. "Lovely is my best friend."

The next morning we set out to visit Muspan Montessori. The construction that Digicel had funded was finished, and the result was astounding. The school was enormous—broad and tall like a government building, its towering walls painted peach.

Gilberte appeared at the door wearing her trademark straw hat and carrying a metal cane with four tennis balls attached to its square base. She kissed us both on our cheeks and started our tour immediately, gingerly leading us up the staircase.

Strings of paper hearts hung from the ceiling and handwritten *Bienvenue* signs dotted the pale yellow walls. The school had just had its grand opening a few weeks before.

Classes were in session. The sound of teachers giving lessons echoed through the open doors. Otherwise, the school was quiet. There was no shouting, no hurling of backpacks, no small children walking the wide halls.

Gilberte led us into the first classroom. It was enormous compared to Lovely's. Kids sat at long wooden desks with plenty of room for each to move and roomy aisles between them. The electricity hadn't been connected yet, so the overhead lights weren't working, but the room's large window let in both light and a breeze. After Lovely's class's chaos, every detail seemed marvelous.

When we entered the kindergarten room, the kids all stood up at their desks. They launched into a song in French, their arms swinging cutely by their sides. Many had their names embroidered on the pockets of their green-and-white checkered uniforms. "*Nous sommes heureux, de vous voir parmi nous*"—"We are happy to have you here with us."

It felt like a parade, but reversed. We marched from room to room and were serenaded in each. Most songs were followed by a flowery message, written neatly on the chalkboard at the front of each class and read by thirty voices.

"*Bienvenue,* Madame Catreen. And thank you for your support," the little kids said. "Keep thinking of us. Thank you. Good work," recited the upper-year students.

There were nine classrooms, so the tour was long, which made me feel proud and awkward at the same time. Lyla felt the same way. She held my hand and cast shy glances around each room.

Finally, we entered the grade-one class, where Gilberte gave an impromptu lecture.

"Do you know what Madame Catreen did for us? You don't know?" she said from the front of the class. A little boy in the second row put up his hand and asked if I was a new professor come to teach.

"If it wasn't for her, we wouldn't have been able to continue the school," Gilberte continued. "We have to pray for her every day, because for two years she helped pay for professors. Would you be able to come to school without professors? No. It's thanks to her and her friends in Canada. There, they made donations for you to go to school. So that's why we say thank you to Madame Catreen."

I didn't need the sales pitch; I had just committed to raising another US$26,000 for this coming school year. I wasn't alone now—a group of girlfriends had offered to help me do it—and this trip confirmed it was the right thing to do. Compared to all the failures I had documented in Haiti, Muspan was one undisputed, unanticipated success. Here, in this one place, Haiti had indeed built back better. I had warned Gilberte, however, it was my final year of providing *èd*. Next year she would be on her own.

After Gilberte finished her speech and retreated into the staff office, Lyla and I stayed behind, taking a seat on a back bench to watch the grade-one class. The teacher was a tall, thin woman who patrolled the rows, her hands clasped behind her back, peppering the children with questions. What were their favorite animals and how did they spell them? After a few answers, she arrived at our desk and announced it was Lyla's turn.

My daughter had been drawing in her journal and not paying attention. So I whispered an answer in her ear: "*Chien.*" The class around us broke into laughter. I had forgotten that dogs weren't normal pets in Haiti; they were either wild in the streets or tied up to guard properties. They were not things you liked.

The laughter embarrassed Lyla, and she said she wanted to go. This school bored her anyway. It was too much like her class back home.

"I liked Lovely's class more," she whispered. "It was more fun."

We said good-bye to the class and Gilberte walked us out the front door. "Next time you come, little lady," she said to Lyla, "you will stay at my house."

We decided to spend our last day in Haiti at the beach. I had traveled to many of Haiti's neighboring countries *just* for the beach in winters past, but here the idea seemed revolutionary. Not only had I never been to one of Haiti's beaches, I'd never even seen one. I'd glimpsed the Caribbean Sea, but only as the fetid border to Cité Soleil's shacks or the flashing backdrop to Titanyen's mass grave site. To me, the ocean seemed like an ironic theater set, pegged up with tacks for a play about despair.

Rosemene had told me that she had never been to the beach before, despite growing up near a beach town. For that matter, no one in her family had ever been, so they were all keen to come.

I hired a van and driver from the guesthouse. Our plan was to pick up Lovely and her family in the morning and then travel north of the city to Wahoo Bay, a private beach some Haitian friends had assured me was beautiful.

That morning Lyla and I climbed in with our swim bags packed. The young guesthouse driver clambered into the front seat and started up the engine. It promptly died and refused to come back to life, no matter how many times he turned the ignition. We wouldn't be leaving the guesthouse driveway, it seemed. Thankfully, the guesthouse manager agreed to loan us the backup van, a clunky blue tank with ancient seats and, we discovered, just one working seat belt, which I dutifully wrapped around Lyla.

The engine groaned to life and we lurched up the steep driveway, dumping black smoke behind us. We made it up to Place Saint-Pierre, where the entire family piled in: Lovely, Jonathan, their parents and cousins, aunt and uncle, and Venessaint, who had brought his best friend, Lovinsky. Lovely immediately settled into the seat beside Lyla and they pressed their heads together, coloring in her notepad.

We cut through the heart of the city and reached the airport, rounding the *Trois Mains* statue and passing the sign and blue gates of the Sonapi industrial district, which Rosemene pointed out excitedly. That was where Lovely had been found, two times—first by *blans*, then by her family. To Rosemene, it was a billboard of love.

The mountains rose softly before us, their edges smoothed as though scuffed with green sandpaper, and the ocean glistened beside us, holding up fishermen in rustic wood sailboats.

Wahoo Bay, like all private property in Haiti, was barricaded behind a high wall.

On the other side, we were met by a Caribbean airlines ad: pink bougainvillea dripping overhead from trellises, a pool surrounded by lounge chairs, and, down at the end of the stone steps, a sandy beach dotted with wooden umbrella stands.

Exquisite. Lyla ripped her clothes off and waded into the ocean immediately, without a care in the world. Lovely and her family were hesitant, standing awkwardly near the water, not quite sure what to do. This was completely foreign for them. Not one of them could swim.

Slowly, they each peeled off their clothes. Lovely was the only one who had a bathing suit, an orange one covered in yellow leaves that Lyla had outgrown last summer. Everyone else wore tank tops and their underwear.

They each sat down tentatively just inside the surf, but the water was so warm and inviting that, before long, Enel and Rosemene began to submerge their bodies and venture up and down the beach in the shallow water like cats, pawing at the sand with their hands.

I took Lovely in my arms and gave her a lesson in floating, the way I used to with my own kids—"Stomach down, kick, kick, one, two, one, two." Jonathan stood on the shore screaming "*Mwen, Madame Katrin, Mwen.*" He wanted his turn.

Lyla dove around the edges of the group, her dark goggles pulled down over her eyes. She asked me to play, but after I'd explained how we were the only ones who knew how to swim, she began to take her lifeguarding role seriously. I spent the rest of the afternoon as a swim coach, rotating between Lovely and Jonathan, and then Rosemene and Rosita. They each closed their eyes and smiled widely while I held their bodies supine in my arms and rocked them back and forth in the water.

Their delight was so huge, it was heartbreaking. This seemed truly the definition of poverty: to live beside a paradise and never experience it.

The rest of the day passed like a dream, everyone relaxing more and more. By the end, all the adults were laughing by the water in a carefree manner I'd never seen. Venessaint was a natural swimmer, plunging his head under the water and kicking around the shallow end. Lovely and Jonathan huddled under my arms and we chased after Lyla, with Lovely excitedly shrieking "La-La, La-La," which had become Lyla's Haitian name.

My pen lay on my notebook under the shade of a beach umbrella, untouched. I had not written a single word all day—a first for me in Haiti. This was my introduction to the country as Catherine, mother and friend, goofy woman who liked to laugh and play. It felt so good.

Perhaps Lovely and Rosemene had never seen me as a human tape recorder and bank machine. But I had. This was Lyla's gift to me. She had shown me a different Haiti, yes. But, more importantly, she had shown Haiti a different me.

I would have stayed until nightfall, but Rosemene took note of the sun's position in the sky and announced it was time to go. We reluctantly crowded into the van's rickety seats and trundled back through Haiti's countryside, happy and relaxed. Lyla fished out a bag of jelly beans from her knapsack and distributed them, one by one. "Wahoo Bay, Wahoo Bay," Rosemene repeated, as if trying to imprint it on her memory.

Enel sang quietly to himself behind me in the back seat. I craned my neck to tell him about an offer I had recently received from a reader who wanted to help him begin a career, paying for his schooling and start-up costs for whatever he chose to do.

"You could become a mechanic," I told him. "A security guard?"

"*Mototaksi,*" he said, smiling. He wanted to be a motorcycle taxi driver.

"You don't need to decide right away," I said. "You can think more about it."

The late afternoon sun coated the banana trees outside our windows with honey, and when we reached Titanyen, a gasp went up from the front: a giant rainbow arched over the site of mass graves. Even the ugliest and saddest site in the country, a symbol of death, poverty, and injustice, was beautiful at that moment. A sense of hope filled my chest. Everything could be remade; anything seemed possible.

Sitting on her mother's lap near the front, Lovely announced she wanted to sit on "*Manman*." She crawled over the back of her seat toward me.

"What are you doing, Lovely?" I asked her. "Your mother is there."

"She calls you *Manman*, too," Rosemene said over her shoulder. "*Manman Katrin*."

It was the second time Rosemene had said this to me, and my thoughts sprinted down the same reactive track. I was not Lovely's mother; having Lyla here with me underlined that. I would never know Lovely's internal world like I knew my daughter's. But Lyla's presence also revealed the depth of my affection for Lovely and the level of comfort I had with her. I *felt* like a mother to her. So while I had previously rejected the idea that I was, in any meaningful way, Lovely's mother, I was now coming to see that there was an element of truth to it.

Jonathan followed behind her, squeezing between Lyla and me, while Lovely nuzzled her head under my chin. Lyla started singing "Down by the Bay," a camp song we often sang in the car at home to pass time. I looked around me at the mosh pit of arms and legs and felt completely, totally at home.

Chapter 12

Fè Byen Se Fwèt
(No Good Deed Goes Unpunished)

It was destined to be a difficult trip to Haiti, because that was the kind of winter I was having in 2012.

I was in the dumps. Things were going right in my life, but I couldn't focus on the happy aspects. I glommed onto the bad, the hard, and the cold. I was determined to be miserable, and my misery became a self-fulfilling prophecy.

It had to do with turning forty, but I wouldn't see that right away, even when it hit me in the face on Christmas Eve, two days before my birthday. I had pulled on winter jogging gear and headed out into the gray, frigid streets to de-stress from work before the holidays started. My intentions were right, but the execution was shoddy. I carried my cell phone to play music on my earphones, but ended up scrolling through email messages while running. I tripped on a bump in the sidewalk and flew headfirst onto the empty street. To save my face, I rolled as I landed and something in my right shoulder popped.

I lay there alone on the hard gray road, howling loudly in pain, so absorbed in the sensations of my animal body, my librarian spirit was incapable of marshaling discretion. A truck approached slowly; its driver rolled down his window and kindly offered to take me to the hospital. He had a huge dog in the back seat that looked at me with its big black eyes and licked my cheek.

It turned out I had torn the ligament in my shoulder. The good news was I wouldn't need an operation. But all I heard was that my shoulder would never be round again: a clothes hanger–like bump would spell the end of my strapless dress days. And I was bound for a difficult recovery: four weeks of shooting pain up my arms and tingling in my fingers. Four weeks of no lifting, no T-shirt wearing, no writing—nothing but Advil-numbed afternoons in bed.

Things got much worse on my birthday, when the phone rang: a dear university friend who Graeme and I had worked with in India had drowned. We were despondent.

Little things were falling apart, too. Our favorite neighborhood bakery closed down. In the grand scheme of things, it wasn't terrible, but it had been our family's Saturday morning ritual to wander over to the bakery for cinnamon rolls and challah. "Who will take over the store?" Noah asked.

"Probably some crappy store will go in," Lyla responded. "They are leaving, and I love them. Everyone I love leaves."

"No more sticky buns," lamented Noah. "No more yummy bread."

I decided I needed a big change in my life. I wasn't sure what it would mean yet, but I was pushing Graeme to move—not to another neighborhood but another country. But first I had some things I had to settle in Haiti.

Two weeks before I arrived back in Haiti in March 2013, Rosemene delivered a baby girl.

She'd known it was a girl because of the way her body filled in at the waist, and she'd intended to name her Mylove. In the end, she chose Ananstania, because a neighbor said it was from the Bible, a claim that turned out to be untrue.

I sat in the dim light of their one-room house and held Ananstania's small body in my lap. She had Jonathan's heavy brow and Lovely's wiry body. She was swaddled in clothing. Rosemene had pulled no fewer than three hats over her little head; the top one was a pink one that I had brought with me in my regular gift bag of *rad kenedi*.

Ananstania looked up at me quizzically, swung her arms around, and opened her mouth and closed it like a hungry little bird.

A feeling of dread hung on my body like the cold mountain air. There was no doubt she was beautiful, and a healthy baby is always a blessing. But that mouth. Rosemene had struggled for so long to feed the three children under her care. Now there was one more. Lovely would likely go back to being hungry. Ananstania's birth seemed like a huge step backward for the family as a whole. I tried to hide my disappointment.

Rosemene lay on the room's single bed, similarly bundled in several layers of clothing, with a thick white towel wrapped over her head. It was a Haitian tradition, she told me. They both would remain like this for three months.

The day of Ananstania's birth, Rosemene went to a *jèn*, an all-day prayer session. On her way home she'd felt cramping in her legs.

"I cooked. I cleaned the house. I made some coffee," she said. "In the afternoon I felt a slight pain in my stomach. I felt ill at ease." I remembered feeling achy and restless the afternoon before I went into labor with Noah. I had moved from the floor to a couch to the bath to bed, fruitlessly trying to calm my nervous body, which sensed the approaching storm.

Enel had offered to take Rosemene to the Baptist mission hospital, where she'd gone for prenatal visits and planned to give birth. But she thought it was too early. So she went to bed instead. The contractions woke her up in the middle of the night. Enel lit a fire to heat some water. He had added some soap so there was foam and rubbed her belly with it between contractions. It was the poor person's version of a bubble bath.

By 4:00 a.m. the contractions were so intense, Enel went to fetch Elistin and Rosita.

"I was so hot. I had to get outside," Rosemene said. "I gave birth right in the front door. Three pushes and she was out."

Rosita caught the baby. Enel cut the cord with a new razor blade. By then, all the kids were awake and Jonathan was screaming in fear: "*Papa tou'em Mami!*"—"Daddy's killing Mommy!"

We all laughed at that. I knew how lucky Rosemene had been that the birth had gone smoothly. If things had gone badly, she could have bled to death right there on the stoop of their home.

In the time Rosemene had told her story, Ananstania had peed and pooed through her clothing. The family had no diapers, which meant she needed to be fully changed and bathed regularly. Rosemene pulled out a tub of cold water—she had no charcoal to light a fire to heat it up—and I watched as she dipped the baby's small, excited body into it. Ananstania flailed her arms. Her facial expressions were wonderful—surprise, joy, consternation. Rosemene giggled and kissed her cheeks.

"Don't go pee," she said. "Ooooh. You peed. Oh, *cheri*."

She rubbed Ananstania's face with cream and laughed at her reaction. "Don't open your mouth. I'm not going to feed you."

I asked her what she dreamed of for Ananstania's future.

"I hope her life is easier than mine," she said. "I want her to learn a profession so she doesn't grow up like I did. I'd like her to wake up and not worry about how to feed her kids."

In my own life, I'd always thought of birth control as a feminist issue—a woman's right to control her own body. Here, I learned it was a development issue, too. The fewer babies Rosemene had, the more each one would get—not just attention but food, schooling, clothing.

The Kreyòl word for birth control, *planin*, was from the English word, since foreign aid groups had delivered most of the supplies. Compared to most development programs in the country, it had proved moderately successful. Twenty-five years before, the country's average family had 6.8 children. Since then, it had dropped to 3.4. One in three Haitian women had access to birth control—including Rosemene, who had gotten free shots of the hormone medication Depo-Provera every three months. But the drug had had severe side effects for her. She tried birth control pills next and found they caused the same problems, so she'd dropped them, too. A month later she was pregnant with Ananstania.

"I wanted two. God gave me three," she said. "Some people want children and can't have children. *Lavi pi chè*. (Life is more expensive.) I have people helping me and I still find it difficult."

One thing Rosemene was certain about: "I'm not having any more kids."

Enel returned to the house in time to greet the kids returning from school. Lovely was dressed immaculately in her school uniform, a little Dora the Explorer suitcase in hand, plastic and purple. She charged toward me and leapt into my arms. I was so happy to see her and I wanted to hear all about her school and friends and life.

Sitting on my lap and drawing in my journal, Lovely told me she could now count to five in English and that she'd written exams the week before.

"I had a rabbit exam," she said. "A leaf exam."

I burst into laughter. She was such a cool kid. And she clearly loved her new sister. I watched as Lovely held Ananstania and kissed her little mouth repeatedly. Still, I hoped Rosemene would not have any more. It seemed critical for Lovely's success.

I asked Rosemene what kind of planning she was using since giving birth to Ananstania. She had sent Enel out to collect the burr-like seeds of the Palm of Christ plant—the same *grenn maskriti* the family used for massages and taming Lovely's curls. Rosemene was now swallowing the seeds like pills.

"I heard about it in the countryside," she said. "It's called natural planning. If you drink ten pills, it lasts ten years. Take twenty, you are good for twenty years."

Perhaps there were some natural birth control properties to the seeds. But it seemed like a folktale to me.

"Listen," I told Rosemene, "that won't work. That isn't *planin*. You will definitely get pregnant again unless Enel uses condoms or you go back on the pill. You need to go back to the doctor and ask about it."

She told me she would. I hoped she was being sincere.

If I thought things were bad at Lovely's home, they were far worse at Muspan. The building was the same. It was what was happening inside that was in shambles.

Gilberte took me on our ritual tour, and it didn't take me long to sense that something was wrong. The teachers, who normally smiled and instructed their classrooms to stand and welcome me, were stone-faced. They shifted their gazes around to avoid looking me in the eye.

Gilberte launched into the speech I'd become uncomfortably ac-customed to: about how I was the Canadian journalist who had paid for the teachers' salaries so the students could all go to school for free. Then she went off script.

"But since she didn't pay enough, I had to pay the rest out of my pocket," she announced.

What was she talking about? I was getting regular emails from Ryan Sawatzky's foundation showing the money had been sent every month. My group of friends and I had just finished raising the US$26,000 to cover the school's costs for a final year. I knew Rea Dol had had a hard time reaching Gilberte and delivering the latest in-stallment. But she'd gotten through and paid her as usual, so what was Gilberte talking about?

As the tour progressed, with more sniping from Gilberte and masked looks from professors, it became clear I'd stepped in the mid-dle of a political war.

We shuffled into the dark administration office and sat down to talk. Gilberte planned to fire all the staff, she said. They were incompetent. They weren't delivering their lesson plans, so she had cut their paychecks. In response, they'd gone on strike the week before.

The root of the problem, she explained, was the government's free education program. The teachers thought the grant money should go to them directly in the form of a raise. But Gilberte pointed out that most made about US$120 a month, which was good for a teacher.

"The money should go elsewhere to create other schools like Muspan," she said. "It should be used to help pay tuition for other children."

This was the first I heard that Gilberte had received money from the government program. She handed me a package of letters that outlined how much they'd given her last year—around US$3,800, to cover the tuition of all the school's grade-one students.

That wasn't the only surprise. The same letter laid out Muspan's annual budget, listing it as US$20,000—US$6,000 less than what I was sending her. Adding the two together, Gilberte seemed to have made an extra US$10,000 last year. What was going on?

I felt sick as I went through the documents in the guesthouse that night. I phoned one of the teachers who spoke English.

"Liar! She's a liar. We were at school all of last week," he sputtered over the phone. "The professors were there; the students were there."

I asked him how many months he'd been paid last year. His response: nine. I had sent money for twelve. It was all fishy. I carefully crafted an email to Gilberte, being direct but polite. Could she please explain? Two days later I received a response. She said she'd only received "maybe 10 months" of transfers. Once the school is over in June, she said, "I don't receive transfers from Rea." I imagined her squinting at the computer screen and pecking out the next paragraph with the fingers on her left hand. The email was all in lowercase letters.

"I must assure you the funds I receive go strictly to Muspan," she wrote. For her the school was *"une oeuvre sociale"*—a charitable work. She'd paid for the teachers' salaries for eight years out of her own pocket, she reminded me.

"I could never profit from the school," she wrote. "It is true that Haitians have a bad reputation. I believe I am an exception."

I called Rea and arranged to drop in a few mornings later to go through the paperwork. Maybe they would show that Gilberte was being honest—that she hadn't been paid for the summer months when school wasn't in session. But when we met, Rea pulled out a folder of receipts, each written out carefully by hand on white paper. They showed that, month after month, Rea had received US$2,000 for Madame Salomon from me, Catherine Porter, and that the money had been given to the undersigned. At the bottom of each line was a shaky signature: "G Salomon."

So Gilberte had received the money for the summer, contrary to what she said. The sick feeling in my stomach spread up to my lungs. I wondered: Is that why Rea had found it so difficult to connect with Gilberte? US$10,000 was enough for a couple of very nice vacations.

Corruption was an emerging theme of the country. The *teledjòl* was still buzzing about rumored graft by the president himself. Frustration among international donors was mounting.

Nigel, who was now the top United Nations representative in the country, had voiced all this in a recent speech, stating that—despite all the grumbling about foreign interference and the United Nations in Haiti—the "political elite" had much to answer for.

"What is sovereignty for the mother who is forced to send her child to the city as a *restavèk*?" he asked. "What is sovereignty if all Haitians are not equal before the law? What is sovereignty if opportunity is limited to the few?"

I felt I owed it to all the school kids, friends, and family who had raised money for Muspan to get some answers. I called local contacts and friends for advice on how to approach Gilberte. One expat who had lived in Haiti off and on for a quarter century was frank: "Don't do anything. Just drop it. She could take you to court."

"She could take you to court or worse," advised a Haitian friend. "She could take you *out*."

Sophia Stransky of the Digicel Foundation said she'd noticed Gilberte was forgetting and confusing things of late, but she didn't think she was corrupt. Instead, she thought she was showing signs of the early stages of dementia.

Sophia suggested I take the oblique approach, gently asking for clarification, and I trusted her advice. I drafted another email to Gilberte, attaching the photos of the receipts from the summer.

"I am really confused," I wrote. "Could you please explain to me what happened to this money during the summer?"

She asked for my mailing address so she could send me the payroll sheets for eleven months, signed by the teachers. "If I had received the transfers, I would not have suggested for you to go look for the receipts," she wrote.

She made a good point. It was of course possible someone else had forged her signature.

As a show of goodwill, the morning I was departing for Canada, Gilberte sent a driver to my guesthouse to drop off letters from a dozen students. Each came with a photo attached and began sweetly with "*Cher ami(e)*." I promised to deliver them to a teacher in Toronto whose class was going to start a pen pal program with Muspan.

A few weeks later the signed payrolls sheets arrived at my office. It appeared the staff had been paid for eleven months—not nine, as the teacher told me, nor twelve, as Gilberte had said when we set up the system. So that meant that only US$2,000 of the money I'd sent had gone missing. It was disappointing but not a catastrophe. Gilberte might have simply put that money into the school in a different way—for books or gas for a generator. I decided to simply swallow it. Compared to other projects I'd documented in Haiti, I had gotten off lightly. There was a Kreyòl expression for the predicament: *fè byen se fwèt*. The literal translation was "Doing good is to be whipped." In English, we say "No good deed goes unpunished."

While I was trying to sort out what had gone wrong with Muspan, I was starting another development project in Haiti. I had brought the

US$1,500—sent by the Canadian reader—specifically earmarked to help Enel start a business. On paper, the plan was perfect, the essence of the "Teach a man to fish" proverb. This wasn't a forced, foreigner-imposed project: after deliberation with Rosemene, Enel decided that running a motorcycle taxi business was the right choice. I insisted he do some homework so that he was prepared and would put some of his own sweat into the idea.

There were some setbacks along the way: he lost his national ID card, and he had to restart his driver's license application when he discovered the bureau had printed the wrong name on it. But he had spent the last month taking lessons from a local *chofè mototaksi*, or motorcycle taxi driver, named Roland. Considering Enel had never ridden a bicycle before nor driven a car, he had learned a lot. He performed some long loops on the freshly paved road near his home for me, demonstrating how he could balance Roland's motorcycle over the speed bumps, switch gears, and come to a wobbly stop.

That last part worried me. Motorcycle taxi drivers in Haiti were like independent hairdressers: they groomed their own clientele, who called them directly. There was no central dispatcher, just the driver and his cell phone. They seemed to be all men; after thirteen trips to Haiti, I had yet to see a woman motorcycle *chofè*. If a driver proved himself to be reliable, he could make US$12 a day from his regulars—twice what Enel made now working on building sites. But a couple of accidents could spell the end of their careers. The *teledjòl* was ruthless—word would get out and their clients would find other drivers they deemed safe.

Enel seemed to think he was ready. "It was hard at first," he said. "But now it's easy."

Richard and I arranged to go motorcycle shopping with Enel the next morning in Pétionville. He brought along Roland for advice. The sunlight filtered through the palm trees onto the burnt-orange and Dijon mustard–colored buildings that lined the street. It seemed like it was finally going to be a good day in Haiti.

The first place we rolled up to was still closed, despite a sign outside that announced it opened at 9:00 a.m. The second had no motorcycles in stock. The third place had two on display, but both had already been purchased, the salesman told us.

We continued to a department store that had everything from beds to generators on display. There were motorcycles for sale there, the clerk told us. Fabulous! But there was just one small hitch. We'd need to get the bike's registration papers from the customs office. And that could take a week at minimum. Likely more.

"You see why this country drives me crazy?" Richard exclaimed loudly. He'd spent more of his life in Haiti than in New York, but he still maintained his American expectations. The country, to him, was purgatory. "It's as if they don't want to be in business."

We went off in search of the next shop, strolling through the market and past a corner with a bunch of guys sitting on their motorcycles. Richard called it the "motorcycle station."

"Where is the station?" I asked. To me, the word conjured a building where you could buy tickets and load your luggage, maybe get a snack between trips.

"That's the station," Richard responded, bursting into laughter. "There is no building."

It seemed another classic make-believe situation. But, mulling it over, I saw I was imposing my own cultural expectations on Haiti, the same as Richard. Why did a station need a building? Why was my North American idea of a station more correct than this assembly of motorcycle taxis stationed together?

As we walked, Roland and Enel fell farther and farther behind Richard and me. At first I thought they were just dawdling. But then it became clear: they didn't want to be seen with the *blan*. Perhaps they were embarrassed, but more likely they were worried the perceived connection would get them robbed once we'd parted ways. I tried to understand, but I took their distance personally. I felt like a mother dragging her petulant children around to go shopping. Compounded with all the other failures of the week, my irritation bubbled over.

We came to the shop that should have been our one and only stop.

It was called Mototech, and all it sold was motorcycles and their accessories. More important, it had tons of machines in stock, parked in neat rows along the sidewalk and deep into the open parking lot beside the store. The owner was an Israeli I found working on a four-wheel motorcycle buggy that sold for US$35,000—more than Enel would likely make in his entire lifetime.

Enel and Roland conferred for a while and picked out a cherry-red Apollo that cost US$960, lock and helmet included. Enel stroked it like a little kid getting his first bicycle. "It's beautiful," he said.

"Why this one?" I asked him.

He giggled and said simply, "The design."

Roland had practical reasons for the choice. It would serve Enel well up in the chewed-up roads of Fermathe, he said. "It's not afraid of mountains; it's not afraid of rocks."

While I stepped inside the office to pay the bill, Roland and Enel remained by the bike, where Roland started chastising Enel, venting all the criticisms that had been brewing inside me. I eavesdropped through the screen door. "How can you lose your ID card and not report it? How could you not read your license and notice they'd put the wrong name down? This is why you are spending all this money," he said. "You don't act like an adult!"

Rather than placating me, hearing the criticisms voiced stoked my growing anger. How many people get an offer to restart their lives? It was like Enel had won the big prize in a game show, and all he had to do now was invest his winnings wisely. If he was smart and cautious, this gift could mean he could feed his children three times a day, every day.

Once I was finished paying, the vendor told Enel to return in two hours so his staff could fine-tune the bike. As we departed, I handed Enel around US$12 for gas to get him home. Then, quietly, he asked me for lunch money for him and his friend.

Lunch money for his friend? Was he kidding? I started ranting in my pidgin Kreyòl but quickly shrugged it off for more comfortable English, spraying out words like bullets—*rat-tat-tat-tat*. Richard began to translate, then stopped. "Don't get angry," he said, raising his eyebrows.

"I *am* angry!" I exploded. "What happened to the US$25 I gave him two days ago? What does he take me for? I'm not made of money."

I walked away to clear my head, and Richard sent Enel off on his own. I hoped he could manage to arrive home without getting in an accident.

Back in Canada, my family's plans cemented. We were moving to Dakar, the capital of Senegal, for a year. I couldn't have placed the country on a map before Graeme texted me to say his business partners would be keen for him to move there, since their company did so much work in West Africa. Once I started researching it, though, I got very excited. Senegal was among the most stable countries in Africa. Since its independence in 1960, it had not suffered a coup d'état or civil war. There was no history of ethnic strife between its many tribes. By big-city standards anywhere, Dakar was considered safe. It was the capital of international business and the aid industry in western Africa, so there were good schools, and it had a thriving cultural scene. And the city was spread across a peninsula, with beaches on three sides, which would entice the kids. They could learn how to surf!

Most exciting for me, however, was how different the country was from Canada. It was hot, Muslim, and French-speaking. I was amazed to read that it had been a major departure point for slave ships in the seventeenth century, loading kidnapped West Africans into their holds and sending them off to what was then known as Saint Domingue: Haiti. Dakar, it seemed, would offer both the adventure I craved and a connection to what had become my second home.

Even the preparations were exciting. The first step was to take the kids back to our travel doctor. Noah was so nervous about the yellow fever shots, we spent a week carefully assembling a plan to calm him: I'd go first, then Lyla, and then, once Noah saw how little pain the needles caused, he would take his turn.

But the doctor clearly wasn't used to kids. He insisted Noah should go first and ordered me to hold him in my arms. Noah instantly transformed into a snotty, squealing, bucking farm animal. The doctor unloaded the first needle and then, without warning, jabbed a second one into his other arm.

Noah went from a pig to a bronco. He burst from my arms and charged out of the examination room. I raced back into the doctor's office to find him ransacking the place: his little arms swept all the papers and pens off the doctor's desk, and he tipped over two chairs. I managed to lasso him in my arms before he got to the computer.

Lyla, in the meantime, had left the doctor's office altogether. I found her in the hall, waiting for the elevator. "I don't want to go to Senegal anymore," she said.

When we were back in our car, on our way home, each of the kids sucking on a huge lollipop consolation prize, Lyla and I laughed about what had happened. It would take Noah weeks to stop brooding about it, though.

"He said he was going to give me just one needle," he said, "but he gave me two." He felt the doctor had pulled a dirty trick on him.

As my excitement mounted about the year of adventure ahead, I had one lingering regret: Lovely. I doubted I would get to visit her from Senegal. I checked plane fares from Dakar to Port-au-Prince online and they seemed prohibitive. Not much chance the *Star* would foot the bill, I thought.

So, in June, I went for one last visit before the move. This time I wouldn't be alone. I brought with me one of the regular contributors to the *Star*'s Lovely project, a man named Paul Haslip. Of all the people who had donated to Lovely and her family, Paul had contacted me the most over the years. He was the one who had sent me the surprise C$2,000 Christmas check, and also the one who had proposed funding a new career for Enel. I figured he should come to see where all of his money had gone. He'd be a representative of all the *Star* readers who had donated over the years. For Lovely and her family, they would finally meet one of the strangers from across the world who had been moved to help them.

Paul was a sixty-year-old investment broker from a sleepy French-Canadian village in southwest Ontario. His favorite hobbies were working on his century-old home and cleaning his and his wife's matching Jaguars by hand. He had never been face-to-face with poverty in the developing world before. But he projected a serene calm, dressed in a purple paisley shirt at the airport check-in counter where I met him for the first time. I figured he'd be okay.

When we arrived to Lovely's place, we found out she had moved again. We were climbing out of the car, when we heard Rosemene's voice call out across a small field of towering corn plants, their husks glowing magenta in the afternoon light, "*Misye Richard, nou la*"— "Mr. Richard, we are here."

Lovely appeared along a thin path that skirted the corn, wearing one of Lyla's old dresses and her purple sandals. She took my hand and led me to her new home. Except it wasn't a house; it was a grotto. Like the family's former place, this was just one room, but the floor was rough, unpaved concrete and the ceiling sagged down overhead, rusty rebar poking out here and there like bony ribs. It was a dark death trap.

After greeting Paul and me with kisses on both cheeks, Rosemene handed Paul her bundled baby as if she'd known him for years and took a seat in a plastic chair.

"I don't like this house. It's not finished. It's not pretty. But our landlord raised the rent in the other place," she said. "We couldn't find another place."

The rainy season was well under way and everyone had snotty noses and fevers. The family was struggling. Enel's *mototaksi* business had not taken off. He'd made only two regular clients—*timachanns* who called him to transport their tomatoes and cabbage to and from the market twice a week. That earned him just US$3 a day, once he subtracted gas costs, so he'd found another job working on a construction site.

Paul wasn't disappointed. He was impressed by Enel's doggedness and flexibility. "It's a start," he said, holding the baby bundle on his lap. "It will take time for him to figure it out."

A couple of days later, Paul and I met Nigel for breakfast up at the Montana Hotel, which had been rebuilt to only a fraction of its former self. There were a few rooms, a pool, and a large patio restaurant and bar, which offered a stunning view of the city below. Small birds darted between nearby trees.

Nigel arrived pressed and groomed for another day of high-powered meetings. He wore a blue suit, and when he took off his jacket to hang on the back of his chair, he revealed a pink dress shirt without a single wrinkle. A patch of dry skin had appeared beneath his left eye. He was only ever supposed to be in Haiti for two months, but he'd remained for three and a half years, and the experience had clearly taken a toll on him. He still had his twinkle, but his upbeat, Scout leader enthusiasm had dimmed.

"Yes, there has been progress," he said. "But it could have been much more and the cost has been too much."

He tried to untangle the many reasons for the lack of development. First, he didn't think the government deeply cared about its people, and the public administration was too weak. The country's elites needed to take a course in civics, and there were far too many donors and volunteer groups doing their own projects without coordination.

"Haiti is littered with the carcasses of successful projects," he said. "It has to stop being a charity case."

But the greatest problem, he said, was the pervasive culture of criticism and blame among Haitians themselves. He used the Kreyòl expression "Se pa fòt mwen"—"It's not my fault." It made getting basic things done difficult. Even Afghanistan had been easier to work in, he said.

"Don't tell me it's only the foreigners to blame," he said.

This would be our last meeting, as Nigel's term as the head of the United Nations mission here was ending in two weeks. He was planning to move back home to Canada—at least temporarily, until he got his next offer to move into another disaster zone. He was leaving the country feeling proud of the progress he'd been part of, but sorry, too.

Back in the car, Paul was having none of Nigel's pessimism. Paul didn't see the disorder and filth in the streets; he saw the neat piles of green bananas and mangoes laid out carefully in rows by *timachanns* on their blankets on the road. The mother of all *blokis* that absorbed our car didn't faze him. Instead, he remarked on the patience and courtesy of Haitian drivers, making way for one another.

He reminded me of myself on my second trip to Haiti—full of wonder and goodwill, unendingly optimistic, and buzzing from the adventure of it all. He was far out of his comfort zone, and he was loving it. I realized that I was the fixer in his midlife crisis.

On our last day in Haiti, we rented a minivan from the guest-house and picked up Lovely and her whole family early in the morning at our usual meeting spot in Pétionville. We were going to the same beach we'd been to with Lyla. It was quickly becoming our reunion tradition.

The day was magical in all the same ways it had been the previous fall. The moment we got there, Lovely whipped off her clothes to display one of Lyla's old bathing suits and grabbed my hand, jumping in the water and shouting, "*Wi, wi!*" The other kids raced down after her, swarming me in the warm water, touching my hands, shoulders, arms, legs, demanding that they be next for a turn out in the deep to feel what it's like to swim.

After lunch, I sat between Lovely and Sophonie, with little Jonathan's legs straddling me from behind as if we were heading out for a toboggan ride, and we let the waves wash over us, squealing with delight.

Lovely cooked up her favorite meal of cornmeal porridge, *mayi moulen*, from sand for me.

"I am stirring in tomatoes," she said, adding some pebbles.

"What can I add?" I asked, grabbing my own pile of rocks.

"Potatoes. Carrots. Cabbage and peppers," she said as I dropped each stone into her sand meal.

I felt like I was up at my family cottage with my own kids. None of the pesky questions about identity, my complicated role in the family, how my generosity was becoming a trap for both them and myself—none of that clouded my mind. I was fully, deliciously present.

A few hours later, Rosemene called down from her beach chair under an umbrella that it was time to go. She wanted to beat the afternoon showers that arrived during the rainy season like clockwork.

"Five more minutes," I begged her, just like my kids always did. She nodded her head. Five more minutes.

"Madame Katrin, when will we come back to the beach?" Sophonie asked.

"*M pa konnen*"—"I don't know," I responded. My eyes, hidden behind my sunglasses, filled up with tears.

I was sandbagging the shores of my heart. My own midlife-crisis adventure was looming, and it meant I wouldn't see my second family for at least a year; likely quite a bit longer. It suddenly seemed a terrible tradeoff. I knew I would return to these last lingering moments during the months ahead, so I wanted to stretch them out as long as I could.

We ran into the water one last time, all three of the kids squealing atop me—on my shoulders, my back, my arms. I was their raft as we floated, heads in the water, eyes tight, smiles enormous.

When our five minutes were up, we all reluctantly pulled ourselves up from the water's embrace and trudged up the stone stairs to the outdoor showers. It was only the second time any of them had experienced a shower; Rosemene, in particular, soaked it in. *Imagine what her reaction would be to a hot shower,* I thought. She wore just the bright yellow bathing suit bottoms I had brought with me and began to lather herself with soap.

All right then, I thought. *When in Haiti* . . . I carefully undressed both Lovely and Jonathan, folding their clothing and tucking it up on a ledge, took a breath, and removed my own bikini. Then the three of us stepped under the water spout beside Rosemene.

I felt her hands on my buttocks before I saw them. Rosemene was washing me.

"You need to clean that," she said, rubbing away the sand.

Once we were finished, Lovely stood up on the ledge, my pink wrap draped over her head and around her body, a vision of beauty. As I changed into my underwear and shorts, I felt her little hands on my face. Gently, tenderly, she was rubbing *krèm kawòt*— skin-lightening cream popular with Haitian women—onto my face.

Lovely and her mother were caring for me. They were feeling the same heavy tenderness I was.

By the time we rolled back to my guesthouse, a few blocks from our regular meeting spot, the rain was coming down as if we were driving through a car wash. I couldn't see out the windshield, even with the wipers manically darting back and forth.

"When will we see you again?" Rosemene asked from the middle row of the minivan.

"*M pa konnen,*" I said weakly.

"I will miss you *anpil,*" she responded, kissing my cheeks.

"We'll talk on the phone," I answered. "I will miss you all, too."

I kissed them all, one by one.

With that, I hauled open the minivan door. Paul and I were immediately soaked by the pouring rain. By the time we scooted into the building, my tears were crashing down just as hard. I pressed my eyes, embarrassed to be crying so unabashedly in front of a man I had just met.

Nothing was settled in Haiti, nor would it ever be for me. Over the years, my feelings for Lovely and her family had become complicated and messy and deep. My mental spreadsheet of aid, which had started so simply, was now decorated with curling lines and blackened-out sections and calculus equations that kept changing with each visit. My mind finally understood what my heart had been screaming at me: I loved them. There was no way I could be away from them for a whole year. I would have to figure out a way to visit from Senegal.

Chapter 13

Lave Men, Siye Atè

(Wash Your Hands and Wipe Them in the Dirt)

Dakar was exactly what I'd been hankering for. Every day was an adventure.

Most of the year, the landscape was a parched brown, but because we'd arrived in the middle of the rainy season, the hillsides were a brilliant emerald green. Large brown hawk-like birds of prey called kites circled in clouds overhead, crying and diving and striking each other with their yellow talons. The trees were scrubby except for the giant baobabs, whose thick gray trunks reminded me of elephants' legs.

We moved into an apartment on the city's main promenade, with a long rectangular pool in the back garden. White egrets visited, standing on the fence to watch us swim, and iridescent blue swallows darted into the pool around my children. Each day, by late afternoon, the street transformed into a marathon of runners—in sneakers, soccer cleats, and my favorite, jelly sandals. Most were men, although women walked in bunches and did fitness classes on the sidewalks, too. Exercise was a national pastime. I kept asking fellow runners why they did it, and they invariably responded with a perplexed look and a variation on the answer "It makes me feel good." Of course it did. Everyone in North American knew that. It's just that very few people acted on it. Again my cultural windshield became more evident.

I delighted in all the differences. Our first morning in the city, we headed off to the grocery store for supplies and had to pull over onto the side of the road to allow a herd of longhorn cattle to pass. Walking to school each morning, the kids and I skirted goats along the sidewalk. But some things felt eerily familiar. I could see Haiti everywhere. The local buses, called *supers*, resembled *tap-taps*; they were painted colorfully and so densely packed with people that many hung off the back doors and stood on the bumpers. The high walls barricading private property and the little boys darting between cars with bare feet and begging for money wouldn't have been out of place on the streets of Port-au-Prince.

The streets felt alive in the same way as Haiti, a carnival of commerce and traffic, including horses pulling loaded wooden wagons. Few roads had street signs, which I came to view less as a symptom of disorganization and more as a brilliant design intended to foster healthy human communication and interdependence. Even the local translators I hired had to stop strangers regularly to ask for directions. It reminded me of what Dimitri had once said: "In Haiti, you have to know, to know."

Our first weekend excursion was to Île de Gorée, a small island three kilometers from downtown Dakar. From the ferry window, the island seemed like a village plucked out of Tuscany and plopped down into the Atlantic Ocean. Old ocher-colored buildings with wooden balconies and terra-cotta tile roofs crowded its cobblestone laneways. But the beauty masked a sinister reality: each of the Renaissance-style houses had served as a slave prison for more than four centuries.

One home had been turned into a museum called the Maison des

Esclaves. We hired a guide who led us around the small stone rooms on the ground floor, describing how the kidnapped children had been separated from their mothers and the women from their husbands. After months of fattening, they were shuttled through the "door of no return" and onto boats, where they were chained head to foot to the floors of the galleys, for the three-month voyage to the colonies. Display maps showed where most of the kidnapped people were sent. One giant arrow swept across the Atlantic Ocean and pointed to Brazil. Another led to Haiti.

One morning in early October, I woke up with red, swollen eyes. The next morning Lyla's and Noah's eyes looked the same. We'd gotten the Apollo virus, the street name for acute hemorrhagic conjunctivitis—pink eye on steroids. Our eyes were itchy and pus-filled and heavy. Sunlight made them sting. We stayed indoors and took turns lying on the bathroom floor to administer the red antibacterial drops that transformed us into vampires, crying blood.

The kids' eyes cleared up before mine, and they returned to school. I stayed inside, miserable. Eduardo, a short, happy man who arrived on his Vespa each morning to clean the pool while singing songs from his native Benin, knocked at our door to ask why I wasn't on the patio, typing on my laptop. I peered at him with my bloody eyes.

He told me not to worry. It would pass. "This is scary for you because you've never had it before," he said. For locals, it was like the flu. I thanked him for his wisdom and he repeated a refrain that was so common, it seemed the national saying.

"*Nous sommes ensemble*. We are together."

Over the next few months Eduardo would teach me a lot about how Senegal worked, both directly and inadvertently. He taught me how to bargain and offered advice on how to bribe police officers, which I could never bring myself to do. But his biggest lesson came after the morning he knocked on my door and asked if he could borrow money.

He had a cousin who had been rushed to the hospital for an acute illness, and he needed to pay for his treatment. Eduardo's request triggered a familiar reaction in me. This was why he had started to knock on my door, I thought. All those conversations were a means to an end. I wasn't his friend; I was his big white ATM. This would be the first of many requests, I feared.

I retreated to the war bunker in my brain and found my trusty, well-worn shield. Despite appearances, I told him, I didn't have an endless supply of money. I couldn't pay for his cousin's operation.

He looked surprised, but not for the reason I expected. He wasn't asking me to pay for all of it, he said. He was calling all his friends and asking for contributions that, together, would cover the medical bills. Twenty dollars would be great. That's how it worked in Senegal, where there was little state-sponsored safety net. Instead, families and friends worked together always to stitch it.

A light switched on in my head. In Canada, I had grown up with the unspoken cultural rule of thumb that friendship should never be polluted by money. Sure, I might pay for a friend's lunch, but never had anyone asked me for money to go to university or cover the mortgage. That's what bank loans were for. Our system was built on the idea of independence.

As North Americans, we don't send remittances overseas to people. Instead, we remain removed by donating to NGOs. Introducing money into a relationship, to us, makes it feel impure and unequal. But in countries where the social safety net was thin, like Senegal or Haiti, people depended on one another more frequently, which meant money and friendship often went hand in hand.

I had been thinking about my relationship with money and Lovely's family—a book I'd bought about Senegalese culture called *African Friends and Money Matters* by David E. Maranz was illuminating— but it wasn't until my conversation with Eduardo that I truly recognized how culturally based my understanding of the rules governing friendship and finances was. I'd been wrong to carry bitterness about the repeated requests for help from Lovely's family. "*Nous sommes ensemble*" was a variation of how it worked in Haiti, too.

I invited Eduardo and his cousin to Christmas dinner in our apartment, along with a mélange of friends who we'd met over the

past few months. A few days later my family headed north to Mo-
rocco to meet Graeme's parents for a vacation. I had a different destination, though. I had pulled together a number of story ideas and sent
them to my editors, along with a budget. Despite the hefty airfare,
they had consented. I was following the fat arrow on the map at the
Maison des Esclaves and heading back to Haiti.

My first night back in Port-au-Prince, I phoned Elistin. He was the
one I could best understand on the phone: he spoke slowly, unlike
Rosemene, who chirped away like a morning lark no matter how
many times I asked her to slow down.

"Madame Katrin!" he shouted gleefully into the phone. "I didn't
know you were coming."

We traded updates about our families.

"I am a new father," he said. "Rosita had the baby last week. A
little girl."

"What is her name?" I asked.

"Lala," he said.

I paused. Was I hearing right? What was her name?

"Lala," he repeated.

"Like my daughter, Lyla?" I asked.

"Yes," he said.

The next morning, on the drive up to Elistin's place, I wondered
if I had misunderstood something. My Kreyòl had come along over
the years, but it was still pretty basic. Would they really have named
their daughter after Lyla?

I arrived at Elistin and Rosita's little house with the tin shed and
rabbit cage, only to find that they no longer lived there. Three months
earlier they had moved down the hill into their new home, which, I
was amazed to find, was almost finished.

It turned out that Paul Haslip had sent Elistin about US$900 after
he got back home. I wasn't surprised. Even before his visit, Paul had
sent a lot of money to help Lovely's family. Now, he had a personal
relationship with them. I had asked, at the beginning of our trip

together, that Paul not give tips or handouts to anyone I was interviewing, particularly Lovely's family. So he had simply waited and sent the money down later through Western Union.

Together with Elistin's savings, Paul's donation was enough to buy the necessary supplies and hire a three-person crew. The house now had stone walls, a metal roof, and two rooms. Elistin had even hired someone to string up a live wire and tap it covertly into the electrical network, so he had intermittent stolen electricity, which powered a single overhead lightbulb. Elistin's dream had finally come true.

So had Rosita's. For years she'd told me she'd longed for another baby, but pregnancy had eluded her. Now she'd given birth to a healthy little girl in their new house.

I expected a joyful air, but the mood in their new house was funereal. I arrived in the late afternoon, when the sun was hanging over the far horizon, offering little light. The hanging bulb was dead. I sat with them on wooden chairs in their dim salon, trying to get to the bottom of the baby's name.

Rosita was dressed to go to the gym in an oversized gray sweatshirt and sweatpants, with a white shawl wrapped around her head. Her daughter lay on her lap, similarly bundled. Lala had fat cheeks and thick patches of black hair that stuck out from under her knit cap.

Elistin was listless. He was drained of energy. He rummaged through a wooden drawer in search of the baby's birth certificate, since he couldn't remember her official name.

"We call her Lala," he said. Lypse had been the one to propose it: he'd so loved his time with my daughter, he wanted to name his sister after her. I was moved almost to tears. But why weren't they rejoicing?

And then the story of what they called the *Zafè Ti Bòs*—the Little Boss Episode—began to emerge. A few weeks before they finished the new house, the property owner had called Elistin. She was angry. "Who authorized this house construction?" she had bellowed over the phone. She gave him a month to get out.

"I thought she'd respect her word," he said forlornly.

Rosita hadn't slept or eaten since last week, when the owner had called again threatening to use force if they didn't leave this month. She would arrive with a justice of the peace, the police, and likely a gang of thugs to attack him and destroy the place.

"I'm scared Elistin will be shot. People here kill each other for land all the time," she said. "If he gets killed, I'll be dropped in hot water."

They were resigned to moving, but how and where?

They had poured all their savings into building this house; they had no money left to pay a year's rent, which had to be paid in full in advance. Plus, they were losing Elistin's three farm fields, which provided part of his income.

They'd been trying to get ahead, but the *Zafè Ti Bòs* would leave them worse off than they'd been before.

Elistin tried to be philosophical about it. "It's part of life," he said wearily. He cited a Kreyòl expression: "You think you are going to sleep well, but the house is hot."

But I thought another was more suiting: "*Lave men, siye atè*"— "Wash your hands and wipe them in the dirt."

I had been mulling over the idea of buying land for Lovely's family. But land ownership was a controversial issue in Haiti. Corruption and shoddy records meant that most pieces of land had more than one owner with legal papers. It was one of the reasons international development workers with organizations like Oxfam and Habitat for Humanity had been unable to build much new housing for earth-quake victims: no one was sure who owned the land. There was a joke among locals that if you put all the legally owned land on paper, Haiti would be the size of Canada.

I had heard that a columnist from Montreal named Agnès Gruda had managed to buy some land for a Haitian family, and I phoned her for some advice.

Her story proved a cautionary tale. Leading up to the earthquake's first anniversary, Agnès had been assigned to find a young boy who had been pictured on the front page of her newspaper the year before. She'd had nothing to go on but the photo, showing the boy's dusty head and shirt, red with blood. No name, no address, no number.

Agnès had phoned a Haitian-Canadian documentary filmmaker in Port-au-Prince and asked her if she could find a fixer to track down the boy. The filmmaker had delivered a counterproposal: she would find a fixer, but if he found the child, the newspaper had to do more than just write a story. They had to help the boy and his family.

The filmmaker called my fixer Richard, who managed to find the boy. Agnès was determined to live up to her end of the bargain, and she raised money to buy the boy's family a small piece of land. She hired Richard to help the family set up a bank account, only to later discover that he had taken a cut of the money she'd sent to the family.

"Richard screwed me," she said. She didn't feel comfortable asking readers to fund corruption costs, so she replaced the lost funds with her own money and fired Richard.

The whole process took more than a year, and she still didn't think the family's ownership papers were legitimate.

"I gave up," she said. "It was mission impossible. You have to be modest. You do what you can."

In the car, Richard and I fought like siblings about what he'd done. According to him, everyone in Haiti got a cut and there was nothing wrong with that. He gave me an example. Once, when working logistics for a North American company, Richard got three bids for their rental cars. A year after he lost his logistics job, he continued to receive a check every month from the winning rental company with his commission, and he wasn't about to correct them.

The way Richard saw it, he hadn't forced the family to give him the money. He hadn't held a gun to their head or threatened them. He had just made it clear he expected *pa m*—"mine."

"Without me, there would be no house, no land, nothing," he said, his voice rising. He was getting passionate now. "Without me finding the boy, they would not have attained all these funds."

I shook my head. "But, Richard," I said, "you grew up in North America. You know people there will see this as corruption. You were paid for your work, and then you took more."

"I'm living here," he replied. "I have to survive things happening here. This is Haiti. This is how it works here."

His reasoning was clear: if everyone took a cut, then it couldn't be corruption because it was a built-in part of the system. I might have been more indignant had I not discovered that petty corruption was similarly endemic in Senegal. When we first moved to Dakar, I traveled back and forth to the Affaires Étrangères police station for my permanent residency permit no fewer than seven times. Each time an officer told me that I hadn't "*bien compris*" and that, yet again, there was something missing from my fattening file. When I vented my frustrations to taxi drivers, they repeatedly smacked their heads and asked how could I not see: the officers were expecting a "sacred handshake." One went so far as to demonstrate how I should fold a bill in my right hand and then slap it into the officer's palm upon greeting him. I wasn't sure what was worse: bribing a police officer or returning again to sit among the dusty plants outside the permit office. I decided to hire someone to get it done for me and eventually received my bloody card. Corruption wasn't a moral failing; it was simply how you played the game.

The thing was, I could afford to bribe. Elistin's family couldn't. And neither could Lovely's. I wondered if Richard had taken *pa m* from every transfer I had sent for Enel's preparations to become a *mototaksi* driver. He promised me he hadn't. But he also said the family insisted on giving him phone cards as acknowledgment of his work.

Even before Elistin's *Zafè Ti Bòs*, the prospect of buying land for Lovely's family had become less and less appealing. Now it seemed an impossibility.

Enel held Baby Ananstania on his lap, sitting in the family's rough, dark cell of a home. He spoke so softly that I had to lean toward him to hear his explanations for the two motorcycle accidents he'd had since I'd last seen him. The first one occurred when he'd dodged out of the way of a police car that had been hurtling at top speed down a country road. Enel had lost his balance and fallen into a ditch, banging up his hand, knee, and head. Another motorcycle driver rushed him to the Baptist mission hospital, where he was stitched up.

Thank God I had set up an account there, I thought.

Then, in November, another motorcycle driver slipped across the center of the road and crashed into Enel head-on. Enel got off lucky that time—he hurt only his ankle—but the bike console was smashed.

Paul had sent Enel money for repairs, but the word on the street had been punishing. Enel got even fewer customers than before. Some days he returned home with less than a Canadian dollar after many hours of waiting in one of the local *mototaksi* stations.

By December, things had gotten so desperate that Rosemene left baby Ananstania with Enel and descended all the way down into the city center to buy curtains. She spent the night down there with her brother and the next morning had taken two more *tap-taps* back up into the mountains to sell them in the Fermathe market. Her profit from those two long days of hustling was less than US$4.

"I'm so ashamed," she said. "We haven't put money in the bank."

Just when the family should have been more comfortable, they were poorer than before. It might have just been bad luck. But they had a grander explanation: *maji*. Sorcery.

After the second crash, Enel had discovered a plastic bag stuffed in the compartment behind the bike's pedals. In it were two matches, some corn kernels, and a handful of dirt they thought had come from the cemetery.

"Someone had him *mare*—tied—to stop him from making money," Rosemene explained. "They poisoned the bike. It was a *malfektè*—an evildoer—to stop him from succeeding."

Enel and Rosemene believed someone had gone to an *oungan*, or Vodou priest, to buy the spell. They had no theories as to whom; it could have been any of their neighbors, who were jealous that Enel had a new motorcycle.

"Haitians are like that," Rosemene said. "They hate each other for any little thing."

Enel and Rosemene were strict Pentacostalists. They didn't practice the Vodou religion, but their belief in evil eyes and evil tongues wasn't about the religion. It was cultural. Before I moved to Senegal, this contradiction confused me. Now it seemed less strange. In Dakar, the population was devoutly Muslim, unfurling large carpets throughout the downtown streets on Friday afternoons to pray together. But my friends there also believed in the evil eye, the evil tongue, and evil spirits, called *djinn*. They hung *gris gris*—leather amulets fashioned by spiritual leaders—around their children's necks to protect them against unseeable evil.

On one of our first trips, to Dakar's miserable zoo, I was offered a bottle of lion urine, which, the zookeeper assured me, would cure asthma if poured in a bath and ward off robbers if kept on a bedroom dresser.

I now understood how syncretic religion could be, braiding together ancient African beliefs with Western or Middle Eastern ones.

"Have you gone to get a counterspell?" I asked.

Rosemene shook her head adamantly. "Real Christians don't go to *oungans*," she said. "Evil cannot cure evil."

Instead, Rosemene had bathed the motorcycle in a homemade cure for the magic poison, made with lemon, some local leaves, and oil blessed by a priest. But she wasn't sure it would be effective. She thought the *maji* might be too powerful. She wanted Enel to rent out the bike or sell it and go back to working construction sites. The jobs there were irregular and held no chance of career advancement or raises, but they were safe. Enel was reluctant. Even though he was making no money, he liked the status the bike gave him and how passersby would say hello.

"Why don't we get you some more lessons?" I suggested. It seemed to me that he just needed more practice. My friends who rode motorcycles told me it was difficult to learn—and they had ridden bikes from childhood and driven cars. Enel had done neither. But he dug his heels in stubbornly.

"I don't need more lessons," he said. "It's the *maji*."

We were at an impasse. I couldn't make them disbelieve in *maji*. And I worried again about the jealousy my mere presence in their neighborhood had clearly caused. But mostly I wondered about the larger cultural trap I had inadvertently stepped into. How could a country develop if every small individual advancement was cause for jealousy? It was the inverse of the development theory that a rising tide would raise all boats. Instead, it seemed, any boat that rose up would be dragged back down to the bottom of the ocean.

It took all my energy and determination to visit Muspan. I had stopped funding the school the summer before, as had been the plan all along. I had always meant for my help to be temporary, the intention being to get the school back up on its feet, not to hold it up forever. Gilberte needed to do that on her own.

But I also knew she hoped I'd change my mind.

After all our emails back and forth last spring, I knew I would never get to the bottom of what had happened to the missing US$2,000. Anyone could have taken it—the groundsman, the driver who had picked it up, a secretary at the school. I had dropped the issue and continued the payments until August 2013, the last month of the school year. Given what I'd learned about *pa m* and corruption, one month of missing funds seemed like a small loss compared to the larger gain: the school was up and running, and the kids were in class for free.

Gilberte had sent me an email in the fall, asking whether I could help her find other donors. The government's money had not come through, and she didn't know how she would continue. I had been polite but firm: No. I didn't think I could find the right people from Senegal, and I was tired.

My donations to Muspan might have ended, but I still felt attached to the school. I phoned Gilberte a number of times, trying to schedule a visit, but she never responded, so I just dropped in one morning. A surprise visit would produce more honest results anyway, I figured.

I braced myself to be confronted by a brochure for aid failure: dirty, half-empty, teachers missing. Instead, what greeted me was full classes, teachers instructing, the floors more or less clean.

The building sounded the same, too. The singing voices of the grade-three class rang through the halls. They weren't performing for me, though; it was part of their lesson.

On the door of the administration office was a list of twenty-two students who had written the national grade-six exam; only one had failed. Clearly the new teachers were working out.

Gilberte wasn't there, so I headed downtown to Institut Louis Pasteur in search of her. Where there was once a large pile of rubble, I now sized up a three-story building made of concrete and turquoise metal siding. Students in beige nursing uniforms lined the thin halls, waiting for their next class. Gilberte had done it: she'd rebuilt her college.

I found her in a small office made entirely of wood, working at a desk cluttered with papers, a computer, and a television. Photos of her grandkids were tacked to the wall behind her, along with the school's certificates. She was wearing a long white dress, and a big red cross hung from a cord around her neck.

She saw me in the doorway and gasped. "You're here! It is great to see you," she said.

She gave no sign of resentment from our argument the previous year, nor a guilt trip about money, as I had feared. Instead, Gilberte directed one of her staff to go out and buy me lunch, and as we ate, she laid down one piece of good news after another, like a blackjack dealer. The gap between her front two teeth beamed from her smiling lips.

She had rebuilt both schools using her old system: her profits from the nursing college were funding most of Muspan. She was still hoping the government would fund all six classes at Muspan, and if that happened, she'd use her money to build another school for poor children.

"We have a Haitian proverb," she said. "'*De lajan pa goumen*. Two monies don't fight.'"

She had recently turned seventy but wasn't slowing down.

It had all worked out. My instincts four years before had proven right. I'd found a committed local activist and my money and efforts had greased her wheels long enough to get her cart moving again. Instead of being crestfallen, as I had expected, I felt like I could fly.

When I asked Gilberte how she had done it, she said she would be happy to go through the accounting books with me—but only if I committed to be her partner again. I shook my head and she laughed.

"I know, Catreen," she said as we hugged good-bye. "We will never forget what you've done."

So the project I thought had crashed and burned—Gilberte's school— was a full-on success, and the project I'd thought was proceeding well—Enel's business—had crashed and burned. The more I learned about Haiti, the less I knew.

I decided to spend the earthquake's fourth anniversary with Lovely and her family. They were going to church, so Richard and I met them there, dressed in appropriate church-going attire at 7:00 in the morning. We were an hour late.

The family's church was so simple that it felt only half-built. Wide-brim straw hats and leis made from plastic flowers nailed to the rough concrete pillars were the only adornments. Two clocks at the front were broken, stopped at different times.

Women sat on the simple wooden pews, listening to a Bible lesson about moneylenders. The men and children were downstairs, in the school—the same one where Elistin had once considered enrolling Lypse.

I sat halfway back with Rosemene and her family. Partway through the talk, Lovely climbed onto my lap. If the locals wondered about me, no one showed it. But soon after the pastor began to deliver his sermon, he asked about Richard's and my presence.

Rosemene stood up and announced: "These people helped save my daughter on January 12."

Sitting on that hard bench, in the middle of a church that would surely fall if there was another earthquake, I wondered: *Did I really help? What are the fruits of all my love and concern and efforts? Are Lovely and her extended family any better off than they were four years ago, when I met her for the second time and first offered to pay for her schooling?*

The group around me prayed loudly, waving their arms in the air, shouting their thanks to God and shaking their bodies. I stayed seated and bowed my head in my own humble way. Haiti's earthquake had sent me to church, and four years later I was still going. I still wasn't sure what kind of a God I believed in, but I did believe in a connected universe. Inside my head, I asked whoever had set me on this path to show me how to proceed.

Chances were good that Lovely's life would never be easy. She might step out of misery, but she'd likely remain poor. So what were my reasons for giving more? And when would I stop being a benefactor and return to being a pure journalist again? What would I lose if I did that?

I'd been wandering around the forest of development for the past four years, with only my guts and heart to guide me. I had broken the journalistic rules of detachment and objectivity. Now it was time to set some new ones—for my own benefit.

In my head, I decided I would form a small security net for the family by continuing to send their children to school and maintaining the hospital account indefinitely. But that was it. I could not fix all their problems or buy their way out of poverty. That trap was too great for one person to overcome.

After church, we returned to Lovely's house, where I sat alone with Rosemene in the shade of two banana trees, just the two of us. The kids were playing, and Rosemene washed their white uniform T-shirts in a big plastic tub.

In my rudimentary Kreyòl, I told her how sad I was that my help had not changed things for them. I wondered, in fact, if the jealousy my presence had created had done them more harm than good.

Rosemene dropped the wet shirt in her hand, shook off the soap, and reached over to touch my shoulder.

"Oh, Katrin. We love you," she said. "You've done so much for us. Our life is so much easier than it would have been."

Sure there was *maji* and jealousy. But the good was more powerful. Every time she made food, Rosemene sent a plate to her neighbors, and they did the same.

"God is greater," she said.

Rosemene was right: she would always remain poor, but perhaps Lovely would not. Success stories did happen. I had to pace myself and take a longer view.

I asked Rosemene an echo of the question I'd asked four years before, the one that got me into this mess: If she had the money, how would she celebrate today? Her answer was much simpler than enrolling her daughter in school.

"I'd buy some pop and lettuce and tomatoes and black mushroom rice and French peas and chicken, and we'd have a big feast," she said.

That seemed like a pretty easy thing to do. I gave Richard some money and asked him if he could go buy us lunch at the Fermathe market. He returned carrying Styrofoam containers heavy with all the things we'd asked for.

Just as we were about to dig in, Elistin arrived.

"My head is so full, I forgot it was January 12," he said. He poured a glass of pop and raised it to the table. "Here's to Lovely's party."

After we'd finished eating, I grabbed my phone and played a moody song by Adele. Then I grabbed Lovely's small hands and we danced.

She flashed a wide smile at me, revealing three new adult teeth—each one white and huge.

Chapter 14

Coming Home

No one was expecting me back in Haiti other than Richard. It was January 2015, and I had returned for the fifth anniversary of the earthquake. I had phoned both Rosemene and Elistin repeatedly since Christmas, when my plans had crystallized, but I hadn't gotten through to either of them. It seemed they had lost their phones or their batteries had died, because they never even rang.

So, my first morning back, Richard and I drove up to Fermathe to drop in on Lovely unannounced. We were barreling down the gloriously paved main road from the Fermathe market, when I spotted Jenanine, Lovely's neighbor, walking with a jug of water balanced on her head. We slowed down to say hello and an adult-sized frown spread across her face until she recognized who we were. Then she smiled like a kid again. She told us Lovely had moved, then climbed into the back seat to direct us.

It had been a year since my last visit. A lot had happened in my life. Graeme, the kids, and I had moved home from Senegal, and I'd returned to the newsroom. I'd called Rosemene every month or so—until her phone was disconnected—and she had never mentioned the move. Mind you, the family seemed to move every year, so maybe she didn't think it was news worth mentioning. Her stock response to almost every question I asked was "It's good, thanks to God."

Jenanine directed us up the dirt road that led to Elistin's old home. We continued past the place where the mysterious white man had rescued the car between sips of red wine, and she told us to park at a fence made entirely of corrugated metal. This was it.

I pushed through the fence to find a large freshly swept dirt yard bordered on two sides by banana trees whose heavy seeds hung around their necks like pendants. The house was modest, but grace-ful: a sturdy brown box adorned simply by some finished concrete stairs leading up to a black metal door.

Standing there and taking it all in, I sensed some movement from the corner of the yard. Lovely was crouching on the ground beside Venessaint, staring at us. Her eyes were dark and hard, taking me in suspiciously as an intruder. But when she recognized us, her mouth untwisted and stretched into a grin, and she rushed into my embrace.

We laughed and spun around. I was amazed at how much her body had grown and her face had lengthened. Her hair was carefully braided into little cornrows and she was wearing one of Lyla's cast-off pink dresses that finally fit, a year after I had given it to her. She smiled widely, revealing even more new teeth.

What had she and Venessaint been doing?

"We were pretending to make a big lunch," she said.

What were they cooking?

"Rice and beans," she responded.

Suddenly, Jonathan was there, smiling shyly and revealing two empty spaces where his front teeth had been. He took my hand. He had been in a nearby yard playing soccer and heard the commotion.

"Where are your mom and dad?" I asked them.

"Dad is at work. And Mom is at the hospital," Lovely said.

"Why is she at the hospital? Is she sick?" I asked.

"No. It's for the *bebe*," she responded.

By "baby," I assumed she meant Ananstania, who was now near-ing two.

Lovely and Jonathan took both of my hands and gave me a tour of their new place. Inside the door was a small parlor, its walls painted a cheerful pink and its floor smoothly polished. There was a kitchen table and the four chairs I had bought, and their kitchenware was neatly laid out across a shelf. A door led into the bedroom, with their single bed pushed to one side.

On it lay Ananstania, sprawled facedown and fast asleep.

So, the *bebe* at the hospital with Rosemene clearly wasn't her. Richard hauled my duffel bag containing *rad kenedi* from the car, and I pulled out a soccer ball I had brought for Jonathan and a puzzle for Lovely. It was quickly apparent that Lovely had never seen a puzzle before, so I spread out all the pieces on the kitchen table and showed her how to look for ones that fit together. She was pounding at mis-matching pieces when Rosemene arrived.

One look at her, and I understood what Lovely had meant by "the *bebe*." Rosemene was pregnant. She was wearing a dark dress, which clung to her swelling belly.

I felt deflated. How was Rosemene going to care for another child? My dread quickly morphed to anger. How could she let this happen again? She had promised that Ananstania would be her last child! She knew she couldn't afford another baby. How foolish of her!

I tried to swallow my emotions and greet her warmly with kisses on each cheek. She smiled weakly and sank her cheek into her hand.

She was seven months pregnant. Seven months! Why hadn't she told me?

"I was embarrassed," she responded. She knew I would be disap-pointed, and, in truth, so was she.

"Enel cried when he found out I was pregnant," she said. "So did I. I didn't want any more kids. We don't have the means to take care of them."

Her wrists looked swollen to me. And now that I took a closer look, so did her ankles and feet. Was she feeling okay?

"My head hurts," she said. "And my neck."

My anger turned to concern. What had the doctor told her at her checkup?

"They said I had preeclampsia," she said.

No one I knew in Canada had suffered from preeclampsia during their pregnancy. But it was common in Haiti and extremely danger-ous. The high blood pressure could cut off circulation to the growing baby, causing developmental delays or brain damage. That was if the mother didn't have a stroke, killing both of them.

Doctors weren't sure why the rates in Haiti were so high, but they guessed it was genetic, and the Haitian diet of salt and grease didn't help. While poverty wasn't the cause, it did mean the disease often went untreated, as women couldn't afford the prenatal checkup fees. It was the main culprit for the country's devastating maternal mortality rates.

The only cure was delivering the baby. Usually, doctors tried to reduce the pregnant woman's hypertension until her fetus was de-veloped enough to be delivered by C-section. Sure enough, the nurse had told Rosemene she needed an operation. What concerned me, though, was that the local hospital couldn't treat her.

"Did they refer you somewhere?" I asked.

"*Non.*"

This made absolutely no sense to me. I knew the hospital had planned surgeries; I had seen the operating rooms. And the account I had set up there would cover the cost. So why wouldn't they admit her?

I grabbed my cell phone and emailed the hospital administration for an explanation. Then I sent Rosemene to bed and told her I would look after the kids until Enel got home from work. She needed to rest and keep her blood pressure down until we could figure out which hospital to admit her to.

The kids and I dug through my bag of treats and clothing, pull-ing out clothes and books and pens. Lovely put on a fashion show for me, trying on each new dress and sashaying back and forth across the floor. We chewed through my supply of granola bars.

Enel returned dusty and tired from a construction site. He'd had another motorcycle accident last summer and decided to park the bike indefinitely. He wanted to sell it and buy another one that had no curse on it. Rosemene chirped from the bedroom that she wanted him to sell it and buy a cow.

"You can do what you like with it, Enel," I said. I wasn't happy it hadn't worked out, but I accepted that I wasn't in control. "It's your motorcycle, your business, and your responsibility."

When I crept into the dark bedroom to say good-bye to Rosemene, she was lying on her side on the room's single bed, a scarf wrapped tightly around her head. The hospital hadn't even given her Tylenol for her headaches. What use was an account at a hospital if they didn't treat you? I was going to get to the bottom of this.

The next morning the hospital administrator called. There had been a mistake, he said. Rosemene should come back to the hospital immediately. I couldn't uncover why she'd been turned away initially, but at least I could rest easy knowing she would now be safe.

The same couldn't be said of the reconstruction of Haiti in general. The center of Port-au-Prince was dotted with fences like the one penning in Lovely's yard, each of them painted red and stamped with the government's slogan: *"Haiti Ap Vanse"*—"Haiti is advancing." But only a couple had any signs of construction on the other side. *Tòl wouj*—red barricade—had become a Kreyòl saying for a bluff.

Richard and I drove north through Cité Soleil's shacks to visit Haiti's housing dreams: a 2-hectare (4.9-acre) housing expo that had opened in the summer of 2011 with the name "Building Back Better Communities."

That year some sixty-five international and national firms had been selected to erect their model homes, each of which would be given to a carefully selected family of earthquake victims. I wanted to check if that had happened. It didn't take long to discover it hadn't. The site seemed like an abandoned theme park, with each house more bizarre than the last. There was a wooden log cottage that seemed straight out of the Swiss Alps; a Florida-style beach cabin up on stilts so the tides presumably could pass underneath; a house with two concrete roofs that stuck up in the air like upside-down ice cream cones. Each one had a family living in it, but none of the ones I interviewed were earthquake victims. They had simply come and taken the house, and no one had stopped them.

It made no sense. Of the 160,000 new homes the government had hoped to build after the earthquake, fewer than 10,000 had gone up around the country, and those precious commodities had not been safeguarded. And it wasn't just housing that had been a complete bust. I asked Richard to drive to a sewage treatment plant I had toured a couple of years before. Sewage plants were not the kind of thing that excited me, but cholera had shown me how crucial they were for human health.

The plant consisted of six vinyl-lined pits that used nothing but sunlight, wind, and natural bacteria to transform human waste into compost and clean water. It had seemed the perfect design for a poor country: low-tech, eco-friendly, relatively cheap to operate.

But the plant was clearly no longer operating. Peering through its brown metal fence, I saw no sewage trucks, no de-sludging workers in rubber boots, nothing but a couple of parked tractors and brittle, knee-high weeds. A custodian stepped out of the glass office by the entrance to talk to me, along with a thin security guard toting a shotgun. "The plant has been closed for over a year," the custodian said. It had operated for only six months before the vinyl liners had ruptured, and they had not been repaired.

People were back to dumping their excrement into canals and streams or waiting until the rains washed out their simple latrines for them. During the torrential rains the previous fall, cholera cases had spiked, and once again the government hadn't been able to respond. If Médecins Sans Frontières had not been in Port-au-Prince and swiftly opened 180 cholera-treatment beds, the country's death count would have shot up again.

All the setbacks would have been enough to irritate the journalist in me before. But development in Haiti was long past being just a professional interest for me. It was personal.

I drove up to Fermathe the next afternoon to check on Rosemene and meet with the hospital's lead doctor. I found him in his office at the end of one hospital wing, surrounded by medical students in their white jackets, stethoscopes hanging around their necks. He was holding court.

There was hardly room for another body to squeeze into his room, but he waved me in and paused in his lecture to brief me about Rosemene's case in front of them all.

Her hypertension was extremely high. He'd admitted her for bed rest and prescribed some medication in an attempt to bring down her blood pressure. The hope was that she could stay in the hospital for another month, until the baby was considered full-term, and then he would schedule a C-section with an obstetrician.

"It depends on how she responds to the medicine," he said. "What worries me a bit is the baby. If there is too much pressure on the cord, it will die."

Rosemene's blood pressure was 220 over 130. Hearing this, the students in the room shifted and widened their eyes like spooked horses. Normal was 120 over 70, one whispered to me. Her blood pressure was deep into stroke territory.

"Wouldn't it be best, then, to take Rosemene to the Médecins Sans Frontières obstetrics hospital?" I asked. I'd visited the hospital a couple of years earlier for a story and knew it specialized in high-risk pregnancies just like this.

"There's no reason to take her to a specialist hospital," the doctor said. "I will continue to follow her. If her case becomes *urgent* urgent, we can take her there by car."

I found Rosemene in a private room just down the hall. Enel was in the chair beside her, and her brother Arnold was nearby. Rosita sat at her feet, with her head in her hands.

"She's worried if I have a cesarean, I'll die," Rosemene said. "I'm not scared. I'm with Jesus."

She'd just moved out of the general ward, she explained sheepishly, because last night two women in beds near her had died.

"My stress went up," she said. She was also worried about drawing on the family's account at the hospital. A private room was much more expensive than a bed in the general ward, which looked like a scene from *Annie*—the beds stretching down each side of the room in two long rows.

"Don't worry about money," I responded. "There is enough in the account to cover this."

After a while, the room emptied and I sat in Rosita's spot, stroking Rosemene's calves and swollen feet.

"I thought they were so swollen because I walk so much," she said wanly.

A half dozen people arrived from Rosemene's church. They crowded around her bed, held their hands up to their shoulders, and began to sing hymns. They were praying for her. I slipped out of the way and stood just outside the door so I could watch.

"*Every day, every hour, we need you, Jesus,*" their voices rang out.

Rosemene half sat up, resting her shoulders and head against the wall. She held her hands up as if she were cupping a basketball, closed her eyes, and accepted their prayers. Both of her legs trembled noticeably beneath her floral skirt.

Protests had become a weekly occurrence in the city. I watched one that surged through the slums—mostly men running and shouting slogans and dancing to the music played by *rara* bands that peppered the crowd. "Martelly has stolen the country," one man behind me yelled. "We are hungry."

President Martelly was now ruling by decree. He was on his third prime minister, who'd been appointed without parliamentary approval because there was no parliament to approve him. Martelly blamed the opposition for blocking his most recent electoral plan; the opposition claimed that it had been Martelly's plan all along to claim absolute rule.

I was at a press conference downtown, listening to two prominent Haitian lawyers talk passionately about what they saw as corruption by Martelly, his family, and his government, when Richard showed me his phone. It was a text message from Rosemene asking if we could bring some blood pressure medication to her, since the hospital's pharmacy was out. Clearly it wasn't stocked with medication for preeclampsia.

We got into the car and made our way up to Pétionville. We couldn't find the medicine at the first couple of pharmacies, but we finally found it at Giant, the upscale supermarket. I picked up some groceries—pita bread and cheese and pear juice and Lovely's favorite salami—along with the medication. I figured we'd quickly drop off the meds at the hospital and then have lunch with Lovely and her siblings. We weren't in a rush. Rosemene hadn't indicated this was "*urgent* urgent."

When we were back in the car, on the winding road up the mountain, my phone rang. It was Rosemene, wondering if we were bringing the medication.

"The doctor is asking," she said.

"We're almost there," I said.

Her room was dark when we arrived. Enel was standing by the door. He grabbed the medication bag I was carrying and ran down the hall, looking for the doctor.

Rosemene lay in a nest of duvets and pillows. She had the white scarf wrapped tightly around her head. She was feeling awful. The swelling in her feet and hands had gone down, but her head throbbed and now her chest hurt. Her brother had descended into the city to get the medication himself, but he had purchased the wrong one, and the doctor hadn't let her take it.

A nurse entered the room to take Rosemene's blood pressure, which had gone up even more, to 240 over 140. A young female doctor burst into the room shortly after.

"We can't keep you here," the doctor announced frankly. "We need to get that baby out, but we can't do that here right now. You could have a seizure any minute."

Rosemene sat up in her bed and asked about the urine tests she had just paid for. Shouldn't she wait until the results came back?

"Would you prefer to wait for the results and die?" the doctor snapped. "Or just lose that money?"

"I don't want to die," Rosemene responded softly.

We were clearly in the "*urgent* urgent" zone. The doctor promised that the hospital would organize Rosemene's swift delivery to the Médecins Sans Frontières obstetrics hospital using the Baptist mission's single ambulance, donated by an American evangelical NGO after the earthquake. But the ambulance had broken down again, and the American parts were difficult to find in Haiti. There was a new ambulance service in Port-au-Prince, stocked with a few dozen vehicles, but its central yard was located near the airport, and it could take hours to get there and back—if it was dispatched at all. No, we'd take Rosemene immediately in my rental car.

The stillness of the room popped suddenly, as though pricked by a pin, and we all sprang into action. Enel and Arnold yanked free Rosemene's bedding and stuffed it into plastic bags. I emptied her side table and looked under her bed. Richard ran out to get the car and we all raced after him, arms full.

Rosemene remained calm. She rose slowly from her bed and stretched her arms out in the shape of the cross in the empty room.

"Jesus," she said. "Please protect me."

She drifted down the hospital's main hall and floated briefly into the general ward, where she'd stayed her first night, to say good-bye to the women who'd been her neighbors.

"Pray for me," she chirped to them, her voice high and singsongy.

Each second felt infuriatingly long. Finally, we got her into the back seat of the car, and Richard roared out of the parking lot.

My hands were soaking wet. Sweat leaked down my wrists and dripped off my fingers. I was panicking.

What if Rosemene died in our car? What would we do? I dried my hands on my lap and punched the number for my editor back in Toronto into my cell phone. I had to let her know that, once again, I'd stepped into the story. When I heard her voice on the line and started explaining what was happening, my throat constricted with emotion and my voice cracked.

"You have to remain calm!" Richard bellowed beside me. He gripped the steering wheel, weaving around slowing *tap-taps* and giant potholes. Whatever happened, he'd been through worse. For all his faults, Richard was a rock in the storm. He calmed me by getting philosophical about Rosemene's situation.

"If you go back to the beginning of this story, you have to go way back," he said. "Go back to the poverty, the weak infrastructure, the broken state, the Duvaliers . . ."

"Slavery," I added, "the restitution agreement, the American occupation . . ."

We stopped behind a dump truck full of construction material as it turned into the driveway of one of the nearby mansions.

"The corruption, the class system," I continued.

The back seat was stone silent. Enel and Arnold sat like statues, eyes forward, saying nothing. Rosemene leaned her head against the window. Her eyes were closed but her lips were moving. She was quietly praying. I rubbed my left hand dry on my pants and reached back to grab hold of one of hers, just like I often did with my kids.

"Breathe," I said aloud, to both her and myself. "Breathe."

The minutes grudgingly nudged by. There were more dump trucks and braking *tap-taps*. Even if we had been in an ambulance, we wouldn't have been able to go much faster. The road was so narrow, there was no room for cars to pull over.

We made it to Pétionville, where the *blokis* got even worse. I wanted to unroll my window and start screaming at people. Didn't they see this was an emergency? We were trying to outrun death!

Breathe. Breathe.

Time slowed to a trickle, and while my mind was hollering at it to hurry up, my eyes snapped vintage photographs out the window that I still carry in my mental album today. Snap: a newly expanded luxury hotel with drivers all standing by the entrance, waiting for the politicians they were chauffeuring to emerge. Snap: another renovated city park, with mosaic tiles and businessmen in suits sitting on the benches. Snap: a man on the side of the road with a puppy in his arms and, beside him, a white van with an A-frame sign on the roof declaring, *Foreign dogs, buy and sell.* Snap: women with baskets on the side of the road, selling mangoes and secondhand shoes.

I pleaded with God for Rosemene's life. *Take the baby,* I thought, *but please leave her alive.* If she died, Lovely would be left with nothing. Rosemene was the family's *poto mitan.* Without her, all the children would be lost.

The faded MÉDECINS SANS FRONTIÈRES sign appeared and we pulled up to the hospital's brown gate. A guard came out and peered into the car, then nodded. The gate was heaved back and Richard edged the car into the gravel parking lot.

I checked my phone. It was 3:37 p.m. The trip had taken us exactly forty-nine minutes.

My body was flooded with relief. My limbs felt like they were deep underwater, they were so heavy. My hands were still slick with sweat.

Rosemene stepped slowly out of the back of the car and gingerly walked inside the hospital with Enel and Richard beside her. She was admitted immediately.

Richard overheard the intake nurse say she was lucky to be alive.

The baby was born the next afternoon at 2:00 p.m. It was a little boy, weighing just over 3 pounds.

I gazed down at him through a glass window. He was tiny and light-skinned, with a large head and little frog legs. He looked malnourished, with ribs poking out down his chest. The doctors said he would be fine, and compared to the baby in the bassinet next to him, he seemed huge. Both were lucky to be in one of the few hospitals in the country with a well-equipped and functioning neonatal unit. If they were going to survive anywhere in Haiti, it was here.

The hospital was made entirely out of blue shipping containers joined together into a modular one-story building, with a couple of small green gardens in the center. It was plain, simple, and very clean, with running water and electricity and gleaming operating rooms.

Unlike most other hospitals in Haiti, Médecins Sans Frontières had very strict protocols. There were visiting hours and a two-visitor limit for each patient. There was even a press relations officer to make sure journalists couldn't just walk in and start interviewing patients. He had met me in the gravel parking lot out front that morning and given me a choice that perfectly captured my perennial predicament in Haiti: I could visit Rosemene as a reporter, in which case I would be accompanied by him, or I could visit as a friend, which meant I could go in alone, albeit without my camera or notepad.

It was a clarifying moment for me. The choice was obvious. For too long, I'd been a divided person in Haiti—part social worker, part journalist. But increasingly I was playing a third role that seemed more important than either one: friend. Careening down that pot-holed two-lane road, I'd been sweating and praying for Rosemene, not for my deadline or my project.

I stepped through the hospital gate and into the visitors' line, pinched between cell-phone-minute salesmen in their red pinnies and *timachanns* selling egg sandwiches and meat patties.

I found Rosemene in a small ward with only a handful of other patients. She was sitting up weakly, wearing one of my old dresses. Her feet were still swollen, and she said her head throbbed; but now that her baby had been born, her blood pressure was falling.

I sat down on the edge of her bed and we held hands as we whispered to one another.

"You saved my life," she said. "If I had stayed in the other hospital, I would have died."

I looked down at her and smiled. It was true. I had worried that she was going to die.

"You were crying in the car," she said. I nodded again. We sat there for a moment in silence.

"I will get *planin*," she said. "They do it here. It will last ten years. I can't trust Enel to do it."

"You can't have another baby," I concurred. "You can't afford it."

Most money I sent went to feed Rosemene's kids, who were always hungry. Lovely, in particular. When they were out of money, they bought on credit, so any new cash was gone almost instantly. I gave her the US$200 I had tucked into my pocket.

"This is for food, then," I said.

Rosemene hadn't seen her baby yet. The doctor told her maybe tomorrow, once her blood pressure was down. "Will you take a photo for me?" she asked. When I brought back the picture on my phone, she craned her head to look at it and commented on how small and pale he was.

"What are you going to name him?" I asked.

She wanted a biblical name. Even this morning the doctor had said her case was touch-and-go and that they almost had to choose between her life and the baby's.

"Jesus kept us both," she said.

She asked me to think of some names from the Bible. I scrounged around my brain, uncovering and dusting off the obvious Old Testament characters. How about Moses? Or Noah with the flood? There was Abel . . .

She didn't like any of those. So I started to dig deeper. Peter? Paul? They were apostles. Zachary? I couldn't remember who he was, but I was pretty sure he was in the Bible.

"Zachary," she said. "Yes. That one."

And just like that, the little boy was named. I couldn't remember who Zachary was in the Bible. I hoped he was a good man. Later, I was relieved to read that he was a Catholic saint, the father of John the Baptist. His name was actually Zacharias. It meant "The Lord has remembered."

After visiting Rosemene, we drove Elistin home. He'd lost the house he had spent so many years building, but his landlord had shown him mercy and given him some money to leave. It didn't cover his costs, of course, but it was enough to pay for a year's rent. The family was now living inside a single room at the back of a house about ten minutes from where they once lived.

Inside, there were two beds, a night table with their valuables in a drawer, a small table piled with kitchenware, and a laundry basket bursting with dirty clothes.

Rosita, Lala, and Ananstania were all napping together. Rosita woke up, and I sat down on the bed across from her so that Elistin and I could fill her in on what had happened with Rosemene and the hospital.

"They take your money and do nothing," Elistin said, speaking about the hospital. "Haiti is like that."

It was a warm day, and sunlight splashed onto the floor through the open door. Chickens darted by, followed by a kitten. Lala woke up, and Rosita plopped her onto my lap. She raised her hand to my neck and left it there.

Elistin sat in a chair by the door and rubbed his head with his long fingers, as was his habit. "*Bon,*" he said. "We want you to be her *marenn.*"

I didn't know how to respond. The word *marenn* meant so many things in Haiti. It translated to "godmother," but it meant much more than that did in Canada, where godparents were largely just symbolic. If I accepted, I would be expected to offer wraparound support—not just with Lala's education and health care but with bigger things, such as helping her get a job later in life. My impulse was to say no.

I sat quietly for a moment and then asked him why he wanted me to do this.

"You are the head of the family," he said.

"No," I responded. "You are the head."

Elistin smiled, revealing a mouth that had lost even more teeth. He rubbed his head again.

"I am the *bòs,*" he said. "But you are very important to us."

Just over a month later, at the end of February 2015, I was back on a plane from Toronto to Haiti, staring down at the soft green mountains covered in what looked like white scales: Port-au-Prince. It was Saturday, around 2:00 p.m. Lala's baptism was the next day.

For the first time in five years, I had no performance anxiety in my belly. Every other time I'd traveled to Haiti, I found myself searching for a story at some point. Even when Lyla had traveled with me, I knew I would have to write about it, as well as report on another subject. This time, though, I wasn't worried about missing a story. The only story I had ahead of me on this trip was a personal one. Richard greeted me outside the airport doors, his eyes shielded by mirrored sunglasses and his bulldog frown transforming into a smile when he caught sight of me. He hugged me and took the bag off my shoulder.

As soon as we were inside the rental car, I yanked off my running shoes and socks and pulled out my flip-flops. I rolled down the window and delighted in the familiar sights flashing by, whooping out loud with joy. I was happy to be home.

We rushed right up to Fermathe, not bothering to stop at the guesthouse. I had less than two days in Haiti and I wanted to make the most of every minute.

When we arrived, Elistin's new home was bursting with people. There was Lovely and Jonathan, Lypse, Sophonie, Elistin, Ananstania, Rosemene, and Rosita, holding Lala. And on one of the beds, no bigger than a water bottle, lay Zachary, swaddled in bonnets and blankets. His face was thin, making his eyes look large and round. His mouth was like Lovely's, twisted in a little bow.

Richard pulled my bag, stuffed with presents for everyone, out of the car. Lovely crawled up on my lap for the distribution ritual. Rosita picked up Lala and plopped her on my lap, too.

I had decided to accept the offer to become Lala's *marenn*. It seemed I was unofficially all the children's *marenn*, anyway. I was paying for all of their school costs and, for the past few months, had hired one of Sophonie's former teachers to tutor and feed them lunch each day after class let out.

But Zachary's birth and nearly losing Rosemene had crystallized something for me. My life was entwined with theirs now, far beyond what any story could ever have done. It was time I stopped struggling with that and simply embraced it. I wanted to be in their lives, not because of some bargain with my conscience or a duty to my readers, but because I cared for them. They had become my Haitian family. I wouldn't write another story about Lovely for the newspaper, but her story would continue to grow and change, and I would document it as part of my own life.

I reflected on what had happened over the past five years and all of the choices I'd made in Haiti. In the end, my foray into foreign aid had been limited to two projects. One had been a success. Muspan was up and running and more than three hundred kids were learning for free. After just over two years of funding the school, my commitment had ended cleanly. I had worked myself out of a job there, which I believed was the true role of an aid worker.

The other project had been a failure from a development perspective. Rosemene's family had eaten all her merchandise. Enel had started his new business and destroyed it. Elistin had built his house and lost not just his home but also the three fields he had farmed. They had no steady income and even more children to feed.

I hadn't worked myself out of a job there. In fact, I was more and more embroiled in supporting the family. There was nothing sustainable about it, except for the connections. I had thought our relationship would be clean and easy and distant, with me sending money from afar and getting reports from teachers. But it was the opposite: close and messy, a pile of children around me on the bed, all arms and legs.

If I were given the chance to twist back time, there were some things I would change. I would have talked to Rosemene first about her business plans. I would have been clearer about my expectations and asked what her expectations of me were. I would have insisted Enel take more motorcycle lessons and been firm when I didn't think he was ready. But I was not in control, and in Haiti neither were they. The country had not afforded them any safety net. How could they rise up without one? Like many who had funded projects big and small across the country, I had expected too much. In the end, I should have looked at my donations the same way the catastrophe missionaries had—as acts of kindness and solidarity.

The next morning, I arrived early in my Sunday best to find Lala dressed up like a 1980s bride in a puffy white dress and white fishnet stockings beneath lacy socks and white shoes. On her head she wore a white tiara that pointed down her brow. Rosita and Elistin plopped her in a chair and stood beside her in stiff frontier-era postures, demanding I take their photos. Then every single person in the family squeezed into the rental car to make the short trip to church.

I spent most of the service nervously sitting in a pew, worrying that I'd be called to the pulpit and asked to say some words. But it never happened. Instead, after what felt like an eternity of impassioned singing and stern sermon giving, the pastor called Elistin up to the front with his family and announced that, as everyone in the congregation knew, "introductions to God" were always done on the last Sunday of the month. But since Lala's *marenn* had come all the way from across the ocean for this, he was making an exception. I realized I had mixed up the dates and arrived a week late, but Elistin had been too polite to say anything. I smiled in my pew.

Later that afternoon, five women arrived at the family home to squat over charcoal fires and cook the feast. They made rice and grilled chicken and shredded salad and macaroni. Elistin's landlady had converted her parlor into a party room for the occasion, laying a nice tablecloth across the table and clearing out furniture. When the meal was ready, people I had never seen before surfaced as if by magic to carry out plates heavy with food. Richard popped a bottle of champagne.

Afterward we dragged our chairs into the sun-speckled front yard. Lypse pulled out the soccer ball I had brought for him and we played monkey in the middle with Lovely. She squealed and gasped, racing around me and shouting "*Madame Katrin, mwen mwen*"—"Me me." I loved moments with Lovely like this, when she transformed from a tough, wizened little woman into a carefree child.

The afternoon passed like a summer dream, with kids climbing on and off my lap and Rosemene parading the clothing I'd brought for her and Rosita up and down the yard. Just a month ago Rosemene had been so close to death. Now here she was, vibrant and happy. I was in awe; it seemed another miracle.

Near the end of the day, we all curled up on the two beds like a pack of kittens, with Lala in the middle sitting upright, her hair an Afro halo around her face. Lovely lay beside me, writing a letter to Lyla on my notepad in her flowery French penmanship.

"*Chère amie Lala,*" she wrote. "*C'est ton amie Lovely.*"

I smiled, remembering the first time Lovely had taken my notepad, just three months after the earthquake. That was the afternoon that started it all: the day I'd seen her potential and decided to cross the line.

I still wondered if it had been the right choice. As a foreign correspondent, many of my stories would inspire readers to help the people I was writing about. I saw the wisdom of most journalists who directed their readers to NGO workers who functioned as intermediaries. The professional line of impartiality was there for a reason, protecting journalists in big ways and small ones. But I also understood that that wouldn't prevent moral dilemmas from surfacing in more acute ways throughout my career, as they had the first afternoon I met Lovely, or a month ago when Rosemene's life was in danger. And in those cases I would always cross it. The mantra I'd devised five years ago hadn't changed: I was a human first, a journalist second.

If I hadn't decided to help Lovely, what would her life be like now? I wondered. She'd probably be back in Fort National, living in a tin shed. She wouldn't be in school; that was for sure. She would never have learned to read or write. Her only prospect would be the life of a *timachann* selling bouillon cubes or mangoes in the market. She would be poor and hungry. By those standards, my development project hadn't been a failure. It was just ongoing. I'd have to wait another ten years to see what Lovely would make of her life. Maybe she'd be a cook, like she said she wanted to be, or a writer like me.

Her mother pointed out how much she loved to read and write stories, sure that it was my influence.

She had so many things going for her: her loving family, her grit, her determination. She was smart and hardworking. She was tough. And she had me. As long as she kept studying, I would continue to pay for her schooling.

I doubted she could be the president. I now knew enough about Haiti to understand she'd been born in the wrong class for that. But I did see that she could lead a full, meaningful life. And I was so glad that I would be there to watch it unfold.

Epilogue

The path down to Lovely's new home was so steep, I had taken my shoes off to navigate it barefoot, my toes curling around the shards of damp rock to prevent me from slipping and falling.

It was early October 2017. The rainy season was tapering to its end, which meant the red earth beneath my feet was still moist. The sun was high, cooking the heavy air like a sauna. Banana trees in the valley just below us gleamed an emerald green, and the voices of Lovely's neighbors echoed around us.

I'd left the *Toronto Star* earlier that year for my dream job—a foreign correspondent for the *New York Times*. I was the Canada bureau chief, based in my home in Toronto, so I got to see my kids more. But I also covered the entire country, flying to places so different that, although they were within my country's borders, they gave me the sense I always craved—of being a visitor in a strange land.

Before I started the new job, I'd traveled to Haiti to visit Lovely and her family, thinking it would be the last I would see them for some time. But Haiti had me *mare*—tied. No matter how far away I was, the country worked some magic to bring me back. In this case, my new editor at the *Times* had launched a series about death around the world and asked me to tell a story from Haiti, since I knew it so well. So, I'd traveled back three more times throughout the year, to the point that, on my last trip, Elistin exclaimed, "You are here again! I thought they were joking when they called to say you were at my house."

I discovered that Lovely's family had moved again. They'd rented a small piece of land on the edge of a steep, rocky valley in Fermathe and built a house on it. The house was made entirely of scraps of tin, nailed together like a quilt. From the outside, it looked almost as terrible as the hovel I'd seen at the bottom of Bobin, albeit without the surrounding trash. But inside, the home was cool and roomy. There was one single bed and the frame for a second, a little shelf filled with all their kitchen supplies, and a television, which miraculously turned on for a couple of hours a day when the electricity was working. At night, they rolled out bits of carpet on the floor, which was rocky dirt, for the kids to sleep on.

The fact that the family owned the home, on rented land they aimed to buy at some point, gave them a sense of security they'd never had. Rosemene saw it as progress. She and Enel had bought a cow with the proceeds from the motorcycle he'd sold, and the cow was now pregnant. They planned to sell the calf and buy a concrete floor for their home.

"The city wasn't built in one day," Rosemene said, as a parable for patience. "It's been seven years and look at it. It still hasn't been built."

She was right. Seven years after the earthquake, the country's reconstruction had paused indefinitely for lack of funds. The world had moved on. Haiti had not been "built back better." Aside from a few good projects, it had returned to what it had been before the earthquake.

I still considered Muspan as one of those few good projects, particularly because it had withstood a huge tragedy. Gilberte Salomon had died. She'd been visiting her family home in Les Cayes when she suffered what seemed to be a stroke. Her son Anthony told me she'd had diabetes for a long time and had not been managing it well. He lived not far from me, in the suburbs of Toronto, but was now running his mother's school remotely, flying down to Haiti regularly to check on it and the nursing college. Even though he told me he didn't share his mother's thirst for social justice, he still carried on her legacy, charging just US$30 tuition so that poorer children wouldn't be priced out of an education.

Lovely's family had suffered its own tragedy of sorts: Sophonie was pregnant. The news had stunned and infuriated Rosita in particular. Sophonie, just sixteen, had more education than she and Elistin put together, and now she seemed destined for their lot—piecemeal labor. She would not be helping the family out of poverty, as they'd hoped. The local high school wouldn't accept her pregnant, so she was lounging about at home, casting back her parents' anger.

I was disappointed, too. This was a barrier to progress I had considered when it came to Rosemene, but foolishly had not contemplated for her children or nieces. I hoped Sophonie would return to school once the baby was born, but it seemed depressingly unlikely. *Please, Lovely*, I thought, *learn from this lesson*.

Lovely had just started grade six. She still had the toughness and grit that drew me to her when we'd met, but she was softening with age, adopting some of her mother's lightness and delight in life. It made her all the more lovable.

She was guiding me down the path, pointing out the best places for me to step. I held my shoes in one hand, and her hand in the other. I looked down at her with pride and wonder.

How was it that she survived six days under the rubble? But more importantly, why had she survived? It was a question I'd mulled for years now. All the death I'd seen in Haiti, all the poverty and dejection, and yet here she was—not just surviving, but thriving. Lovely was only ten, but she had already been granted three lives.

I wondered how she carried that. Was it a heavy burden?

"Lovely," I asked her, as she jumped down to the next step, "do you remember the earthquake?"

"Yes," she responded.

"Do you remember being under the rubble?"

"Yes," she said. "A man helped break the building."

"What do you think about it?" I asked.

She paused for a moment, and we stood quietly on the edge of the rocky valley.

When she finally answered, she said, "I don't know."

I squeezed her hand, she turned to face me, and we smiled at each other.

I didn't know, either. Some things, I figured, we would never know. But we'd also never tire of thinking about them.

Kreyòl Glossary

(Haitian Creole)

anpil: a lot
bayakou: latrine cleaner (often derogatory)
bidonvil: slum
blan: foreigner
blokis: traffic jam
bon bagay: good stuff
Bondye: God
boutik: small store
bwat: box; in most cases a lunch box
byen chè: very expensive
chofè: chauffeur/driver
dlo: water
èd: aid
ekip: team

fèt: party

gade: look (verb)

goudougoudou: The onomatopoetic word created by Haitians after the earthquake to impart the sound the earthquake made. It is now synonymous with "earthquake."

goute: snack

jèn: all-day prayer session

kay: house

kenbe kontak: keep in touch

kleren: high-proof sugarcane liquor

kraze: smashed, broken, collapsed, destroyed

lekòl bòlèt: literally "lottery school," but in a Haitian context it refers to low-quality private schools

lougawou: a demonic shape-shifter

machinn: car

maji: magic, sorcery

manman: mother

mare: tied, bound

marenn/parenn: godmother, godfather

mototaksi: motorcycle taxi

oblije: obligated or required

oungan: Vodou priest

pa gen kòb: there's no money

poto mitan: central pillar, generally a reference to the central pillar of a *peristil* (Vodou temple), but figuratively a cornerstone or foundation (e.g., "the *poto mitan* of the family")

rad kenedi: old-fashioned term for secondhand clothes sold on the street; named after former US president John F. Kennedy, because the first shipment of gently used clothing from the United States to Haiti occurred in 1961, around the same time he founded the government's international development agency, USAID

recho: small metal charcoal stove

restavèk: a child domestic worker

tap-tap: privately run buses, usually made from pickup trucks with benches thrown down the back, and metal awnings usually painted with bright colors and decorated with mottos like *Jesus watch over us*

teledjòl: literally "mouth television"; refers to word-of-mouth information

timachann: market woman/small-scale merchant

timoun: child/children

Acknowledgments

I began to write this book as a conversation with myself—a way to unravel what happened in my personal and professional lives as a result of my many visits to the devastation of Haiti and to understand how it had changed my view of the world.

Most of the unraveling and resewing took place before 6:00 a.m., while the demands of my work and daily life were still asleep. It continued for three years.

It made me unbearable to many people I hold dear, for an awfully long time—particularly because I get emotional and short-tempered when I am tired.

So, this note is equal parts thank-you and apology.

My husband, Graeme, took care of our children during my more than twenty trips to Haiti, without complaint. He never let the fatigue and irritation creep into his voice when I called home. He never made me feel guilty, which, you will know by now, I have an aptitude for.

My family stepped in often to carry the load with him. My mom, Anna; and dad, Julian Porter, in-laws, Janet and Tony Burt; little sister, Julia; and brother-in-law, Cameron Ainsworth-Vincze; were regular babysitters—most of the times voluntarily.

My grandmother, Maria Des Tombe, has taught me since childhood that being a refugee might form you, but not define you. Her stories planted seeds of compassion in me. I always remember that I am the grandchild and child of refugees.

Then there are my kids, Lyla and Noah, who lost me for weeks at a time during much of their childhood. I am so grateful for their understanding and love, and I am proud that both have inherited my wanderlust.

Good editors become like parents to a writer. They watch your tantrums and witness your most vulnerable moments, because the act of writing is essentially peeling your skin. My editors at the *Toronto Star* were great parents, alternating between the roles of cheerleader, guide, coach, therapist, and critic. They include Pat Hluchy, Glen Colbourne, Lynn McAuley, and Michael Cooke. I shall always be grateful to Michael for wholeheartedly supporting my decision to act in Haiti. And then there is Alison Uncles, a woman as wide in heart as she is tall in stature. She welcomed me into her office after every trip and was always eager to hear my stories, often with a box of Kleenex between us.

You might think leaping from newspaper writing to books would feel natural. It might for some, but not for me.

My mother was a huge help. A former book publisher and author, she counseled, coached, and commiserated with me. She was also my model of how to have a rich career and rich family life.

My mother's best friend, and my godmother, Sylvia Fraser, read my first chapters and offered much-needed encouragement.

My agent, Sam Haywood, was a steely negotiator, and my editor at Simon & Schuster, Brendan May, was deft, astute, and upbeat. He would make a great companion in a crisis.

Funding two years of Muspan would have been impossible without an army of huge-hearted readers, most of whom I never met.

Many regularly sent cards and hand-written notes of encouragement, which I still treasure, along with their checks.

A number of teachers made Muspan their classroom project, raising money through drives and inviting me to speak to their students. Thank you all, particularly Marissa Revzen-Ellis from Stephen Lewis Secondary School, and Mary Egan from Holy Name Catholic School.

In my second year of fundraising, I was joined by my "Mummy's group"—the group of women I met when Lyla was just a baby. They voluntarily threw themselves at the task with joy and zeal, even though none of them had ever been to Haiti. Thank you Dorianne McKenzie, Danielle Oaks, Karen Harkins, and Janine Hopkins.

I'd like to thank the Sawatzky family. Ryan agreed to fold my little project under his foundation's umbrella and his mom, Edie, patiently kept the account ledger and sent me regular reports of how much money we had left.

Since that first trip together, *Star* reader Paul Haslip has become my dear friend. In fact, he's returned to Haiti three more times. The country has evolved from a midlife-crisis venue for him to part of his life. The night we stepped out of the pouring rain, he clasped my hands and vowed to help me financially support Lovely's family for the rest of his life. He's remained true to his word.

Then, there are those from *lòt bò dlo*—the other side of the water—and my second home.

As a foreigner parachuting into a place, I needed to learn everything—from the language and history to how to change money and hail a *tap-tap*. It really takes a village to raise a foreign journalist. First, my official guides, some of whom you met in this book, and others who I didn't write about: There was Samuel in his winter toque, David the English teacher, Wilnes the tennis pro, and Jean, with his long T-shirts and shy smile. Dimitri Bien-Aimé will always be kindred to me, for the horrors we experienced together and the kindness he always showed to Lovely and her family. I still laugh when I think of him turning to me in the car, holding up a granola bar and asking, "Is this what you all eat in Canada for lunch?"

Joseph Farly worked with me for more than a year, until I couldn't face another car breakdown, particularly in Cité Soleil. I lost a fixer but gained a dear friend, and every time I arrive in Haiti, I go to the yard before his T-shelter, which he's transformed into a little bar, and have drinks with him and his friends. And then there is Richard Miguel, who remains steadfast, faithful, and makes me explode with laughter. We both admit, perhaps grudgingly, that we have become siblings.

Gail Buck was the manager and den mother of Healing Hands For Haiti Guesthouse. Any time there was a riot in the city, she would call to alert me, and every time I came home from witnessing something terrible, she would sit down beside me, rub my back, and offer me a beer and cigarette. Gail was my first friend in Haiti, and I am grateful for her tenderness and understanding, as I am to Gaëlle Delaquis, the attaché at the Canadian embassy, whose insights and friendship have been invaluable.

The guesthouse became my second home, and I met many people there who helped me over the years—as sources and friends. To start with, the women who run the place and always made me feel part of the family: Syltane, Mercia, Suze, Myrlene, and Louna. The drivers Dade and Noel saved me a number of times.

Both Al and Deb Ingersoll provided a wealth of knowledge about the workings of nongovernment agencies in Haiti and were an inspiration for how to live a good, meaningful, and adventurous life. Andy Ripp patiently taught me the engineering magic of structures built to withstand earthquakes.

Jean Angus was the lead administrator of the Baptist Haiti Mission in Fermathe. He always made time for my questions, despite the incessant ringing of his three phones, which he answered in three languages. He graciously set up Lovely's family account at the hospital and oversaw it for years.

A number of Haitian journalists helped me along the way, particularly Milo Milfort, who tracked down sources and linked arms with me during street protests. Georges Michel, newspaper columnist, radiologist, and celebrated Haitian historian, was my analyst, teacher, and source of contacts and story ideas over the years. He also carefully read through a draft of this book.

I broadened my understanding of Haitian history through the books of Laurent Dubois, Amy Wilentz, James Ferguson, Michel-Rolph Trouillot, Bernard Diederich, and Paul Farmer—all of which I'd heartily recommend. Dr. Farmer's book *Aids and Accusations* deepened my understanding of the essential role of Vodou in the Haitian culture, regardless of a person's religion, as well as of extreme poverty being the ultimate source of *maji*.

"In such a zero-sum setting," he wrote, "one person's fortune is manifestly another's ill fortune."

Laura Wagner was a saving grace—cross-referencing my pidgin Kreyòl in these pages with the official *Akademi Kreyòl*.

I learned much about the pitfalls of international aid in Haiti from Timothy Schwartz's *Travesty in Haiti: A true account of Christian missions, orphanages, food aid, fraud and drug trafficking*, and three books by American associate anthropology professor Mark Schuller: *Killing with Kindness: Haiti, International Aid, and NGOs*; *Humanitarian Aftershocks in Haiti*; and a book he co-edited with Pablo Morales called *Tectonic Shifts: Haiti Since the Earthquake*. Other books that helped form my thinking were Linda Polman's *War Games* and Naomi Klein's *The Shock Doctrine: The Rise of Disaster Capitalism*.

As a parachuting journalist, I relied on the reporting of others to keep me abreast of news from Haiti while I wasn't there. Clearly, the Haitian newspaper *Le Nouvelliste* was my regular go-to, but I must also pay tribute to the dogged Jacqueline Charles from the *Miami Herald*, and Jonathan Katz and Trenton Daniel, two hardworking former bureau chiefs in Haiti for the Associated Press.

Countless people were continually generous with their time, agreeing to long interviews at the end of long days, none more so than Nigel Fisher, Université Quisqueya's Jacky Lumarque, and Dr. Louise Ivers, the country lead for Partners in Health.

You have met Rea Dol in this book—with her booming laugh

and indomitable spirit. Rea was my model and touchstone for how aid could work in Haiti. She also was the reason I could help with Muspan, setting up an accounting system and overseeing the payments every month.

Finally, I need to thank the members of my Haitian family, for sharing their lives with me: Rosemene, Enel, Rosita, Elistin, Sophonie, Venessaint, Jonathan, Lypse, Ananstania, Lina, Sadrac, Lala, and, of course, Lovely. I still don't know what you truly make of me, this strange woman who descends, often without warning, into your lives and pokes. But I'm eternally grateful for your patience and love.